STOP *the* ISLAMIZATION *of* AMERICA

D1379522

STOP *the* ISLAMIZATION *of* AMERICA

A PRACTICAL GUIDE TO THE RESISTANCE

PAMELA GELLER

STOP THE ISLAMIZATION OF AMERICA
A Practical Guide to the Resistance
by Pamela Geller

Published by WND Books
Washington, D.C.

Copyright © 2011, 2016 Pamela Geller

All rights reserved. No part of this book may be reproduced in any form or by any means, electronic, mechanical, photocopying, scanning, or otherwise, without permission in writing from the publisher, except by a reviewer who may quote brief passages in a review.

Book designed by Mark Karis

WND Books are available at special discounts for bulk purchases. WND Books, Inc. also publishes books in electronic formats. For more information call (541) 474-1776 or visit www.wndbooks.com.

hardcover ISBN: 978-1-936488-36-0
paperback ISBN: 978-1-942475-44-6
eBook ISBN: 978-1-936488-73-5

Library of Congress information available.

Printed in the United States of America.

THIS BOOK IS DEDICATED TO

THE INDIVIDUAL

"Honor is self-esteem made visible in action." —**Ayn Rand**

CONTENTS

INTRODUCTION

Make no mistake: We are at war. Our mortal enemy has made no secret of its goal and stated aim: "eliminating and destroying Western civilization from within and sabotaging its miserable house," and installing a universal caliphate.[1] Pretending that fourteen-hundred years of Islamic imperialism and expansionism didn't happen doesn't change reality either.

Ayn Rand said that you can avoid reality, but you cannot avoid the consequences of avoiding reality. If you refuse to fight, you forfeit. If you forfeit, you lose. And I mean, lose everything. The stakes couldn't be higher.

Saul Alinsky had *Rules for Radicals*. I'm giving you "Rules for Infidels." Consider this your handbook to win the war. Keep it with you at all times. There is more than one way to be armed and dangerous.

Why *Stop the Islamization of America*? The very name evokes a visceral reaction in people—particularly in those hard-wired for delusion. Uninformed people might assume that an organization with such a name, and a book of the same name, would only be of interest to racist, Islamophobic, anti-Muslim bigots. When the Southern Poverty Law Center, a hard-left propaganda group, defamed the Stop Islamization of America organization (SIOA) as a "hate group" in February 2011, the spokesman for a real hate group, the Hamas-linked Council on American-Islamic Relations

(CAIR), Ibrahim Hooper, commented: "One need not go beyond the name of this hate group, Stop the Islamization of America, to recognize the validity of the Southern Poverty Law Center's designation."[2]

What Ibrahim Hooper really means is that no one should go beyond the name and expose the Muslim Brotherhood agenda of their proxy groups in America. CAIR, of course, was named an unindicted co-conspirator in the Holy Land Foundation trial; the Holy Land Foundation was the largest Islamic charity in the United States, and was shut down for funding the jihad terror group Hamas. CAIR has had several of its officials convicted of terror activity and has opposed every anti-terror measure devised since 9/11. And so criticism from CAIR is high praise: CAIR fronts for the Muslim Brotherhood and Hamas, and so CAIR is the real hate group, not SIOA.

In reality, and in stark contrast to CAIR, Stop Islamization of America is a human rights organization dedicated to the freedom of speech, which is under attack, as well as to the freedom of religion and to individual rights. These are basic, fundamental principles of the American republic, and they are in danger of being stripped away and seized from us. The violent jihad is the most obvious manifestation of jihad. (Remember the Fort Hood jihadist, the Times Square car bomber, the Christmas day underwear bomber, the Christmas Tree Lighting bomber in Portland, the Fort Dix Six, and so many others?) But the real war on America is also being waged in the universities, the public schools, the courtrooms, the Internet, the workplace, the grocery store, the neighborhoods, and on the airwaves. That is the stealth jihad, the hidden war.[3] And it is to teaching you how to fight that war—where and how and on what grounds—that this book is dedicated.

Why is it that today Islamic supremacists are more assertive in the United States than they ever have been before? They're building large mega-mosques in communities where the local Muslims can neither fill nor afford them. They're demanding—and receiving—special privileges for Muslims in workplaces, and special installations for Islamic prayers in public universities, as well as in airports and other public facilities. (Islamic law places Muslims in a special class, giving them rights that non-Muslims do not have.)

They're bringing back prayer in public schools—but only for Muslims, while insisting that Christians, Jews, Hindus, and Buddhists can assert no such Constitutional privilege under our law; they are seeking special legal status for Islam. They're shutting down the national debate that we urgently need to have about Islam and Islamization. They are demonizing as "bigots," "racists," and "Islamophobes" anyone who suggests any anti-terror measure, or who asks the Muslim community in the United States to do something effective about the jihadists and Islamic supremacists in their midst. (Islamic law considers any critical examination of Islam to be blasphemous and subject to the death penalty.) They're persecuting anti-jihad activists in the courtroom and private citizens who dare to report suspicious behavior by Muslims.

They're working as hard as they can to shut down the rapidly growing anti-Sharia movement nationwide, and to prevent any more states from passing anti-Sharia laws like the one 70 percent of Oklahomans voted for in November 2010—only to see the will of the people overruled by a liberal activist judge who maintained, contrary to obvious fact, that Sharia was merely a private religious law, and not the authoritarian political system involving dominance and the subjugation of unbelievers that it really is.

They're working to muzzle free speech, criminalizing criticism of Islam by means of "hate speech" laws that they will manipulate to shut up their opponents and anyone who dares speak out against their Islamization agenda. This is in line with the international war on free speech that is being pursued by the Organization of the Islamic Conference (OIC).[3] The Muslim Brotherhood, a global organization dedicated to the establishment of Islamic political law in all the countries of the world, is also working through its supposedly "moderate" front organizations like the Muslim American Society (MAS) and CAIR, which tries to intimidate Americans (as in the "Flying Imams" case) into being afraid to oppose jihad activity or even report suspicious behavior by Muslims. And these very organizations have infiltrated senior levels of the Department of Defense, the Department of State, the Department of Homeland Security, the Department of Justice, et al, to advance their agendas and make them law.

Stop Islamization of America is dedicated to stopping that stealth jihad, exposing the Islamic supremacists, and preserving the freedom of speech, the freedom of conscience, and the equality of rights of all people before the law. We are not against Islam or Muslims as such, but against the political and supremacist character of Islam as enunciated by Muhammad, the Muslim prophet who declared, "Islam must dominate, and not be dominated." Separation of mosque and state is the mandate, and should be the rallying cry for all Americans. In stark contrast to the Islamic drive to control all facets of our society through imposition of Sharia, the separation of religion and state is the mandate of our constitutional law, and the continued primacy of our law should be the rallying cry, the continued legal standard, for all Americans.

Muslims are working in the United States now to make sure that Islam dominates by destroying our Constitutional freedoms. How do I know that? Because they've told us.

The Muslim Brotherhood, according to a captured internal document of that international pro-Sharia organization, is dedicated in America to "a kind of grand Jihad in eliminating and destroying the Western civilization from within and 'sabotaging' its miserable house by their hands and the hands of the believers so that it is eliminated and Allah's religion is made victorious over all other religions."[4]

Omar Ahmad, the cofounder and longtime Board chairman of the nation's leading "Muslim civil rights group," the Council on American-Islamic Relations (CAIR), also once let the mask slip in a speech he gave to a Muslim audience in California in 1998. Ahmad said, "Islam isn't in America to be equal to any other faith, but to become dominant. The Koran should be the highest authority in America, and Islam the only accepted religion on earth."[5]

CAIR spokesman Ibrahim Hooper expressed the same desire in a 1993 interview: "I wouldn't want to create the impression that I wouldn't like the government of the United States to be Islamic sometime in the future."[6]

And one of the leading Muslim spokesmen in the United States, the imam Siraj Wahhaj, who in 1991 became the first Muslim cleric to give an invocation to the United States Congress, has warned that the United States will fall unless it "accepts the Islamic agenda." He has also said, "If only Muslims were clever politically, they could take over the United States and replace its constitutional government with a caliphate."[7]

I also know that Muslims are working in the United States now to make sure that Islam dominates by destroying our Constitutional freedoms because of the actions of Muslims themselves. Just look at their feverish attempts to restrict free speech and enact hate speech and hate crime laws, their relentless litigation jihad against truth-tellers and fearless patriots, and so much more. When used by Islamic supremacist groups, such phrases as "hate speech" and "hate crime" in reality mean honest discussion of the Islamic supremacist imperative to impose Islamic law over the world. They do not want critics explaining the actual goals of political Islam; they do not want their aggressive aims exposed, and they obfuscate those aims by labeling the truth about them "hate speech."

SIOA is dedicated to defending America's constitutional government. Every free citizen must join this fight. The separation of mosque and state is essential to preserving American freedom and our way of life. Yet the Islamic supremacists have made real inroads. Over the last few years, we have seen the encroachment of Islam on the secular marketplace.

The gravest threat this Islamization poses is the restriction of the freedom of speech. Under the guise of charges of hate speech leveled against freedom fighters who dare to tell the truth about Islam, the dark shadow of the Sharia looms ever so large. The OIC has labeled the speech of people who speak the truth about Islam, such as Geert Wilders, a world leader and one of the leading contenders to be the next Prime Minister of the Netherlands (and head of its third-largest party), as "hate speech." This is an attempt to squelch the truth about the Islamic agenda in the West. In Islamic law, *slander* (*ghiba*) doesn't refer to telling falsehoods about someone, but to saying things that may well be true, but that a person does not want known or spoken of:

> Slander (ghiba) means to mention anything concerning a person that he would dislike, whether about his body, religion, everyday life, self, disposition, property, son, father, wife, servant, turban, garment, gait, movements, smiling, dissoluteness, frowning, cheerfulness, or anything else connected with him. (*Umdat al-Salik*, r2.2).[8]

As absurd as this is, it has seeped into the public discourse in America and Europe as well. In the West, insulting or defaming Islam is also a societal crime, punishable not by death, but by character assassination.

I'm not suggesting that non-Muslim authorities are consciously and deliberately enforcing the Sharia (specifically, the blasphemy laws of Islam), but in effect, that's exactly what they're doing. Just because they're not aware of the name of what they're doing doesn't excuse them. Sharia tends to be self-enforcing, because people will impose restraints upon their own opinions and beliefs for fear of recrimination and attack. Here in America, we witness the media practicing Sharia (self-censorship) on a daily basis, whether knowingly or not. The effect is the same.

Ignorance of Sharia law is no excuse. Every effective voice against Islamic supremacism has been smeared, libeled, and marginalized with the assistance of a media that is behaving as if it is already subjugated under Islamic supremacist rule. Even someone as notable as Wilders is on trial for what amounts to blasphemy against Islam. It is, in fact, a heresy trial. Even Dutch authorities said that it didn't matter if Wilders was telling the truth; it mattered that it was illegal.

If world leaders are subjected to such medieval and draconian treatment, then no one is safe. And when Muslims advance privileges that are owed to Muslims under Sharia, in defiance of the limitations placed by the Constitution on the establishment of religion, they advance Sharia. And if they advance Sharia, what they are in effect attempting to advance is an agenda that will result, some day in the future, in making the speaking of truths about Islam that Muslims don't wish you to know punishable by death.

Do you want to live in a country where you could be put to death for saying what you think about Islam? Or about Catholicism? Or any other religion?

Do you think this is impossible?

If you do, consider this: What I am suggesting as a consequence of Sharia is happening right now in the world in places where Islamic law reigns supreme. Right now a woman is in prison in Pakistan and awaiting death for blasphemy. This is Islamic law, and this is the Islamic law that Muslims want to bring West.

The very idea that truthful speech about Islamic supremacism and jihad could be categorized as hate speech and/or criminalized is the equivalent of shredding the Constitution. The fundamental principle of free speech is the protection of all speech, not just speech we like. Because who decides what's good and what's forbidden? CAIR? The United Nations? The Organization of the Islamic Conference?

That is precisely the role that CAIR and the OIC would like to play in American society. We cannot and will not allow them to do so because free speech is the line in the sand. Once free men have lost that basic human freedom, they have no other recourse but to resort to violence.

The march of Islamic supremacists enjoined by their Leftist enablers has been going on for decades, long before 9/11, under the radar screen: quiet, unnoticed, stealthy. Muslim Brotherhood front groups had prepared both political and cultural initiatives in anticipation of jihad attacks. And so they were at the ready on 9/11 to direct the efforts of our most senior government and law enforcement agencies—that one of their utmost concerns had to be not initiatives in the Islamic community to teach against the beliefs that inspired and motivated the attacks, but rather preventing a backlash against Muslims. Yet no such backlash ever materialized. But the fallacious meme, "anti-Muslim backlash," became a familiar mantra on the airwaves, in print media, and from the silver-tongued stealth jihadists.

In her book, *A God Who Hates*, Wafa Sultan, a U.S.-based author and former Muslim raised in Syria, describes the threats and intimidation she suffered from Muslim Brotherhood–tied CAIR because of her frankness in exposing Islam in her columns published in the Arab press—and this was *before 9/11*. Wafa wrote frankly and critically about Islam in the Arab press, and the result was predictable:

> Muslims withdrew their advertisements from the paper in protest against what I wrote, and the publisher called me about two months before the September 11th terrorist attack to ask me if he could give my telephone number to CAIR (the Council on American-Islamic Relations), because one of its members wanted to talk to me. I agreed, of course, and on that same day I received a telephone call from Mr. Hussam Ayloush of CAIR. Mr. Ayloush was courteous and did his best to restrain himself during our conversation. He expressed his displeasure at what I had written, and said that I had come close to overstepping the line. When a Muslim—especially if he is a member of CAIR—tells a writer that he or she has come close to overstepping the line, his words, naturally, carry a veiled threat whose dangers can be understood only by those with an excellent command of Arabic and a profound understanding of Islam. After they heard what he said, a number of my loyal friends asked me to ease up and be patient, as things did not bode well.[9]

So even then, in the immediate aftermath of the 9/11 attacks, when the blood had not yet dried, the Islamic supremacists were marching over our dead. Their only concern was advancing their fallacious narrative of victimhood so that they could essentially have a free hand to victimize Americans again.

And so here we are, ten years later—ten years after it was raining bodies on 9/11, and we have Muslim footbaths in universities and airports. We have textbooks that read like a CAIR press release on Islamic history. We have Islamic anti-Semitism infecting the whole soul of the world. We have the mosqueing of the workplace and the public school. We have the United States Treasury Department giving seminars in Sharia finance.[10] We have a Muslim Brotherhood-linked Congressman.

Meanwhile, our universities and our college campuses have become hotbeds of Islamic fundamentalism. At such campuses, leading scholars and thinkers such as Ibn Warraq, Bat Ye'or, Robert Spencer, and David Horowitz (to name just a few) are not only not welcome, but the few courageous souls who invite them to speak are the object of scorn and derision, and have to provide a security apparatus rivaled only by the secret service. When Noam Chomsky, Daisy Khan, Imam Feisal Abdul Rauf, or Michael Moore speak at the same universities, you can be sure they don't need any security guards.

In her remarkable and essential book, *The Decline of Eastern Christianity Under Islam: From Jihad to Dhimmitude*, the historian Bat Ye'or analyzes what she describes as "the numerous processes that had transformed rich, powerful Christian civilizations into Islamic lands and their long-term effects, which had reduced native Christian majorities into scattered small religious minorities, now slowly disappearing." Those Christian civilizations were invaded by Islamic armies. We have to understand that while the invaders are using different means in the United States today, their goal is the same as the goal of Islamic jihadists throughout history: the Islamization of non-Muslim societies.

You may think it ridiculous that many Muslims are working toward this same goal in the United States today by means of the stealth jihad, and that Islam cannot insinuate itself into a dominant role in our society by such methods. But you need only to look at recent history and consider the inroads Islam has made since 9/11 into our government, law enforcement, educational system, financial system, and more—all by stealth jihad tactics, without suffering a single battlefield casualty.

This book will explain why what is happening is happening, and how you must fight it. Trust me, when you see a giant mosque going up on your tiny tree-lined street, where there are no churches and there are no synagogues and there are no businesses and there are no Muslims, it's no accident.

And there are ways you can fight back. Do it. Paraphrasing Ayn Rand: The question isn't who is going to let you; it's who is going to stop you.

CHAPTER I

THE AWAKENING

One dramatic series of events did more than anything else to awaken the American people to the reality of Islamization, and to the connection between the 9/11 attacks and the stealth jihad. That series of events revolved around the attempt by Islamic supremacists to erect a triumphal mosque upon the sacred site of the attack on the World Trade Center towers. And not coincidentally, the whole sorry spectacle of Muslims seeking an advantage from the attack upon the World Trade Center followed a well-established Islamic historical pattern.

In early December of 2009, the *New York Times*—on its front page—heralded the arrival of a fifteen-story mega-mosque going up at Ground Zero. It was shocking. I don't know what was more grotesque: the jihadists' triumphal mosque, or the *New York Times*' preening of it.

Yes, a triumphal mosque, built on the site of an Islamic victory, no less unmistakable than the Dome of the Rock and the Al-Aqsa mosques on the Temple Mount in Jerusalem, which assert the victory of Islam over Judaism. There are thousands of triumphal mosques marking the site of Islamic victories all over the Islamic world. The Ground Zero Mosque would be yet another.

The location was no accident because the imam Feisal Abdul Rauf, the cleric leading the project, said, "New York is the capital of the world, and this location close to 9/11 is iconic."[11] And even that was deceptive, because the building slated to be torn down to build the mega-mosque, the former Burlington Coat Factory at 45 Park Place, was partially destroyed on 9/11, when a piece of the landing gear from one of the planes that crashed into the World Trade Center towers crashed through its roof.

I was enraged, and blogged on it, as did several other counter-jihad blogs. The media virtually ignored it. As the months passed, the powers behind the Ground Zero mosque proceeded to host horse-and-pony shows for the clueless and complicit politicians and various puppets on lower Manhattan's Community Board One, which did not have to approve the project, but would serve the propaganda campaign of the stealth jihadists. When we got wind of the fact that the financial committee, a small subcommittee of Community Board One, had unanimously approved the project, we moved to action.

At my urging on AtlasShrugs.com, and on Jihad Watch, we called patriots and freedom lovers to attend the Community Board hearing scheduled to discuss the project. Hundreds showed up. Robert Spencer reported that:

> The atmosphere was rowdy, with tempers running high. The mosque proponents and the politicians were primarily responsible for this, as they immediately began to brand the opponents of the mosque initiative as racists and bigots. The local city councilwoman [Margaret Chin] characterized all opposition to the mosque as hatred and bigotry, and said that to support the mosque was simply a matter of tolerance and pluralism. Mosque proponents distributed a written statement from [Manhattan Borough President Scott] Stringer, favoring the mosque and saying: "I for one never want to see our country or our city abandon religious tolerance as the result of an act of violence, even one as unspeakable as the 9/11 attacks."[12]

Each person who wanted to address the Board had to fill out a form in order to speak. And on this form, the speakers had to give the topic of their remarks. So in order to be heard early on, I wrote "outreach" as the reason for my being there and wanting to speak. And sure enough, I was called third, after two speakers in favor of the mosque, and long before any other opponents of the mosque project were given an opportunity to say anything. Imagine that. But that's how they stack the deck. Here are my remarks at the Community Board meeting:

First, I'd like to say that it's interesting to me that the elected officials do not represent all of the people. Every elected official has one perspective. Also: Cordoba Initiative. It's important to remember that Cordoba is symbolic of the Islamic conquest of Spain, where Christians and Jews lived as dhimmis, where they lived under a sub-class status, and that is the message in the word "Cordoba." I want also to say that the opposition to the mosque is against bigotry, against racism, against Islamic anti-Semitism, and against kafirophobia. We, too, want outreach with the Muslim world. We, too, are sensitive to the sensibilities of the Muslim world. We ask that Muslims be sensitive to our sensibilities. This is an insult, this is demeaning, this is humiliating, that you would build a shrine to the very ideology that inspired the attacks of 9/11. We feel that an Islamic Center dedicated to the hundreds of millions of victims of over a millennium of jihadi wars, land appropriations, enslavements, and cultural annihilation would be more in order. An Islamic Center dedicated to expunging the Koran of its violent texts would be appropriate on the hallowed ground of 9/11. I encourage all infidels, kafirs, and non-Muslims to join me—and Muslims with a conscience—decent Americans on June 6 to protest the mega-mosque going up on sacred ground. Thank you.

The largely anti-Cordoba crowd cheered, as they did when 9/11 family members were eventually given the opportunity to speak. A black Coptic Christian priest from Egypt would blow the shofar when people asked for mercy from the mosque builders. But the fix was in. After the lopsided vote in favor of the mosque, printed remarks were distributed from Stringer congratulating the Board for its vote. How did he know how the Board would vote? Was the fix in from the start?

And the pushback began. So loud and fierce was the opposition that the media could no longer ignore the story—especially when thousands showed up at my AFDI/SIOA rally on D-Day, June 6, 2010, to protest the Ground Zero mosque. Free people came from Washington state, California, Texas, Ohio, Michigan, Pennsylvania, Connecticut, New Hampshire, Maine, South Carolina, Florida, and elsewhere. They were Christians, Jews, Hindus, Sikhs, Buddhists, atheists, Muslims of conscience. They were lovers of freedom. Police estimated that 5,000 people were there, and other estimates ranged as high as 10,000. The crowd carried signs expressing their love for freedom, their contempt for Sharia, and their anger at Islamic supremacism and the insult to the memories of those murdered on 9/11 that this mosque represents.

On September 11, 2010, even more people showed up for our second rally. The people came to be heard. And so the media favored the construction of a fifteen-story mega-mosque at Ground Zero and charged that those who opposed it were racists and bigots—a claim as absurd as their suggestion that the 70 percent of Americans who opposed the building of the mosque did so out of hatred of Muslims.

Media Coverage

The mainstream media began blaming me for the conflict, as if millions of Americans didn't know right from wrong and had no mind of their own. Salon said that "the controversy was kicked up and driven by Pamela Geller, a right-wing, viciously anti-Muslim, conspiracy-mongering blogger."[13] CNN blamed me also—as did Daisy Khan, Hamas-linked CAIR's Nihad Awad, and others. They consistently ignored the fact that the vast majority of Americans were against this mosque. Americans didn't want a victory mosque marking the site of the 9/11 attacks. They didn't want an insult to the 3,000 Americans who were murdered there by Islamic jihadists and for whom Ground Zero is a cemetery.

From the media's perspective, the Ground Zero mosque was an historical phenomenon. For the first time, a major news story became the most important national and international news story without the media. Think about that. The Ground Zero mosque was not shaped by the media, not covered by the media—not at first anyway. The media scrambled to cover the story. They had no narrative, at first. They would put me on and let me speak. Of course, they always had some Islamic supremacist liar on to destroy me, but they never could. And despite all the handicaps, I had the opportunity to present America with concretes on Islam.

FOX had me on with Hamas-linked Nihad Awad of CAIR and CNN had Ahmed Soliman debate me.[14] I got in the ring with Ibrahim Ramey on CNN, and again with Ramey on the Canadian Broadcasting Centre.[15] There were lefty apologists like Nicole Neroulias, faculty member of the Columbia School of Journalism, who got into the ring with me on *FOX and Friends*.[16]

Palestinian hip-hopper Will Youmans spewed pure fiction in our debate, and I also debated with Robert Salaam on RLTV and other hostile talking heads, including a nasty Bill O'Reilly (who *had* to have me on to refute a virtual fatwa, an incitement to violence that Nihad Awad of CAIR had issued on my head on his show the night before).[17] Joy Behar took her best shot (and missed), joined by Daisy Khan and Roy Sekoff, founding editor of the *Huffington Post*.[18] That panel was thus stacked with three mosque supporters against me alone, but even that was still not skewed enough for them.

I faced off against David Lane and Michael Gross, ACLU and civil rights lawyers who took their shots at me on *Hannity*.[19] And there were classic moments with Ibrahim Hooper of CAIR.[20] CNN's *Anderson Cooper 360* show went so far as to do a whole segment accusing me of ginning up the Ground Zero mosque controversy, saying that if it hadn't been for Geller, there would have been no issue (talk about condescending to the American people).[21]

There were skirmishes with Safaa Zarzour, Secretary *general* of the Muslim Brotherhood front the Islamic Society of North America, and Hussam Ayloush of the Muslim Brotherhood front CAIR-Los Angeles.[22] Not to mention a brisk brush with Michael Ghouse.[23] Across the pond I debated Shahed Amanullah on the BBC.[24] Geraldo did a hit piece on me.[25] I took on Malik Shabazz of the New Black Panthers.[26] I went head-to-head with whoremonger Bob Beckel and hate sponsor CAIR-Chicago's Ahmed Rehab.[27]

Each TV segment was like a short bout in the boxing ring. Every jab, every insult, every lie only strengthened my resolve. Every attack fine-tuned my argument. This is the approach you should adopt too. Never get discouraged. Take every experience, good, bad, or worse, and learn from it. It makes you stronger and smarter. Learn the enemy's strategy—beat him at his own nefarious game. It certainly toughened me up to the rough-and-tumble of this kind of fight. You have to get used to it, and you have to expect it. It will sharpen your abilities and your defense of freedom. Adversarial media treatment is not to be feared, but welcomed.

It is also instructive to contrast these battles to the kid-gloves, fawning treatment the media accorded to Feisal Abdul Rauf and Sharif El-Gamal of the Ground Zero mosque. Rauf even claimed credit for "training" a particularly compliant *New York Times* reporter.[28]

I was not deterred. Each appearance was "a teachable moment." And I was glad of it.

It was a unique opportunity for counter jihadists. Right after 9/11, the media didn't have its story straight either, and there were moments where you heard and saw things you would never hear or see now. The media was surprised and wasn't ready for that terrible act of war against America. But they dusted the human remains off their jackets and began to shape a suicidal narrative about how the West was ultimately responsible for the conflict. We have gone so far down the rabbit hole, 9/11 images are embargoed and not shown. They are dusted off but once a year and then secreted back into the vault of things the media won't talk about.

The dirty smear merchants over at Media [anti]Matters understood what was happening and issued a directive to the leftwing lemmings: "do not have Geller on national television."[29] The very same day that Goebbels-inspired post ran, Chris Matthews canceled my TV appearance for that evening.[30]

And the media, both left and right, has generally followed suit. They will only have me on if they have no choice. If I make news vis-a-vis a lawsuit or rally or some other newsmaking event and they are forced to, they do so reluctantly. If they can get my lawyer instead, they will because they have become so fearful of the truth.

Despite this, the left could not contain the story. The American people would not back down.

In the continuing Ground Zero mosque story, the media hoped the "opposition would just melt away" (to quote Matt Lauer in his puff piece on thug Ground Zero mosque developer El-Gamal). The media tried to play catch-up. They settled on the tired "racist–islamophobic–anti-muslim–bigot" narrative, but it didn't fit. The 9/11 families, like all Americans, were entitled to their pain and their grief. The *ummah* couldn't cry about sensitivity to Muslims when their leaders showed such callous heartlessness toward the pain and sensitivity of non-Muslims and Muslims of conscience. The more they tried to destroy the opposition, the more intolerant they looked.

The alphabet networks stayed out of it for as long as they could without looking completely out of touch. And when they finally weighed in, the heavyweights like *60 Minutes* shilled for Islamic supremacists, and consequently came under enormous fire from the American people, the blogs, and talk radio.

But a *20/20* episode was a turning point. They found their card, the *dawah* card. Dawah is Islamic proselytizing, and the media decided to proselytize for Islam. Dhimmi Diane Sawyer's show on Islam was a horrible lie. Overwhelmingly terrible. I don't imagine that even Hamas-linked CAIR would have dared to write such a fallacious and dangerous script filled with obvious lies.

ABC followed up the propaganda hour with Sunday morning's notorious stealth jihadist, Christiane Amanpour, whose obvious Jew-hatred and predilection for submission has become the hallmark of her embarrassing career. She did not disappoint. Amanpour framed and packaged this hot-button issue for Al-Jazeera audiences, not American ones. But America wasn't buying—Amanpour was bombing, dead last.[31] A very great sign of things to come.

The mosque story has been a game-changer. The media is now working on preaching Islam, spreading the historically inaccurate white-wash of Islam. That is how they are using their considerable power to disarm the American people against a mortal enemy that seeks our destruction. They ask, why are we fighting? That is the role the media has chosen, and it's no accident. Beware, America.

The bias was relentless. Tens of thousands attended the Rally of Remembrance for the 9/11 victims and against the Ground Zero mega-mosque on September 11, 2010. The crowd was so large, it stretched as far as the eye could see; you could not see the horizon from our stage. Yet AP reported that the pro-mosque counter-demonstration drew around a thousand "activists," while "a smaller group of opponents rallied nearby, chanting, 'USA, USA.'" The *New York Post* was only marginally more honest, numbering our rally attendees at 2,500: "The estimated 3,000 pro-mosque demonstrators outnumbered the mosque opponents by about 500."

New York 1 did a story on the rallies, but only showed footage of the small pro-mosque rally. The *Post* likewise only published pictures of the pro-mosque rally. AP ran an aerial photo of the rally, but one that was so poorly framed that one-third of it was dominated by a large gray building, and the crowd was cut off on the other side.

No one ran accurate photos of the rally, showing the full size of the crowd stretching beyond the horizon. Why didn't anyone think to take aerial shots of both rallies? That would have settled all questions. The pictures don't lie, but the media does. AP and the *Post* were not alone in their depiction of our rally and the pro-Islamic supremacist one as "dueling rallies." Their coverage of our immense rally versus the tiny counter-protest is dangerous and absurd.

The media operates under the narcissistic assumption that if they don't report it, it didn't happen. The Ground Zero mosque story has shattered this fundamental belief of theirs. The Ground Zero mosque story is the first news story of not only national but international proportions that emerged as the leading news story day after day, week after week, month after month, without the propulsion of the mainstream media. They scrambled to cover it late. They were playing catch-up, and then tried to force it, shape it, and destroy it.

The people were having none of it. The people drove that story. And they will continue to drive the story.

Why not a Ground Zero Mosque?

There were numerous reasons to oppose the mosque. First, there was Imam Feisal Abdul Rauf, the initial leader of the mosque effort, and still a member of the mosque initiative's Advisory Board. Rauf has such a sterling reputation as a moderate that both the Bush and Obama Administrations sent him on goodwill tours to Muslim countries. Yet it is clear that Rauf and other mosque leaders are not as moderate as they claim to be. Rauf has close ties to the Muslim Brotherhood, a group that is dedicated, in its own words, to "eliminating and destroying Western civilization from within," while those who claim he is moderate just keep telling us that he is without giving us evidence.

Rauf's book *What's Right with Islam* says on the copyright page that "This edition was made possible through a joint effort of the International Institute of Islamic Thought (IIIT) and the office of Interfaith and Community Alliance of the Islamic Society of North America (ISNA). Funding for this project was provided by IIIT." Both IIIT and ISNA are Muslim Brotherhood fronts, and ISNA was named an unindicted co-conspirator in the Holy Land Foundation Hamas terror funding case.

All of these groups have been identified as Threats to Freedom on AFDI's "Threats to Freedom" list.

The mosque organizers, the America Society for Muslim Advancement (ASMA), have worked hard in the media to portray themselves as Islamic moderates working for peace on the exact spot where their belligerent coreligionists perpetrated murder and mayhem in the name of their religion. They claimed that the Ground Zero Mosque would offer "the opposite statement to what happened on 9/11." Rauf has also said, "We need to take the 9/11 tragedy and turn it into something very positive."

Something positive? For whom? Islamic jihad? How does building a giant mosque at Ground Zero address the problem of moderate Muslims not speaking out against terrorism? How does this mosque honor those who were "harmed"—i.e., brutally murdered—on September 11? Whom does a mosque at 9/11 really honor: the Americans who lost their lives or the jihadis who murdered them?

Meanwhile, Rauf's words and deeds suggested a more ominous reality: he was a master of deceptive, Orwellian use of language, manifesting a deep contempt for non-Muslims and full accord with the supremacist goals of the 9/11 hijackers. Rauf's group gave this statement to Mike Huckabee's *Huckabee Report* radio show:

> For over a decade, the Cordoba Initiative and American Society for Muslim Advancement have worked tirelessly to build bridges with other faiths, while condemning violence, extremism, and prejudice of any sort. Our mission is to be a beacon of hope, peace, understanding and harmony to those who join us in condemning hatred and violence of any kind. Too often the question arises of why moderate, peace-loving Muslims do not speak out. We cannot think of a more wonderful expression of our religion than the Cordoba House, where American Muslims stand together with our fellow citizens to condemn extremism and terror. It is a project to honor those who were harmed on September 11th. It is a project to proclaim our patriotism to this country and to stand side-by-side all men and women of peace.

Orwell would be proud.

It's understandable that many have greeted such words with skepticism. Even the name of the initiative—Cordoba—spoke volumes. While Islamic Spain is held up today as a proto-multiculturalist paradise, in reality non-Muslims there suffered under the discrimination prescribed in Islamic law for dhimmis, non-believers who were subjugated as inferiors and denied equality of rights. When we started calling attention to the true meaning of the name Cordoba, the name of the mosque initiative suddenly changed to Park51—with the media lapdogs immediately falling into line. They never mentioned Cordoba again, just like that.

They ignored all the evidence of Rauf's jihadist sentiments. Rauf has blamed the West, rather than Islamic jihadists, for terrorism on several occasions. He has said, according to Australia's *Sun-Herald*, that "the U.S. and the West must acknowledge the harm they have done to Muslims before terrorism can end." He has also claimed that "Western active involvement in shaping the internal affairs of Islamic societies has contributed to the creation of terrorism done in the name of Islam."

In other words, stop fighting back. Let the jihadis do as they please.

Rauf has said, "We tend to forget, in the West, that the United States has more Muslim blood on its hands than al Qaida has on its hands of innocent non Muslims." Revealing his true beliefs, Rauf said on *60 Minutes* shortly after 9/11 that Osama bin Laden was "made in the USA," and that the United States was ultimately responsible for the jihad attacks of that day, because its foreign policy victimized Muslims.

The Arabic translation of Rauf's book is a call to conversion from the pile of human remains at Ground Zero, disturbingly entitled, *A Call to Prayer from the World Trade Center Rubble: Islamic Dawa in the Heart of Post-9/11 America*. In line with this revealing alternate title, Rauf has stated that he wants to bring people to convert to Islam by means of this Ground Zero mosque.[32]

Journalist Alyssa A. Lappen reports that "Rauf promoted the book in December 2007 at a Kuala Lumpur gathering of Hizb ut Tahrir—an organization banned in Germany since 2003, and also outlawed in Jordan, Syria, Lebanon, Egypt, Tunisia, Turkey, and Saudi Arabia, among other places—and ideologically akin to the Muslim Brotherhood (MB.) Both seek to replace the U.S. Constitution with Islamic law (sharia), and eventually impose Islam and sharia law worldwide."

In his book, Rauf supports and justifies Sharia law, and calls for restrictions on free speech in America. He has written another book that has gotten little notice: *Islam: A Sacred Law—What Every Muslim Should Know About Sharia*. In it he explains why God's law is superior to man-made law, or that is, why Sharia is better than democracy:

> God places a high premium on judging in accord with His dictates, and for developing a nation where laws apply to all equally, and where those who are in charge of upholding the law do not set themselves or any other group above the law—for them corruption sets in. The corruption of the individual or a society that abandons Sacred Law is amplified in one of the key Koranic passages regarding the relevance, evolution and meaning of Divine Law, (5:41–50) where Allah speaks frequently of the act of "judging." In this passage, God criticizes previous generations who "raced toward disbelief, among those who say with their mouths 'We believe' while their hearts done believe;" who "altered God's Words from their placements;" indicating somehow that they altered their divinely ordained Shari'ah, placing their own values above that which God had established. The Koran continues to describe them as "listeners of lies, devourers of ill-gotten property," an accusation that a Muslim tries carefully to avoid incurring.

This passage is based on a section of the Koran (5:41–50) that talks about "judging" peoples. It's clear from the context that the "previous generations" are Jews and Christians who have now become "listeners of lies, devourers of ill-gotten property." In other words, Rauf was condemning Jews and Christians in America and arguing obliquely that America should ditch the Constitution and adopt Sharia.

Rauf describes himself almost relentlessly as a "bridge builder." Muslim Brotherhood theorist Sayyid Qutb explains what bridge-building means to Islamic supremacists in his jihadist manifesto *Milestones*: "The chasm between Islam and *Jahiliyyah* is great, and a bridge is not to be built across it so that the people of the two sides may mix with each other, but rather only so that the people of *Jahiliyyah* may come over to Islam."[33]

Rauf has also called Archbishop of Canterbury Rowan Williams' endorsement of the implementation of Sharia courts in Britain "forward thinking"—despite Sharia's denial of basic freedoms including the freedom of speech, freedom of conscience, and equality of rights of all people before the law. He has called upon Barack Obama to emphasize "the commonality of Western and Islamic values," claiming that "if the United States lives up to the values in the Declaration of Independence, the Constitution, and the Bill of Rights, and if Muslims can live up to the principles of Islamic law, then we will find we have fewer points of conflict and more common ground." Then all will be well: "Muslims no longer will fear Western domination and the West no longer will fear Islamic expansion."[34]

Does Rauf really think that the devaluation of a woman's testimony and the institutionalized discrimination against non-Muslims, both mandated by Sharia, are really compatible with the Bill of Rights? Does he really think that stoning people to death for adultery or amputating their hands for theft are compatible with the Eighth Amendment's prohibition of cruel and unusual punishments?

Whatever he thinks of those elements of the Constitution, he doesn't appear overly fond of the freedom of speech. Rauf has compared the West unfavorably to the Islamic world, since the West "protects the right to say anything, no matter how insensitive or scandalous," while Islamic cultures "balance freedom of expression with respect for elders, traditions, and modesty. The idea of respect and honor to elders is deeply ingrained in their psyches."[35] He has criticized the Swiss ban on minarets as a restriction on religious freedom without saying a word about the severe restrictions on non-Muslim religious practice in Islamic states such as Saudi Arabia, Pakistan, Iran, and Sudan.

The morphing mosque narrative

Rauf and Daisy Khan were also repeatedly deceptive about whether the Ground Zero Mosque would be a mosque at all. Initially, the Cordoba Initiative's Web site stated forthrightly that it would be a mosque, and Daisy Khan said the same thing at the Community Board One meeting: "There are two hundred mosques in New York. Another one is not a big deal."[36] After the American people started to wake up to the implications of a mosque at Ground Zero, however, they began insisting that it was not a mosque, but a "community center."

It is worth noting that in the Muslim Brotherhood's document delineating its strategy for Islamizing the United States, it calls for the establishment of "centers" that will function in American cities after the fashion of Muhammad's base in Medina. From Medina, Muhammad conquered and Islamized the Arabian Peninsula.

Mosque organizers and the mainstream media were also deceptive about the location of the mosque at Ground Zero. While Rauf called the location "iconic" and Daisy Khan spoke of a divine hand leading them to a location at Ground Zero, Sharif El-Gamal, when confronted with pressure over the mosque's location and character as a triumphal mosque at Ground Zero, insisted that the "community center" would be "nowhere near" the World Trade Center site. One thing was obvious: the location was tremendously important to them, as they brushed aside numerous offers—from Donald Trump, New York Governor David Paterson, and others—to buy the property at far greater than market value, and move their mosque elsewhere.

The media also followed the twisting line of the Islamic supremacists regarding whether or not the project was a mosque at all. Ultimately, the Associated Press issued guidelines ordering its reporters not to refer to the project as the "Ground Zero mosque," saying falsely that it was neither at Ground Zero nor a mosque.[37] *The other mainstream media leaders fell into line accordingly.*

Rauf was a prominent member of the Perdana organization, a leading funder of the jihad flotilla launched against Israel in 2010 by the genocidal Islamic terror group, IHH.[38] And he was a slumlord. Despite numerous citations for fire, building, and health code violations and reports of vermin and rat and roach infestations, the Imam left his tenants to live in abject squalor and filth. He claimed he didn't have money to hire an exterminator, but he has the *jiyza* (tribute to be paid to the Muslims by infidels, as mandated by Islamic law) to build a $150 million Ground Zero triumphal mosque on hallowed ground?[39] Worse still, Rauf snagged over $2 million in public money to fix his apartments. He took the money, never did the renovations, and forced good people to live with vermin and dilapidation. He was also sued for mortgage fraud, settling the case in June 2008.[40]

Rauf told the American media that money for the mosque would come entirely from Muslims here. Then he told the Arab media that funding for the mosque was coming from many Muslim countries. Also telling was the fact that despite their much-repeated commitment to dialogue, Rauf, Daisy Khan, and Sharif El-Gamal ignored our invitation to conduct a public discussion with us about the mosque at the Conservative Political Action Conference in February 2011. This followed their ignoring my open letter of June 28, 2010, in which I wrote, "Imam Rauf, please withdraw this plan and show the world real understanding and kindness and empathy."[41]

This was no real surprise, however—contradicting all his stated aspirations for dialogue, Rauf told the Arabic press: "I do not believe in religious dialogue."[42] Rauf, Daisy Khan, and El-Gamal routinely demonized their opponents. Khan referred to my "Leaving Islam?" freedom bus ads as "deeply offensive," claiming that they were designed "to provoke" and "to polarize."[43]

Funny, that sounds like an apt description of the 9/11 mega-mosque. Daisy Khan made the argument against the mosque unknowingly.

Rudolph Giuliani remarked that the mosque "sends a particularly bad message, particularly (because) of the background of the imam who is supporting this. This is an Imam who has supported radical causes, who has not been forthright in condemning Islamic (terrorism) and the worst instincts that that brings about. So it not only is exactly the wrong place, right at ground zero, but it's a mosque supported by an imam who has a record of support for causes that were sympathetic with terrorism."[44]

Rauf even threatened America over this project, saying that if the mosque were not built, "if we don't do this right, anger will explode in the Muslim world....If we don't handle this crisis correctly, it could become something very dangerous indeed."[45]

There were numerous questions about the mosque project and its organizers that remain unanswered to this day. So anxious was Soho Properties, mosque developer Sharif El-Gamal's development company, to secure the location at Ground Zero that it bought the Burlington Coat Factory building for $4.85 million in cash, with part coming from Rauf's group, the Cordoba Initiative. El-Gamal, who up until only a few years ago was a waiter, has never explained where that money came from. El-Gamal is a thug who has been arrested several times and has said, "when you beat someone up physically, you get exercise and stress relief."[46] He is also a deadbeat. This man who plans to build a 150-million-dollar mosque was evicted from his office for non-payment of rent.[47] It also came to light in the summer of 2010 that he owed $224,270.77 in back property tax on the mosque site, and failed to pay its bills in January and July.[48] In October 2010, Valley National Bank sued him for an unpaid $95,778 loan, and in December 2010, Citibank sued him for an unpaid loan of $99,489.[49] Most outrageously, in August 2010 it was announced that the mosque was being considered for tax-free financing, and mosque organizers had the audacity to apply for $5 million in federal grant money earmarked for the post-9/11 rebuilding of lower Manhattan—nearly a third of the $17 million that is currently available for that purpose. Yet Daisy Khan declared, "we don't want to use taxpayers' money."[50]

These mega-mosques are making a supremacist statement. Most people assume they're just like synagogues or churches. They don't realize that Islam has political goals that are expressed through the mosques, and that the mosques often symbolize that Muslims are claiming a particular territory as their own. In Europe, the "no-go" areas for non-Muslims in France, Sweden, and elsewhere show what these claims lead to.

For the Muslim Brotherhood, mosques aren't just houses of worship. They're centers of political power, from which plans are made to increase that power in various ways. Veterans of Iraq and Afghanistan know this well.

When you hear Muslims speak of tolerance, you should understand that Islamic notions of "tolerance" arise out of Koran 9:29, where tolerance means that non-Muslims are to be tolerated only as those who submit to Islam as inferiors, without equality of rights with Muslims. Many oppose the Ground Zero mosque for just this reason. After all, we do know that this is what is taught in mosques that are designated "Islamic Centers"—the ones that some people ignorantly claim are not mosques. Certainly the Muslim Brotherhood in America's goals in outreach have nothing to do with successful outreach or achieving Western standards of tolerance, but rather with bringing over converts and getting us to subvert our way of life—primarily by working with them.

Is it really "racism" and "bigotry" to oppose the mega-mosque because of all this? Of course it isn't. It's just common sense—common sense and love for America.

One might think that the Muslim community would have been

capable of some sensitivity, considering how maniacally sensitive they are about any perceived insult to Islam. Every time there is a jihadist attack, which is happening with increasing frequency, the *ummah* (global Muslim community) starts wailing on us infidels about Muslim sensitivities and anticipatory and imaginary affronts and insults. Yet what could be more insulting and humiliating than a "mosquestrosity" in the shadow of what once was the greatest multicultural community center in the world: the World Trade Center buildings?

Imam Rauf and his wife and partner Daisy Khan, along with the Ground Zero mosque developer Sharif El-Gamal, said it was a mosque of healing. Yet Rauf, Khan, and El-Gamal cannot control the perception that Muslims worldwide will have of this mosque. That perception will be guided by Muslims' own cultural context. There are thousands of triumphal mosques all over the Islamic world, either converted from churches, synagogues, and Hindu temples, or built over churches, synagogues, and Hindu temples that were destroyed in jihad attacks.

These mosques are designed to mark Islam's victory over and superiority to the religions that Islam views as rivals. Everywhere jihad attacks have been successful, triumphal mosques have been established. The most famous are the Dome of the Rock and the Al-Aqsa Mosque on the Temple Mount in Jerusalem, and the Aya Sofya Mosque in Istanbul, formerly the Hagia Sophia Cathedral, which, for one thousand years, was the grandest church in the Christian world. Historian Sita Ram Goel has estimated that over two thousand mosques in India were built on the sites of Hindu temples.

There are, by contrast, no mosques of healing and reconciliation built at the site of previous jihad attacks in order to reach out to those targeted by these attacks. So when Muslims worldwide see the Ground Zero Mosque go up, they will view it in light of the victory mosques around them—and this victory mosque will embolden jihadists worldwide as no other victory mosque ever has.

The ex-Muslim human rights activist Wafa Sultan explained, "It is crucial to study the supremacist ideology of Islam and to recognize, for example, that the building of a mosque especially at Ground Zero is viewed by Muslims as a decisive victory over the infidels in Islam's march to establish its ultimate goal: the submission of all others to Islam and to Sharia Law."[51]

If this mosque really were about healing, why wouldn't the self-declared Muslim leaders build an Islamic Center dedicated to expunging the Koran and Sunnah of their prescribed violent teachings that inspired the attacks of 9/11? There have been over 17,000 Islamic jihad attacks since 9/11, each one with the imprimatur of a Muslim cleric. What is being done about this?

It should not be forgotten, moreover, that Ground Zero is a cemetery. For many of the 9/11 family members, it is the only place they can go to mourn their loved ones, whose remains in many cases have never been found. And remains are still being discovered: as late as June 2010, the remains of seventy-two victims of 9/11 were found at the World Trade Center site.[52] The Canadian government has restricted access to the site of the shipwrecked *S.S. Edmund Fitzgerald* on the grounds that it is a "watery grave."[53] Do 9/11 family members deserve no similar consideration? They must be confronted with the sight of a mosque teaching the same beliefs held by the 9/11 mass murders every time they visit the site of the deaths of their loved ones?

Sadly, New York City officials were avid to help the Ground Zero mosque organizers get their victory mosque built. They violated protocol in numerous ways to ram the mosque through in warp speed, removing every obstacle to expedite the process.

In July 2010, the city's Landmarks Commission denied landmark status for 45 Park Place, despite the fact that New York City has granted landmark status to the sites of far lesser loss of life, such as the location of the Triangle Shirtwaist Factory, where a disastrous fire occurred in 1911, killing 146 people. Refusing to wait until the entire board could meet, seven board members voted to deny landmark status to the Burlington Coat Factory building. The Lower Manhattan landmark commission unanimously (with one recusal) voted to recommend to the Landmarks Preservation Commission (LPC) that landmark status be denied. Although the Lower Manhattan Community Board actually favored landmark status decades ago, it was now disregarding the increased historical and cultural significance of the property.

This building has special historical significance because of 9/11. It was part of the attack. The landing gear from one of the planes that crashed into the World Trade Center towers fell onto the Burlington Coat Factory building, through the roof to the basement. The fact that the commission ignored that fact is outrageous and disrespects the victims of 9/11.

The stated basis for the decision was that the LPC had not recommended landmark status for other architecturally and aesthetically significant buildings in the neighborhood—which was patently untrue.

Compare, for example, two Lower Manhattan buildings: 45 Park Place, which is the Ground Zero mosque site, and 311 Broadway. Landmark status was granted to 311 Broadway in January 2010 by the Landmarks Preservation Commission. Bob Tierney, chairperson of the commission, said at the time: "It's one of the few remaining palazzo-style buildings on Broadway in Lower Manhattan."[54]

Yet both buildings are Italian Renaissance, palazzo-style architecture in the same neighborhood. Why was one granted landmark status and the other denied it?

Useful and politically corrupt idiots

That was a rhetorical question, of course. The answer was that the Landmarks Commission members were all appointees of New York Mayor Michael Bloomberg, who refused to meet opponents of the mosque, including family members of 9/11 victims, and allowed key decisions about the mosque to be decided on a week's notice in the middle of the summer.

At the very least, due process demanded that such decisions be delayed so that the community could have had a full opportunity to be heard. One phone call from the mayor's office could have gotten this vote tabled, so that the opponents of the mosque could have prepared the case for landmark status. Considering the sudden rush to schedule this all-important vote, it seemed a small accommodation.

The only thing worse than Bloomberg's pernicious callousness in his refusal to meet with the 9/11 families on this issue, was the media's silence. Where were those architectural elitist effetes at the *New York Times*, who took themselves and their expertise so seriously?

Bloomberg framed the mosque as a freedom of religion issue:

I think it's fair to say if somebody was going to try, on that piece of property, to build a church or a synagogue, nobody would be yelling and screaming. And the fact of the matter is that Muslims have a right to do it, too.... What is great about America and particularly New York is we welcome everybody, and if we are so afraid of something like this, what does that say about us?... If you are religious, you do not want the government picking religions, because what do you do the day they don't pick yours?[55]

To this, Sarah Palin made a pointed rejoinder: "This is nothing close to 'religious intolerance,' it's just common decency."[56] And while I agree that that the government should keep its nose out of religion, I also believe that if the mayor really believed government should stay out of it, he shouldn't have publicly taken one side.

But the mayor already had chosen sides before plans for this mosque became public. The *New York Daily News* reported in December 2010 that "Mayor Bloomberg's top deputies went to great lengths to help those trying to build a mosque at Ground Zero—even drafting a letter to the community board for them, newly released documents show. City Hall on Thursday released a flurry of emails between its brass and Feisal Abdul Rauf, the imam pushing to build a mosque near the sensitive site, and his supporters."[57]

It was worse than we imagined.

The release of these documents, emails, and various exchanges between Bloomberg's office and Rauf and his motley crew of Islamic supremacists showed evidence of collusion, inappropriate political support for the Ground Zero mega mosque, and favoritism given to the project.

The documents showed that Bloomberg's office went to extraordinary lengths for the radicals trying to build a mega mosque at Ground Zero—even writing a letter to the Community Board for them. Nazli Parvizi, the Commissioner of the Mayor's Community Affairs Unit, wrote to Julie Menin, Chairman of Manhattan's Community Board 1 while the Board was considering whether or not to approve the mosque project. Parvizi wrote a letter to be signed by Daisy Khan, asking the Board not to consider the mosque project—temporarily—because of the opposition to it. Parvizi explained, "What the letter will do, I hope, is get the media's attention off everyone's backs and give you guys time to regroup on your strategy as discussed…"

Was it any wonder that Rauf and his wife Daisy Khan were so confident at the hearings about whether the site should be designated a landmark? They knew the fix was in.[58]

On May 10, 2010, Daisy Khan emailed Fatima Shama, the Commissioner of the Mayor's Office of Immigrant Affairs. Khan asked Shama: "Is there a good time to chat tomorrow? We need some guidance on how to tackle the opposition." So the Mayor's office was even advising the Ground Zero Mosque opponents on how they should answer…us.

This collusion started early. As far back as September 2009, Shama exchanged emails with Rauf, el-Gamal, and Khan about the status of the mosque project.[59]

Why did the Mayor apparently break ethical rules for a slumlord with radical ties, whose buildings were placed in receivership in November? Judicial Watch filed Freedom of Information Act requests for the correspondence between Bloomberg's office and Rauf concerning the mosque months ago.[60] The Mayor failed to release these documents back in August. It took an additional six months to get Bloomberg to comply with this request.

Now we know why, and what he was hiding.

The emails between the Mayor's office and Rauf concerning the Ground Zero mosque showed that Bloomberg more than once colluded with Rauf and his gang to make sure the mosque project would sail through to get all the approval from various city offices that it needed.

Why did Bloomberg help the Cordoba Initiative write its letter to the New York City Landmarks Commission, altering and making suggestions and revisions to Rauf's original letter?

Why did the city intervene on behalf of Rauf to help him secure the permits from the building department for permission to assemble in a building that had been destroyed in the 9/11 attacks?

The dotty, irrational Mayor has shown no such favoritism towards the rebuilding of the ninety-six-year-old St. Nicholas church at Ground Zero.[61] Completely destroyed in the 9/11 attacks, it remains vanquished by Muslim terrorists, despite a ten-year battle by Church officials who have been frustrated by city officials again and again in their attempts to rebuild.

The revelation of Bloomberg's ethics violations and collusion with the Islamic supremacists of the Ground Zero mosque project ought to put an end to the Ground Zero mosque once and for all—as well as to Bloomberg's political career.

Another instance of the New York City government colluding with the mosque organizers was the Metropolitan Transportation Authority (MTA)'s refusal to allow SIOA's anti-mosque, pro-freedom ads on New York City buses. They said that the images of the burning World Trade Center towers that were part of the ad were offensive. As I said at the time, "what's more insulting and offensive—that image of truth, or a fifteen-story mega-mosque looking down on the sacred ground of Ground Zero?"[62]

The MTA backed off and allowed the ads when we threatened a lawsuit, but the episode illustrated two things: the city government's strong pro-mosque stance, and the necessity to keep fighting until attaining victory. The fact that we even had to fight this battle shows how threatened the freedom of speech is in the United States today, and how anxious authorities are to kowtow to Islamic supremacism.

And so with each outrageous revelation about the mosque organizers, we fought. We called attention to the mosque organizers' dishonesty. We galvanized the opposition to the mosque and used every means at our disposal to make our voice heard. And we were heard. The mosque remains wildly unpopular with the American people, despite relentless media propagandizing for it. And so by the spring of 2011, it was likely that the organizers would not make their initial goal of breaking ground for the mosque on September 11, 2011. And we would keep up the pressure to make sure that it would never be built at all.

The people were awake.

CHAPTER 2

ALL MOSQUES ARE
NOT CREATED EQUAL

A HANDY GUIDE TO FIGHTING THE MUSLIM BROTHERHOOD

A critical front in the Islamization of America, not hard to discern and not so hidden, is the establishment of *rabats* in cities and towns all over the nation—in quiet, innocuous small-town America. A *rabat*, in Islamic theology and history, is a fortified place, a kind of beachhead for the invasion and conquest of a non-Muslim land by the warriors of Islam. Going back to the time of Muhammad, Muslims have conducted raids on infidel lands, designed to "strike terror in the hearts of the enemies of Allah" (Koran 8:60). After the raids, the Muslims would build rabats in the newly conquered land, consisting of a mosque and a military training component. The most obvious modern-day rabat is the proposed Ground Zero Mosque.

The Prime Minister of Turkey, Recep Tayyip Erdogan, is often quoted as saying, "The mosques are our barracks, the domes our helmets, the minarets our bayonets, and the faithful our soldiers."[63] Make no mistake: mosques in America are no different.

September 11 was the Islamic jihadists' largest-scale raid thus far on the United States of America. And after it comes the rabat: the Ground Zero mosque. But there are also other mosques, other rabats, other beachheads, going up all across the country. These are almost invariably monster structures that are completely out of place with their surroundings architecturally, demographically, and in terms of zoning. These are very deliberate structures that are designed to expedite the advance of Islam into unsuspecting communities. In other words, the people won't know what hit them. Interestingly enough, however, even the least informed people are now waking up, because they see that their neighborhoods are changing in the blink of an eye.

Take, for example, journalist Sarah Honig, who wrote in the summer of 2008 about her experiences visiting an old high school friend in Brooklyn.[64] Her friend, she wrote, "still lives at the same Brooklyn address in the cozy middle-class neighborhood where I sometimes visited her way back then." However, "when I climbed up the grimy station stairs and surveyed the street, I suspected that some supernatural time-and-space warp had transported me to Islamabad….Women strode attired in hijabs and male passersby sported all manner of Muslim headgear and long flowing tunics."

This was not a benign demographic shift. Honig's friend flew a large American flag on her front lawn, and explained: "We're besieged. Making a statement is about all we can do. They aren't delighted to see our flag wave. This is enemy territory." Indeed: the imam of the local mosque was, up until the mid-1990s, the Saudi-financed Gulshair el-Shukrijumah, whose "disciple, Clement Rodney Hampton-El, an explosives specialist, possibly helped assemble the bomb detonated in the '93 World Trade Center attack. He was convicted of plotting to blow up the UN, FBI headquarters, and the Holland and Lincoln tunnels." What's more, "Gulshair acted as interpreter for Omar Abdel-Rahman, the 'Blind Sheikh' now serving life for the first WTC bombing, conspiring to use explosives at other NYC landmarks and colluding to assassinate U.S. politicians."

Honig also noted that her friend's "ex-neighbor is now a fugitive and subject of a worldwide FBI manhunt." And then there was the "in-your-face insolence of the immigrants," including the rooftop loudspeaker that the mosque used to call the faithful to prayer.

Honig's friend hastened to assure her that she was "not a bigot," but "the jihadists" weren't there "to coexist but to conquer….Muslims call us infidels and want all infidels out. We're threatened."

Nor was this a singular incident. Yet we have seen communities take action against these rabats in 2010, not only in Sheepshead Bay, Brooklyn, but also in Staten Island; Rutherford County, Murfreesboro, Tennessee; Sheboygan County, Wisconsin; and elsewhere.[65]

Murfreesboro, Tennessee, is just one of a growing list of medium-sized towns all over the country that in 2010 became the center of controversy over a large mosque planned for a residential area. Besides Murfreesboro, there were controversies over mega-mosques in two other towns in Tennessee as well, along with others in various towns and cities nationwide. They're separated by thousands of miles, but they share a common element: Muslims are building huge mega-mosques in communities with tiny Muslim populations—raising important questions about their funding and overall goals.

Citizens are rising up against these suspicious new structures, but often their opposition is unfocused and uninformed, making them easy prey for the inevitable charges of "racism," "bigotry" and "Islamophobia" that CAIR and the mainstream media always deploy in these situations. That's why it's important to know how to fight smart.

I've provided a step-by-step guide for folks across America who find themselves faced with a huge monster mosque proposal in their small towns. Here's how you should proceed.

1. Find out who and what the players are.

The vast majority of mosques are backed by groups that are linked to the Muslim Brotherhood, the group that is dedicated to "eliminating and destroying Western civilization from within."[67] Mosques with jihadist, terror ties must be fought fiercely and defeated. Look for connections to the Muslim American Society, the Islamic Society of North America (ISNA), the North American Islamic Trust (NAIT), which is the source of funding for numerous mosques around the country, the Islamic Circle of North America (ICNA), the Muslim Students Association (MSA), the Muslim Arab Youth Association (MAYA), the Islamic Association for Palestine (IAP), from which came the Council on American Islamic Relations (CAIR), the International Institute for Islamic Thought (IIIT), and other Brotherhood-linked groups. The dossier on the stealth jihadists at CAIR, ICNA, ISNA, MAS, etc., are in the evidence presented at the Holy Land terror trials. Check the group affiliations of the mosque organizers against the list of Brotherhood groups in the captured Muslim Brotherhood strategy document released during the Holy Land jihad charity trial.[67]

The Brotherhood memorandum contains "a list of our organizations and the organizations of our friends," including the Muslim organizations enumerated above or their parent groups.

Usually if the mosque in your area is linked to one or more of these groups, this is public and easily obtainable information, since despite their Brotherhood connections these groups are still regarded as "moderate" and wholly benign by most law enforcement and government officials. Nonetheless, if the mosque is indeed a Brotherhood-linked entity, notify local reporters, and persist. If they ignore the story, ask them why they're not following up on this link between the mosque organizers and the Brotherhood, the parent group of Hamas and Al-Qaeda.

If none of the groups behind your mosque are on the list, find out as much as you can about the groups that are involved: it is part of the Brotherhood's strategy in the United States to create a dizzying array of groups, so that organizational affiliations are obscured and links to unsavory groups and individuals be easily denied; however, often there is a great deal of personnel overlap between various Islamic groups, and so connections can be established. There may be no connection to Brotherhood groups, but don't assume there isn't because there is no obvious connection.

Also find out as much as you can about the mosque's imam and other leaders, if any. Often imams with "moderate" reputations are anything but. Take, for example, the Imam Anwar al-Awlaki. He was the go-to Muslim cleric for reporters scrambling to explain Islam after 9/11; yet it turned out that he was the same imam who guided the 9/11 Muslim attackers to commit jihad. Al-Awlaki was the "spiritual adviser" to three of the hijackers who attacked America on September 11, 2001. He guided the 9/11 jihadis, the Fort Hood jihadist Major Nidal Hasan, and Umar Farouk Abdulmutallab, the Christmas Ball bomber. He was the imam at the *respected* Dar al Hijreh mosque in northern Virginia while being the go-to Muslim for big media for information on Islam—and while aiding the 9/11 jihadists and Major Hasan. Exactly like how the un-indicted co-conspirator, Hamas-linked CAIR's leaders are the go-to guys for media now.

Imams matter. Al-Awlaki wasn't in Yemen when he was aiding the 9/11 jihadists. He was in Virginia. He was born in America. The problem here is not just immigrant Muslims, the problem is the doctrine of jihad and the ideology of Islamic supremacism, which any Muslim anywhere can hold.

Also, be sure to check out not just the organizers, but who is being brought in to speak. A mosque could have no discernible or public connections to the Brotherhood, but then bring in to speak someone like Siraj Wahhaj (a "potential unindicted co-conspirator" in the 1993 World Trade Center bombing case) or Ingrid Mattson (leader of the Hamas-linked Islamic Society of North America).

2. Check on the sources of their funding.

This information will most likely be harder to come by, and that should give you an opportunity to ask questions, and to ask the local media why they aren't asking questions. Most mosques in America are Saudi-funded and stocked with Islamic supremacist Saudi literature. Ask mosque leaders, if they aren't forthcoming about the sources of their funding, what they have to hide. Call for funding transparency. And if they admit to Saudi funding, ask them what assurances they can give the community that Saudi Wahhabi Islamic supremacism, with its contempt for non-Muslims and desire to subjugate them, will not be taught at the mosque.

3. Call for a full curriculum review, access to reading lists, etc.

The mosque and/or the Islamic school's curriculum, as well as its funding, should be transparent. As Ayn Rand said, "Honest people are never touchy about the matter of being trusted." The Mapping Sharia project found that three out of four mosques preach hate and incitement to violence—and that includes the last (chronologically) and most authoritative chapter of the Koran on jihad—chapter nine, "Repentance." This corroborates the testimony of the Muslim Sheikh Muhammad Hisham Kabbani before a State Department Open Forum in January 1999. Kabbani said that 80 percent of American mosques were controlled by "extremists." Also, the Center for Religious Freedom report in 2005 found that hatred of Jews and Christians, as well as Islamic supremacism, were extensively taught in American mosques.

Those are the only surveys of what mosques in America teach that anyone has ever undertaken, and they all agree. Supporters of mosque construction can't point to any competing studies that claim to show that mosques in America teach pluralism, free speech, love for non-Muslims, equality for women, etc. There aren't any.

The Islamic Saudi Academy (ISA) in Virginia used textbooks that called for jihad and labeled Jews apes and Christians pigs. The U.S. Commission on International Religious Freedom's report criticized ISA textbooks for stating that it was permissible for Muslims to kill converts from Islam and adulterers. The results of this teaching are obvious: former ISA valedictorian Ahmed Omar Abu Ali was convicted in federal court of joining Al-Qaeda and plotting to assassinate President George W. Bush. And former ISA student Mohammed El-Yacoubi was carrying a suicide note and was believed to be planning a suicide bombing attack in Israel.

And check out, for example, the proposed reading list that ties the sponsor of the proposed huge Tennessee Islamic facility to the Muslim Brotherhood. The Islamic Center of Murfreesboro (ICM)'s Web site claims that the organization "is not in any way associated or affiliated with any outside organization locally, nationally, internationally or any other way." However, the investigative Web site Global Muslim Brotherhood Daily Report has revealed that the Islamic Center of Murfreesboro's reading list betrays a decided taste for the Muslim Brotherhood perspective on Islam and contemporary politics (GMB = Global Muslim Brotherhood; USMB = U.S. Muslim Brotherhood). The Daily Report notes that the list recommends works by:

- Yusuf Al-Qaradawi (Global Muslim Brotherhood leader)

- Harun Yahya (Turkish "creationist" known for anti-Semitic writings and heavily promoted by the GMB)

- Ahmad Sakr (important figure in early history of the USMB)

- Jamal Badawi (USMB leader)

- Akbar Ahmed (Pakistani American close to USMB)

- Hassan Hathout (deceased leader of the Islamic Center of Southern CA with likely background in the Egyptian MB)

- Ahmad Von Denffer (German Muslim Brotherhood)

- Taha Jabir (likely Taha Al-Alwani International Institute of Islamic Thought (IIIT)

- John Esposito (Georgetown academic and longtime USMB supporter)

The Global Muslim Brotherhood Daily Report adds, "It should be noted that the ICM book list also features 'Silent No More,' the work of ex-Congressman Paul Findley, a long-time harsh critic of Israel and a supporter of the Council on American Islamic Relations (CAIR), an important part of the U.S. Muslim Brotherhood. Mr. Findley appeared at a 2006 press conference at the World Assembly of Muslim Youth (WAMY) headquarters in Saudia [sic] Arabia to support a CAIR initiative. The ICM also has reported that is [sic] sponsored a January 2009 protest against the Israeli 'war on Gaza.'"

Here is a case history of one battle: James Lafferty is an SIOA board member and chairman and founder of the Virginia Anti-Shariah Task Force (VAST), a loose-knit coalition of people committed to stopping the spread of Sharia in Virginia and America. He was an early warrior to the fight, a pioneer in activism against Islamic supremacism. He organized a grass roots fight the expansion of the Saudi-owned and operated Islamic Saudi Academy (ISA), an Islamic school in northern Virginia that taught hatred of Jews and Christians and the necessity to replace the Constitution with Sharia. And while they lost the fight by one vote, it was very early in the information war. Most Americans were unaware of the colonization going on right under their noses.

Lafferty's initiative to stop the expansion of the Islamic Saudi Academy succeeded because of the initiative and resourcefulness of VAST's members. The expansion of the radical ISA required the approval of the Fairfax County Board of Supervisors.

Lafferty explained:

> We were present at every hearing, no matter how small. At the first public information session, the Saudis turned out in force—their lawyers had lawyers. We set the tone for the debate however—how can you square the oath you took as public officials to "protect and defend" the Constitution of Virginia and the United States and then approve the operation and expansion of a madrassah which teaches and operates on Shariah principles? We broke all attendance records for the planning commission.
>
> We lost all of the recorded votes, but we won the war when the Saudis relented and dropped their plans to expand.[68]

VAST credits three elements for outlasting the Saudis:

1. Publicity—Every time there was any hearing or public event, we called the media. In our testimony we used vivid soundbites, which highlighted the criminal legacy of the ISA and challenged public officials to "keep your oath." The ISA hates publicity—even its school busses are marked "ISA" instead of spelling-out the school's name.

2. Confrontation—Unlike their liberal counterparts, anti-Sharia activists are typically polite, rarely "coloring outside the lines." VAST encouraged them to ask tough and accusatory questions during the hearings and take advantage of media coverage to make a point. When one official demanded during a public hearing to know the names of "cowardly politicians" referred to in a VAST flyer, audience members stood and shouted out the names of prominent politicians. The embarrassed official tried to stop the huge audience response with an "I've heard enough," but his name was also included in the long litany.

3. Unrelenting Opposition—"The fight isn't over until we stop fighting" was the principle that brought VAST members to every public discussion of the ISA expansion. Supportive county employees even tipped us when Saudi lawyers/officials performed routine tasks like applying for permits. A VAST member would soon appear.[69]

Lafferty added:

By the end of it, I am sure they were convinced that some of our members actually lived in the county building.

In the end, it has become a large-scale game of whack-a-mole. We stop them here in Fairfax County and they head south to Spotsylvania County or west to Loudon County. We are now a rapidly-expanding statewide group, helping other Virginians organize and develop effective grassroots tactics to stop the spread of Sharia.

It would be sadly ironic if Sharia triumphed in the land of Washington and Jefferson and the Constitution was discarded in favor of a cruel code that seeks to punish those who exercise freedom or liberty.[70]

4. Research zoning laws, parking laws, traffic laws, etc.

The best advice is to assemble a team in your neighborhood to start researching. While this is being done—play the bureaucrats' game. Check zoning, traffic codes, etc. If there is rezoning involved, fight it. If there are some changes to codes, fight them. Keep it tied up. Exhaust them. While the bureaucrat brigade is attacking that flank, research the people and the funding. Try to find pro bono lawyers in your town who understand the problem. If there are none who understand it, make a presentation to lawyers who will listen—giving them facts, not emotion.

At the end of the day, our government is only there to protect us. They steal the rest for their own political purpose, but the point, the goal, the reason for government is to protect our individual rights. Government = force, and if the Muslim Brotherhood intends to open a satellite HQ in your town or neck of the woods, it is up to the government, once presented with the facts, to protect its citizens from Islamic supremacists and jihadism. It could be up to you to present them with those facts. Be ready.

Fighting a Muslim Brotherhood Mosque—A Case Study

In June 2010, as the Muslim American Society, the Muslim Brotherhood's chief front and public face in the United States, prepared to buy a church and convent on Staten Island and convert them into a mosque, the local authorities scheduled a hearing to allow MAS representatives to answer questions from the community, which was growing increasingly concerned about the project. The impending sale of an empty, two-and-a-half story convent in Midland Beach owned by St. Margaret Mary's Roman Catholic Church had neighbors angry.

That same month, lay leadership and tea party leadership in Staten Island approached me, enlisting my support and aid in fighting this mosque. A large Staten Island constituency had come to our first Ground Zero mosque protest on D-Day, and they shared their concerns with me.

The community had long supported the convent, and much of the land had been donated to the church by a parishioner.

Activists Pamela Hall and Robert Spencer and I made our way to the meeting, where it was clear from the beginning that the fix was in.

The Muslim American Society had purchased a convent in what was called a "mystery sale." An underhanded deal had been made for the Church land to be sold to a developer, but then, in a mysterious and shady deal, the land was sold to the MAS. The Archdiocese of New York and the Rev. Keith Fennessy, St. Margaret Mary's pastor at the time of the sale, refused to attend the hearing, or to have anyone there representing the church. The Archdiocese had sold out the parishioners, without so much as basic, cursory recognition of how Christians have fared in Islamic countries—and to the oppressive, violent Brotherhood, no less.

The meeting was cut short when the Midland Beach Civic Association abruptly ended it, after they stopped people from asking questions and brought on shills and propagandists for MAS. The community was having none of it. Not after sitting through a half hour of proselytizing.

Community members took issue with the fact that this took up the speaking time of the residents who had waited patiently in line for their turn to speak, and were now summarily cut off.

I have attended a good deal of these charades and I have to say that the members of this community were the most informed group of concerned citizens I have ever come across. The Q&A was fascinating—every question well researched and educated. The MAS *taqiyya* masters could not snooker this crowd.

Robert Spencer spoke first. He asked the MAS representatives to explain their ties to the Muslim Brotherhood, to renounce its stated goal of "eliminating and destroying Western civilization from within," and to denounce Hamas and Hizballah as terrorist groups. They did none of these things; instead, they dodged and obfuscated. Spencer recounted:

> ...the Muslims began their presentation. They spoke in calm, measured tones. They spoke about their many years in the community, their children, their work (two were physical therapists, one a high school math teacher). They spoke, of course, of the need for "mutual respect." They spoke about the need for both sides to communicate and get to know each other better. They spoke about reassuring someone with a sentimental attachment to the convent building (many of those present had been educated by the nuns who lived there) by saying, "God will be praised in that building." They praised the Muslim American Society as an upstanding civic group with "50 chapters in 55 states across the nation" (yes, you read that right). They spoke of the MAS's commitment to establishing a virtuous and just American society. They denigrated Steve Emerson and his Investigative Project as Islamophobic and claimed that he purveyed falsehoods. When challenged later by an IPT official to name even one specific falsehood in the IPT report on the Muslim American Society and Muslim Brotherhood, one of the Muslim spokesmen said only, "Later on."
>
> I asked them if they were prepared to denounce Hamas and Hizballah, both of which were publicly endorsed by MAS leader Mahdi Bray, as jihad terrorist organizations, and to renounce any intention to bring Sharia to the U.S., in line with the Brotherhood's stated goal of "eliminating and destroying Western civilization from within and sabotaging its miserable house" so that Allah's religion is "made victorious over other religions." In response, the main spokesman for the three hemmed and hawed and emitted billows upon billows of airy nonsense—to the increasing impatience of the crowd. This spokesman, made nervous by the crowd's vocal disdain for his ever-lengthening non-answer, did ultimately call Hamas and Hizballah terrorist groups and renounce any intention to bring Sharia to the U.S. But since these positions are at odds with what are known to be the positions of the MAS, it seems likely that he was only saying this under pressure— otherwise he wouldn't have needed to offer so much empty and con-

descending verbiage to the crowd before getting around to the point.

The other questions were pointed, informed, and full of righteous indignation. Challenged about the MAS's leader, the unsavory Bray, the chief spokesman, a physical therapist named Ayman, called him a "civil rights activist." Challenged on whether he thought the people in the room were the Infidels that the Koran directs Muslims to wage war against, he told the questioner, "No, you are not an Infidel," and explained that the Koranic Infidels were only those who knew the truth and still rejected it. He did not mention, of course, that the Koran doesn't envision any other kind of Infidel, and that it has no conception of people who reject Islam in good faith.

Ayman defined jihad as the right of a nation to defend itself whenever it is oppressed and occupied—a definition large enough to drive a bomb-laden truck through, and that fact didn't elude the questioner, who further asked him whether that definition would indeed make Americans Infidels, because of the wars in Iraq and Afghanistan. He explained that no, he wouldn't be raising his five children here if he thought America was an Infidel. Another one of the Muslims on the dais insisted that Sharia was democratic and protected democracy. Once again, the glaring contradiction of all this with the words and deeds of the MAS leadership and the Brotherhood was left unexplained.

And so it went. Ultimately, one of the Muslim spokesmen, the other physical therapist, whose name was Muhammad, became firm. Asked if the MAS would prove the sensitivity to the community that the spokesmen were insisting they had by leaving the community, he said: "We are exercising our freedom of religion. We will not apologize for being Muslim. We will not apologize for being American."

Ringing words, but ultimately empty—ignoring, yet again, the aspect of Islam that is political, and that would subjugate women and non-Muslims and deny the freedom of speech and the freedom of conscience. And when they were challenged on such issues, the Muslim spokesmen retreated behind their clouds of rhetorical smoke.

Finally, when the local officials tried to stop the questions from the floor while there was still a long line of people waiting to be heard, and to bring on instead a couple of local dhimmis (including a Christian Arab minister in a clerical collar) to explain how wonderful their experience had been living next to the Muslims of another Staten Island mosque, the crowd had had enough of being railroaded and lied to, and wouldn't quiet down. The meeting was summarily ended, prematurely. But it mattered little. The fix was in from the start.

Nonetheless, this meeting exposed the MAS. It was no longer possible for the Archdiocese to justify the sale, and soon Church officials withdrew from their agreement to sell the church and convent to the MAS.

It was a victory that had been won by determined and informed Americans who were able to expose the lies and hypocrisy of the Islamic supremacists and their media shills.

CHAPTER 3

A PRIMER FOR PROTEST

We are at war. And the war of ideas is full on. We are fighting for our nation, for our values, and for the Constitutional principles of freedom that make America great. We are at war for the freedom of speech, the equality of rights of women, and the freedom of conscience—all of which are denied by Islamic law. We are at war, and CAIR and all the other Muslim Brotherhood proxies mean to win. We are in a war in the information battle-space. And all the bullets, bombs, and bloodshed come as a result of what happens in this war of ideas.

The global jihad declared war on America on September 11, 2001. The jihadis attacked you and me and our loved ones on 9/11. We lost moms and dads, sisters and brothers, husbands and wives, decent and fine people who merely went off to work. Children, old people, folks of every race, creed, and color who came to the World Trade Center, the largest multi-cultural community center in the world, were the unarmed victims of jihad. Were these doctors, lawyers, accountants, stockbrokers, fireman, transit workers, and secretaries our soldiers? Were they in uniform? No. But were they combatants in a war, albeit unknowingly? Yes. This is a war on the people, on the infidels who love freedom. This is our war. *We are the fighters.* And we must fight it not only in the battlefields of Iraq and Afghanistan, but in our cities and towns, in the media and the universities.

We must fight it because our leaders are not fighting it. The Obama election was the triumph of style over substance, collectivism over capitalism, statism over individualism, the moron over the informed. The stealth jihadists have cover to advance more than ever.

Each and every one of us is a general in this war. Think like one. Protests and rallies are very effective public awareness weapons against the dark forces of jihad. If you are protesting against the building of a mosque in your area, or any other Islamic supremacist initiative, be righteous, set the example, and do not play into the hands of the enemy. Do not give the enemy ammunition.

Because we are at war, your approach to life must change. Every day when you wake up and throw your legs over the bed and wipe the sleep from your eyes, ask yourself, "What am I going to do today to save the Republic? What can I do today in the defense of freedom?" And plan. First learn everything, then educate those around you. Create networks of people in your neighborhood.

You are the freedom cop on the beat in your neighborhood. Where you see freedom threatened, fight back. If Sharia law is being introduced in the court room, if your kid's schoolbooks whitewash bloody Islamic history, if a mega-mosque is going up in a place not zoned for such things and the supremacists need laws changed to accommodate them, fight back. I will help you.

Get behind candidates who understand the threat. There are patriots of courage who will fight this on the Hill. Volunteer for candidates such as Ilario Pantano in North Carolina, Laurie Pettengill in New Hampshire, and so many others who are sounding the alarm about Sharia.

Even in your social activities—try to fuse your work with your leisure activities. Instead of going to a movie, go hear a scholar or activist on Islamic supremacism speak. Form a group, and try to bring people to your area to speak to your group—people like me, Robert Spencer, and Wafa Sultan. Instead of that card game, protest an antiwar rally. Instead of a tennis game, march against the Million Muslim March in Washington, D.C. You will meet like-minded people whom you'll enjoy talking to and being with, while increasing your reach and expanding your own personal network.

Stage your own events. Don't worry if you only have twenty people there. Take pictures of your event and send them to pamelageller@gmail.com; I will cover it and give the story legs. If you hold a protest and your local news station prints propaganda and lies about it, protest the station. Join SIOA on Facebook. Work with us.

What to do

1.   Be proud and unabashed in your love of country.

2.   Know your Constitution and read *The Federalist Papers*.

3.   Read anything by Ayn Rand that you can get your hands on.

4.   Never back down or be cowed by the liars, destroyers, and radicals.

5.   Always carry an American flag. This is what you are fighting to defend, and it should always have a prized and central place in all your demonstrations and protests.

6.   Focus on the links that the Islamic supremacists who are organizing the initiative that you are protesting almost certainly have to the Muslim Brotherhood, an organization dedicated to "eliminating and destroying Western civilization from within." Most mosques in the United States have some Brotherhood links.

7.   Carry signs with the pictures of mosque leaders and organizers, detailing their ties to jihad killers.

8.   Focus on the organizers of the local mosque, or whatever you're protesting, in their refusal to condemn jihad terror groups, as they almost certainly will. Focus on the fact that they never challenge the jihadists or the ideology that inspires these acts of Islamic supremacism and expansionism in America, the West, and around the world. Focus on their funding, which will almost certainly be questionable. Focus, in short, on the facts, not on emotional or angry appeals or attacks that CAIR will use to shift the focus away from Islamic supremacism and jihad, and onto Muslims as the supposed victims of "bigotry." Remove infiltrators and

plants from your protests—those whose aim is to make you look bad.

9. Be wherever your opponents are. Mosque organizers will probably have to approach zoning boards, building permit committees, and the like. If you are protesting against a mosque, make an effort to show up at any and every public hearing where the mosque issue is raised in whatever context. Be ready to counter their deceptive explanations of who they are and what they plan with verifiable facts about their ties to Islamic supremacist and jihad groups and individuals. Be sure to be unfailingly polite, courteous, and respectful at these meetings, and make no assertions that cannot be verified.

10. Gain access to and study all public documents associated with every mosque project or other Islamic supremacist initiative. There is a wealth of information to be gained on just exactly who is involved in real estate transactions, and almost all of it is public record.

The recorder of the county, the auditor, or the relevant officer in your locality will have sale documents. Trace the lines of title/ownership in order to discover exactly how the property involved has been acquired, and by whom. The county tax assessors will have legal descriptions of the property and other pertinent material. Other county agencies will have information on zoning, and any recorded restrictions upon the use of the land that predecessors in interest may have placed upon it. For instance, in subdivisions and the like, restrictive reciprocal easements and conditions on the use of the land may be in place which make a requested land use prohibited, and these restrictions may be being ignored by mosque organizers and clueless and/or complicit local authorities.

Pay attention to whom is doing the legal work for the Islamic supremacists. If a transaction is complicated, or if it comes before a zoning board, this can often be quite revealing. For instance, Obama benefactor and radical Black Muslim activist Khalid Al Mansour is reputed to advance a great deal of legal work for Wahhabi interests working out of Saudi Arabia. The connection of such a person to a local mosque or other Islamic supremacist initiative can do a great deal to explode the enterprise's "moderate" pretensions and reveal its true agenda.

Another example is the lawyer for the Muslim Brotherhood group that in 2010 began attempting to build an illegal mega-mosque structure (a *rabat*) on a quiet, tree-lined street in Sheepshead Bay in Brooklyn (a street with no churches or synagogues or businesses). Their lawyer was Lamis Deek of the radical organization Al-Awda. Al Awda has been named one of the top ten anti-Israel groups in the country, and made the initial list of Threats to Freedom groups compiled by the American Freedom Defense Initiative.

Al-Awda is relentlessly anti-Israel, and spreads Palestinian propaganda about alleged Israeli crimes, as well as about its history. Al-Awda's slogan is "No Return = No Peace," which shows that it is not interested in compromise or peaceful coexistence, but in the destruction of Israel by the influx of millions of Palestinian "refugees." It has even declared that "the inalienable rights of refugees and displaced people cannot be left to 'negotiations' between Israel and the Palestinian Authority. International law considers agreements between a military occupier and the occupied to be null and void if they deprive civilians of recognized human rights including the rights to repatriation and restitution."

Its logo depicts a key over the map of the whole of Israel, suggesting that it wants all of Israel for a new Palestinian state. It also once featured statements from the now-dead leader of the jihad terror group Hamas, Sheikh Ahmed Yassin on its Web site.

Al-Awda has made numerous other radical, extreme statements, accusing Israel of "massive state terrorism" and of carrying out a "systematic policy of ethnic cleansing"; expressing support for the bloody Palestinian intifada against Israel; and demanding the release of imprisoned jihad terrorists (whom it terms "political prisoners").

Lamis Deek, whom the Muslims in Sheepshead Bay chose as their lawyer, was affiliated with Al-Awda, and was not distant from all this. On videos posted to YouTube, she advocates for the annihilation of the Jewish State. She speaks of a "democratic Muslim state in place of Israel—equal rights for all." She speaks about full equality; yet in what Muslim country is there full equality for non-Muslims? None. And she says that the Jews are welcome to stay in a Palestinian state contingent upon "full dismantlement of all Zionist structures, all Zionist laws, all Zionist institutions." She speaks of Jewish supremacy in a country (Israel) where all people of all races and religions live free in the only democratic society in the Middle

East. Islamic law in the fifty-six Muslim countries in the world is the most extreme racist, misogynistic, and intolerant legal system in the world. And this is the lawyer the Muslims in Sheepshead Bay hired to make their case.

Focus on the players and expose them. Do the homework and send your findings to SIOA, Atlas Shrugs, and Jihad Watch, and we will get your word out.

11. Study all the applications that the Islamic supremacists have filed in connection with their project. In building permit applications, applications for variances, applications for conditions of use, etc., there will be legal work and architectural plans. Look at the letterheads of all paperwork that has been filed; watch for well-known Islamic supremacist groups and jihad terror fronts. Study the names of the architectural firms involved, and research whether they have or have had any connections with Saudi-financed and/or Wahhabi or Muslim Brotherhood-linked entities. Gain access to architectural plans, zoning considerations and the like, and compare them to the considerations and accommodations that ordinary citizens can generally obtain.

Gain access to copies of real estate contracts or other documents of conveyance, which may or may not (but usually do) give a fairly good idea of who is involved in conveying or transferring property.

If possible, hire a lawyer or a law firm with experience in these sorts of things, who knows how to research these matters. Find someone with ties to the real estate trade who can get access to title abstracts, title insurance policies, and histories of the abstracts as compiled by attorneys. There are people in your community who have the skills and expertise to help you. Find them. Don't just hire any lawyer. Find those sympathetic to the cause and who understand what is at stake.

In some states, title companies "read the title" and issue opinions on the title history, and whether the sale can deliver a fee interest free of lien or encumbrance. They issue title insurance policies that say whether or not the seller can deliver the fee/ownership interest he purports to be able to deliver, free of defect. In other states, particularly in the Midwest and New England, lawyers specialize in reading title histories back to the origin of title in the property, for the same purpose. They issue opinion letters as to whether the seller can deliver title/ownership/fee free of encumbrance or lien. Make sure the Islamic supremacists have not been granted special favors in cutting corners on these points.

Send what you find to SIOA; we have begun compiling a registry of dossiers and background sheets on all this kind of information for the use of freedom fighters facing Islamic supremacists all over the country. As time goes by and we augment this resource, it will become ever more useful in the cause of freedom.

12. Get appointments with legislators who are involved in making concessions to Sharia and accommodating Islamic supremacist demands. Point out that granting such demands—for Islamic prayer in public schools, or halal food or footbaths in public facilities, or the like—violates the Establishment Clause of the Constitution. Point out that such concessions violate our basic American concepts of religious freedom, particularly the First Amendment's stipulation that "Congress shall make no law respecting an establishment of religion." Remind the legislators that they would never think of providing such accommodations for Catholics or Jews or Presbyterians or anyone else.

13. Never allow yourself to be physically or intellectually intimidated. Never back down. On matters of principle, never give an inch. Square your shoulders, put your chin up, look 'em in the eyes, and let them know that you will not be cowed, and will never give up and never give in.

14. Again, join Stop Islamization of America. Join on Facebook and subscribe at SIOAOnline.com. We will keep you informed on pro-freedom initiatives and give you ongoing tips on how to fight the battle for freedom in your own area and in your own way.

What not to do

1. *Do not carry inflammatory signs or allow them to be displayed at your rally.* Watch out for signs that bear ethnic slurs, or that call for mass-deportation or imprisonment of Muslims. These are not things that anyone involved in your protest should be supporting anyway; pro-freedom protesters should never let their emotions, frustration, and righteous anger get the better of their common sense. And it is unlikely that freedom fighters would really bring such signs to a rally against the construction of a mosque or the spread of Sharia. People on our side know that we are fighting against Islamization because Islamic law contravenes American freedoms in numerous particulars. Such signs at your protests could therefore be evidence of Leftist/Islamic supremacist infiltration. Move quickly against them: have security personnel on hand and ready to escort people with such signs away from the protest area, if possible. If this cannot be done, then be ready with signs saying "NOT WITH US" with an arrow pointing to the protesters with inflammatory signs. Have people with such signs stay by the inflammatory protesters at all times, so that the predatory press cannot capture a picture of the offensive sign without the disclaimer sign.

2. *Do not bring dogs, or pigs, or pork chops, or other things that Muslims find offensive to the mosque site.* It may be tempting to taunt the opposition; in fact, it is an American tradition at protests. But it is wiser and more effective to stick to the facts. Be righteous. Ask yourself, how will the media and the Islamic supremacists frame this? Will the way they frame it be convincing enough to Americans who are less well-informed and are on the fence about these issues so as to turn them away from our cause? We want others to feel good about joining us, and the shill media and Islamic supremacists have done everything they can do to smear the movement (much like they tried to do with the tea parties). That is deliberate; they want people to be afraid of being tainted. Don't give them ammo.

3. *Do not say things or chant slogans that can be construed as racist or inciting to violence.* This can be a fine line, since the leftist mainstream media considers virtually any protest against Islamic supremacism in all its various manifestations to be hateful and inciting of an anti-Muslim "backlash." But use your common sense: don't say anything that contradicts your own most cherished beliefs and principles. Remember always that you are fighting for human rights and human dignity. This doesn't mean that we say, or that we believe, that we hate Muslims or want to kill all Muslims—contrary to the mainstream media's caricature of our position.

First, learn everything. Understand the battle. We are not at war with Muslims, we're at war with an ideology. Just as we weren't at war with Germans during World War II; we were at war with National Socialism. Once the Nazi government was gone, we began helping Germany get back on its feet. If Muslims sincerely and genuinely renounce jihad, Islamic supremacism, the oppression of women, and the rest of the elements of Islam that contradict American freedoms, we have no problem with them. It bears pointing out that Muslims should be fighting these very same things as well. They should be fiercely opposing the ethnic cleansing of non-Muslims in Muslim countries. They should be fiercely opposing the oppression and subjugation of women in Muslim societies. Yet where are the Muslim groups on these issues? Their silence is telling.

4.   *Do not taunt the Muslims who may be demonstrating in opposition to you.* Do not make fun of them, particularly if they are praying. Do not try to give them literature or to throw things (pamphlets, crosses, etc.) in their direction or at their feet as they pray. Remember again that the mainstream media is predatory, and hates you. Reporters will be looking for anything they can use to frame Muslims as innocent victims and the people at your demonstration as ignorant, racist, redneck yahoos. Even if you are provoked and taunted by the other side, do not respond in kind: remember that even if you are simply responding to insults from the opposition, the media will show only one side of the story, and almost certainly depict you in a negative light.

5.   *Do not build your case on the claim that Islam is not a religion.* This has been tried and has failed; when opponents of a mega-mosque in Murfreesboro, Tennessee, claimed this as part of their case against the mosque, the Obama Federal Government actually intervened to insist that Islam was indeed a religion, and was consequently entitled to First Amendment protections. The media ridiculed the claim, pointing to Islam's mandated prayers and its holy book as just a few of the religious elements of Islam that the Murfreesboro mosque opponents supposedly missed.

It is understandable, however, why people would want to make this claim: when Americans think of religion, we think of a system of beliefs that teaches the love of God and the need to be benevolent and kind to all human beings, not of a program for dominance and the subjugation and oppression of women and unbelievers. Islam has no golden rule. No do unto others as you would have them to do unto you—not when it comes to non-Muslims.

Islam has and has always had a political component that has no parallel in other religions; while Muslims believe that Sharia is the law of Allah, even medieval Christianity at its most politically involved never believed that every law in a given Christian state was divinely ordained. Islam is certainly a political system and not just a religious one; however, insofar as it claims to relate human beings to the divine, it is a religion, whatever else it may be at the same time. Islam is a complete system that encompasses all aspects of life—religious, political, cultural, social, dietary, and financial.

To do all this is not kowtowing to Islamic sensibilities. This is fighting to win.

Also, refrain from proselytizing, unless the point of your event is to try to convert Muslims to Christianity or some other faith. Remember that there are many people of many different perspectives who are threatened by Islamization: not just Christians, but also Jews, Hindus, Buddhists, atheists, and even the people on the left who are busy enabling the advance of the ideology that is more likely to destroy them than any other. Do not risk alienating people on your own side who may not wish to attend future rallies with you if you give them a narrow sectarian focus or a religious objective: If the purpose of your event is to fight for the defense of American Constitutional freedoms against Islamic supremacism, then avoid giving the impression that you have some other agenda.

Our fight belongs to all freedom-lovers.

Preparing to meet the media

When a mainstream media reporter contacts you, keep his or her name. Begin to assemble a list of media contacts. It doesn't matter how hostile these reporters may be to our cause; they need you, and for the moment, you need them.

Whenever you are planning an event, assemble a good press release. Keep it short and to the point, keeping in mind the five w's of good journalism: who, what, when, where, and why. Send it to your list of contacts, and to any other lists that may be available to you. If you have the funds and the event is important enough, send out your press release to local or even national media outlets.

Focus in general on building personal relations with reporters and assignment editors. Then, when you have sent them your press release, make an effort to reach them on the phone, or at least via email, and follow up on your release. Ask them to cover your event and stress to them why it is so important that they do so.

The media is never going to present this argument in a fair or unbiased way. So you're never going to be happy with the tone or the slant. But if a quote from you gets into their story on your event or on the issue in general, you have achieved a huge victory. Even if the news story is slanted against you, many of the people who are reading it think just the way you do, and when they see what you have to say, they will know they're not alone. Some will even join your cause, and your ranks will increase.

Talking to the media

When talking to the media, remember that these predators love to talk to people who are green, who have never done it before. Take every possible step that you can before your rally to make sure that those participating on your side are as well informed as possible.

Develop talking points and stick to them. Do not allow the media to control or direct your remarks. Focus on your top priorities. If you are participating in a rally and don't know the organizers, take some time to inform yourself as much as possible about the issue at hand, getting your talking points off AtlasShrugs.com or JihadWatch.org. Contact the organizers of your event and get as much information as you can.

If you are approached by a member of the mainstream media, bear in mind that these people are your enemy, however friendly, sympathetic, and reasonable they may appear to be. Many times they use a friendly or sympathetic tone to disarm you. The mainstream media is tilted far to the left and is wholly compromised by Islamic supremacists. The media is the enemy. They're aligned with the terror force. When it comes to the war in the information battlespace, the deck is stacked against freedom-loving people.

But so what? That's war. All is fair in love and jihad. Whining about it and complaining about it is a waste of valuable energy; instead, turn it around on them. Use them. The mental image that you should conjure up when you're approaching a media opportunity, whether it's a newspaper interview or one on the radio or television, is that of a boxing ring. You may get two rounds to cinch your victory: thirty seconds apiece. You have to get your head shots in as quickly and cleanly as you possibly can. At the same time, you must do your level best not to give them something that is clippable, that they will use against the rally and the pro-freedom movement in general.

Don't use the word *hate*—don't say "I hate" anything because they'll clip it. You don't hate, you love. You love freedom, you love America, you love the Constitution, you love the Bill of Rights. In reality, of course, there is nothing wrong with hating evil. There is nothing wrong with hating violence against innocent people. There is nothing wrong with hating the brutalization of women, or honor killings, or clitorectomies, or the death penalty for people who exercise their freedom of conscience and decide to leave Islam. But remember that the media establishment and the left are trying to portray our movement in defense of freedom as one motivated by "hate." Don't hand them a weapon they can use against you.

The reporter will try to trick you and trap you into saying something that you don't mean. Focus on getting your points in and formulate five basic points in your mind before you attend any rally, and be ready with them if you're questioned by the media. These can include that you are fighting to preserve the Constitution and help ensure that there is no Sharia in America. No Muslim Brotherhood infiltrators in senior levels of the government. No mosque at Ground Zero. No mosque in the public school system. No mosque in the workplace. No taxpayer dollars for Sharia finance. End Islamic anti-Semitism. Support Israel.

You're fighting so that America will stay the Land of the Free and the Home of the Brave for everybody—particularly for Muslims who are running away from the Sharia. You are fighting the lies and the deception, and giving a voice to the voiceless.

Remember: whatever you say, they're going to try to make it look bad. Speak candidly about Islamic supremacism, without mitigating or watering down your message. Winston Churchill said, "If you have an important point to make, don't try to be subtle or clever. Use a pile driver. Hit the point once. Then come back and hit it again. Then hit it a third time—a tremendous whack."

But give them as little ammo as possible. Always stay on point. Separation of mosque and state. We don't care if you worship a stone, just don't stone us with it. Their objective is to get you off point; your objective is to make your point. Do not fight in public with those on your own side, no matter how vigorously you may disagree with them. It only gives your enemies ammunition, and perception is everything.

Don't rely solely on the mainstream media, either. Educate your neighbors. Communicate with your lists, your church groups, and your reading groups. Make sure you send news articles around to your friends and neighbors—even to those who don't want to hear the truth. Speak to the butcher, the baker, and the candlestick maker. Do not be cowed. Do not be silenced. This is a war in the information battlespace. And this is the age of the alternative media. Become your own one-person media organization. Your email lists. Your forums. Your chat rooms. Social networks. Set up screenings in your living room of *The Ground Zero Mosque: Second Wave of the 9/11 Attacks*. Serve martinis. Make it a happening. You are a guardian of the Republic. Fight to win. And smile while doing it.

Some people favor writing letters to the editor, but this is actually a fruitless effort. Begging the "enemedia" to run your letter is a waste of your valuable time. Post to blogs. Build up the new media. Build up the alternative media. Send material from the new blogs around, not material from the *Washington Post*. Expedite the death of the dinosaur media. Don't stop talking. Never stop asking questions.

Ask why the country's leading imams, such as the Imam Feisal Abdul Rauf, are attacking the defenders of freedom, not the jihadis. Ask why the Imam Rauf, CAIR's Ibrahim Hooper, and other Muslim spokesmen in America never stop complaining about counter-jihadists but are not standing against jihad. In other words, force the narrative. Fight on your own terms. State the truth uncompromisingly, countering the media lies, and stand by it until the narrative changes in your favor. We did it with the Ground Zero mosque. Why can't we do it to save the country?

The pushback

Not unexpectedly, as American citizens start to take a stand against the new proliferation of *rabats* in communities all over the nation, the Hamas-linked Muslim Brotherhood front CAIR is ratcheting up its offensive on patriotic Americans who dare to challenge Islamic supremacism and the creeping Sharia (Islamic law) into secular American life.

In August 2010, CAIR published an Action Alert entitled "Action: Report Harassment by Anti-Mosque Protesters." In it, CAIR (which the Justice Department named an unindicted co-conspirator in the Holy Land Foundation jihad terror funding case in 2007) calls on Muslims in the United States to "report any harassment of worshippers attending Jummah prayers tomorrow and throughout the month of Ramadan."

CAIR was using the methods of Josef Goebbels, Hitler's propaganda minister, to construct false narratives and bogeymen. In reality, there was no harassment of worshippers at mosques anywhere in the country during Ramadan or at any other time.

This Action Alert was all part of CAIR's attempt to fabricate yet again a narrative of victimhood regarding Muslims in the United States. In fact, it is the Islamic machine of which CAIR is a foremost part that relentlessly smears, demonizes, attacks, and attempts to destroy those who are fighting for basic human rights for all.

The Alert claimed that there has been "general Islamophobic hysteria generated in recent months by anti-mosque and anti-Islam extremists" and noted that "on September 11, extremist groups plan to hold a rally in New York in opposition to a planned Muslim community center in that city. The keynote speaker at the rally will be anti-Islam extremist Dutch politician Geert Wilders." (Wilders was actually among a number of prominent speakers, including former U.S. Ambassador to the United Nations John Bolton, journalist Andrew Breitbart, 9/11 family members, and others.) CAIR also referred to protests against mosques taking place in Texas, California, and elsewhere.

The vicious CAIR operatives also warned Muslims about harassment at anti-mosque protests. The Hamas-linked group told its minions to be alert and contact police and CAIR itself "if protesters go beyond the constitutionally-protected right to free speech in a public area—for example, if protesters trespass on mosque property or physically harass worshippers."

This was yet another lie. This kind of thing does not happen at anti-mosque protests. The only protesters who are ever harassed, victimized, or physically assaulted are supporters of Israel, who have been brutalized many times at pro-Israel rallies. There is plenty of evidence and documentation of that.

What's more, we have witnessed a number of "recent attacks on mosques" that turned out to have been perpetrated by Muslims.[71]

Nonetheless, freedom activists should be on guard. You should also regard this smear campaign as a call to action. CAIR directs Muslims to "take video and still photographs of the protest and send to CAIR." Why? Because they want to catch someone doing or saying something that they consider offensive, or holding a sign that they can use to defame the entire protest as "racist," "bigoted," "extremist," and the like.

Remember: as soon as you hit the street, you hit the stage. Act accordingly. Act as if there is a television camera on you at all times. The media is looking for that one moment, that one shot when your guard is down, in order to paint the entire rally with one brush. Do not get sucked in. You represent the family—the American family. Make America proud. We are fighting to defend a civilization dedicated to human dignity and human rights. Let us be worthy in the defense of our great civilization.

CHAPTER 4

WAR GAMES IN THE
INFORMATION BATTLESPACE

Truth is the new hate speech. Just telling the truth is a radical act. And we live in so cheap and tawdry an age that just telling the truth makes you a hero. Yet there are so few heroes.

A big part of the problem facing America today is the obfuscation and disinformation fed to the American people as a daily diet of slow poison. Take, for example, the word "extremist." It is commonly used to describe both Islamic jihad terrorists and those who fight against them and against Islamization in general. So for the mainstream lapdog media, the Fort Hood jihad assassin Major Hasan is an "extremist," and so am I. The word is used to claim that Islam has nothing to do with jihad terrorism—it's all just "extremism," and every religion has its "extremists." This requires the media to label non-Muslims as "extremists" also. They brand me and other freedom fighters with this word, so as to imply that we're beyond the bounds of rational and acceptable discourse.

Ayn Rand brilliantly dissects the concept of extremism in a 1967 essay, "'Extremism,' or The Art of Smearing."[72]

> To begin with, "extremism" is a term which, standing by itself, has no meaning. The concept of "extreme" denotes a relation, a measurement, a degree. The dictionary gives the following definitions: "Extreme, adj.—1. of a character or kind farthest removed from the ordinary or average. 2. utmost or exceedingly great in degree."

It is obvious that the first question one has to ask, before using that term, is: a degree—of what?

To answer: "Of anything!" and to proclaim that any extreme is evil because it is an extreme—to hold the degree of a characteristic, regardless of its nature, as evil—is an absurdity (any garbled Aristotelianism to the contrary notwithstanding). Measurements, as such, have no value-significance—and acquire it only from the nature of that which is being measured.

Are an extreme of health and an extreme of disease equally undesirable? Are extreme intelligence and extreme stupidity—both equally far removed "from the ordinary or average"—equally unworthy? Are extreme honesty and extreme dishonesty equally immoral? Are a man of extreme virtue and a man of extreme depravity equally evil?

The examples of such absurdities can be multiplied indefinitely—particularly in the field of morality where only an extreme (i.e., unbreached, uncompromised) degree of virtue can be properly called a virtue. (What is the moral status of a man of "moderate" integrity?)

But "don't bother to examine a folly—ask yourself only what it accomplishes."

This has been done before. In the 1930s, the media's favorite scare word was "isolationism." It was used in a negative manner, to suggest that an isolationist had his head in the sand about international threats, when in reality the people who were branded "isolationists" were patriots who thought America was getting involved in wars that were not in our national interests. Yet the word was used to smear good people and destroy political careers—the careers of good men who, if they had been heeded, would have saved us from Barack Obama's reckless and destructive internationalism.

Another term used in this way was and is "McCarthyism," which the media uses to refer to unjust accusations and witch hunts. In reality, Senator Joe McCarthy was working against a real threat, that of Communism, and he has never been shown to have unjustly accused anyone. But now his name is used to smear anyone who is concerned about a totalitarian threat, whether of Communism itself or of Islamization.

And today the left is manipulating language to make Americans ignorant or complacent about the Islamic threat. In case you've ever wondered why you never got the straight story on Islam directly after September 11, and still haven't, and why the media seems in the tank for jihad, here's a clue.

A couple of weeks after 9/11, the Society of Professional Journalists (SPJ) issued a directive about how to cover Islam.[73] For sheer propaganda, their "Diversity Guidelines" are hard to beat. In fact, the enemy who attacked our country in an attempt to bring it down may just as well have been writing the narrative.

The Society of Professional Journalists is a critical weapon in the war on information. By deliberately misleading the American people they are disarming us. Forewarned is forearmed.

The "guidelines," adopted at the Society's national convention on October 6, 2001, urge journalists to "take steps against racial profiling in their coverage of the war on terrorism and to reaffirm their commitment to use language that is informative and not inflammatory."

How? Among other things:

• Seek out people from a variety of ethnic and religious backgrounds when photographing Americans mourning those lost in New York, Washington, and Pennsylvania.

• Seek truth through a variety of voices and perspectives that help audiences understand the complexities of the events in Pennsylvania, New York City, and Washington, D.C.

• Seek out experts on military strategies, public safety, diplomacy, economics, and other pertinent topics who run the spectrum of race, class, gender, and geography.

• Regularly seek out a variety of perspectives for your opinion pieces. Check your coverage against the five Maynard Institute for Journalism Education fault lines of race and ethnicity, class, geography, gender, and generation.[74]

Translation: despite the horror, murder, and bloodshed of jihad, don't tell the people. That is what is important: the scrubbing of the truth. In effect, they are aiding in the self-enforcement of the Sharia (blasphemy laws).

There's more.

To deflect attention away from the Islamic character of jihad, reporters should "portray Muslims, Arabs, and Middle Eastern, and South Asian

Americans in the richness of their diverse experiences."[75]

Portray the beheaders, the homicide bombers, and the infiltrators in the "richness of their diverse experience"? You mean the stonings, amputations, Sharia law, clitorectomies, Jew-hatred, Hindu-hatred, the brutal conquests of India and Persia, and the caliphate? Yes, *infidels*, that is the poisonous fruit of the revered institution of multiculturalism.

Journalists should "make an extra effort to include olive-complexioned and darker men and women, Sikhs, Muslims, and devout religious people of all types in arts, business, society columns, and all other news and feature coverage, not just stories about the crisis."

In other words, make an extra effort to depict Muslims not engaged in jihad. And above all, don't talk about the Islamic aspect of terror attacks, especially right after they happen:

> Avoid using terms such as 'jihad' unless you are certain of their precise meaning and include the context when they are used in quotations. The basic meaning of 'jihad' is to exert oneself for the good of Islam and to better oneself...Avoid using word combinations such as 'Islamic terrorist' or 'Muslim extremist' that are misleading because they link whole religions to criminal activity. Be specific: Alternate choices, depending on context, include 'Al Qaeda terrorists' or, to describe the broad range of groups involved in Islamic politics, 'political Islamists.' Do not use religious characterizations as shorthand when geographic, political, socioeconomic, or other distinctions might be more accurate.

Who cares if the jihadis call themselves Muslims and say they're fighting for Islam? What is important is the media's obsession with self-enforcing Islamic law (Sharia). Above all, do not insult Islam. Do not defame Islam, no matter the risk to life, limb, country, or civilization.

The SPJ continues, "Do not represent Arab Americans and Muslims as monolithic groups. Avoid conveying the impression that all Arab Americans and Muslims wear traditional clothing." And "when describing Islam," the guidelines continue, "keep in mind there are large populations of Muslims around the world, including in Africa, Asia, Canada, Europe, India, and the United States. Distinguish between various Muslim states; do not lump them together as in constructions such as 'the fury of the Muslim world.'"[76]

And yet Obama has lumped the Muslim world together in his frequent appeals to Islamic rogue states worldwide, and the SPJ utters not a word of protest.[77] The "Islamic world" itself also frequently speaks this way. The *ummah*—a word you often hear in Muslim discourse—is the worldwide community of Muslims, regardless of national origin.

But instead of speaking realistically about Muslims and Islam, the SPJ directs journalists to focus on largely imaginary backlash: "Cover the victims of harassment, murder, and other hate crimes as thoroughly as you cover the victims of overt terrorist attacks." And so the media dutifully covered the bogus tales of "harassment" just days after 3,000 Americans were brutally murdered by Muslims on our own soil. The same thing happened after the Fort Hood massacre. In fact, every time a jihad plot is uncovered in America, the mainstream media publishes stories about how the local Muslim community is bracing itself for a backlash—and yet it never materializes.

The SPJ is telling journalists to throw Americans under the bus and kiss the adherents to the Islamic ideology that murdered our people and want to take over this country.

Then, of course, they reach for the cheap moral equivalent: "When writing about terrorism, remember to include white supremacists, radical anti-abortionists, and other groups with a history of such activity."[78] There aren't any—except maybe three in an outhouse somewhere in Appalachia. But not to worry: make it up, or pull the Unabomber out of your hat, and Timothy McVeigh while you're at it, too.

And while we have no coherent strategy for fighting the enemy—hell, we can't even name the enemy—they have a war plan that is so detailed and exact that every "t" is crossed and every "i" dotted. That we are not fighting back effectively is, in large part, because the Society of Professional Journalists is doing its best to make sure no one knows there is a war on. As the now-dead jihad leader Osama bin Laden himself said in 1998:

> On that basis, and in compliance with God's order, we issue the following fatwa to all Muslims: The ruling to kill the Americans and their allies—civilians and military—is an individual duty for every Muslim who can do it in any country in which it is possible to do it, in order to liberate the al-Aqsa Mosque and the holy mosque [Mecca] from their grip, and in order for their armies to move out of all the lands of Islam,

defeated and unable to threaten any Muslim. This is in accordance with the words of Almighty God, "and fight the pagans all together as they fight you all together," and "fight them until there is no more tumult or oppression, and there prevail justice and faith in God."

We—with God's help—call on every Muslim who believes in God and wishes to be rewarded to comply with God's order to kill the Americans and plunder their money wherever and whenever they find it. We also call on Muslim ulema, leaders, youths, and soldiers to launch the raid on Satan's U.S. troops and the devil's supporters allying with them, and to displace those who are behind them so that they may learn a lesson.[79]

In contrast to the claims of Western apologists for Islam, who insist that this is not a religious or cultural war, or a clash of civilizations, Osama bin Laden's declaration is a declaration of cultural and religious war. It is a call to all Muslims to kill Americans and plunder their money, and it is a declaration of war on behalf of righteous Muslims against the evil of America.

Every single one of us has had war directed against us, and no Muslim counters the edict of bin Laden to kill us. Not one. I must emphasize that no Muslim cleric or association of clerics, no Muslim political leader, nor the Muslim Brotherhood, nor the OIC, has ever denounced or even disavowed Osama bin Laden's declaration of war. Never. They've issued vaguely worded and loophole-ridden condemnations of 9/11 and of an undefined "terrorism," but have never denounced bin Laden's declaration of war.

The only thing that can be concluded is that Islam adopts bin Laden's view. Period.

But the SPJ won't tell the truth about that or any other aspect of the Islamic supremacist threat. So we have to do it for them. This is our battle. Every single one of us.

Al-Jazeera Expands

Meanwhile, the enemy is advancing its propaganda boldly through its own organs. In March 2011, it came to light that al-Jazeera was planning to expand into the United States, and the chattering classes were treating it as a simple free speech matter.

Let's not let the Islamic supremacists once again invoke the freedom of speech to kill our freedom of speech. The ruse of using freedom of speech to allow propaganda broadcasts over our airways is another stealth attack on the United States of America. The issue of the expansion of al-Jazeera into the United States can only be likened to an expansion of Goebbels' media network into the United States at the height of World War II.

Remember: the Mufti of Jerusalem, Hajj Amin Al-Husseini, was aligned with Hitler and lived in the lap of luxury on Hitler's dime during the height of World War II, while he made weekly addresses to the umma and all the Axis countries, spewing the most vile incitement to slaughter Jews, quoting Muhammad, shrieking Koran verses, demanding the rout of British and American forces. These "holy" speeches whose content came directly from the Koran incited violence across the Axis world and helped al-Husseini raise Muslim armies in Bosnia. Al-Husseini's actions resulted in the deaths of 400,000 Jewish women and children.

The overtly covert (or is that covertly overt?) propaganda war against the West is being waged on all fronts, but no organization has done as much damage to spread hate, lies, and incitement to violence as al-Jazeera. Al-Jazeera is the leading terrorist propaganda organization in the world. Jihad murder-mastermind Anwar al-Awlaki has praised al-Jazeera, and several years ago one of its most prominent reporters was arrested on terror charges. Al-Jazeera also has for years been the recipient of numerous al-Qaeda videos featuring bin Laden, Zawahiri, and American traitor Adam Gadahn. They never seem to be able to trace where these videos are coming from. Yet they have repeatedly been set up at the point of attack right before the bomb went off, so that they could take the picture of the slaughtered, dismembered bodies.

How did they know? Who was their Roger Ailes? A Ouija board? They don't report news. They spread poison. They are no different from al-Manar, the "broadcast" station for Hizballah. And al-Manar is designated as a terrorist organization by the State Department. And yet freedom-loving people have to listen to the Katie Courics and the Matt Lauers and all the other schmucks in the mainstream media laud the coverage of Al-Jazeera, while slamming and smearing Fox News, a center-left news organization.

The global jihad has every news organization at its heel. The BBC. NBC. CBS. ABC. The *New York Times*. The *Guardian*. Where can freedom-loving people get their news? Only from the Net. And now the foremost jihad propaganda arm is coming to America, as if we didn't have enough already.

It's clear to any objective observer that al-Jazeera is sympathetic to the global jihad, and a strong case can be made that it is complicit in those jihadist activities. In November 2010, ninety-one American, Israeli, and Canadian victims of Hizballah rocket attacks filed an unprecedented lawsuit against Al-Jazeera in the U.S. District Court for the Southern District of New York, charging that al-Jazeera "intentionally provided real-time coverage of the locations of missile strikes inside Israel in violation of Israeli security regulations, thereby enabling Hezbollah to aim its missiles more accurately."[80]

The war in the information battle-space is as critical as what goes on in the battlefields of Afghanistan, Iraq, and now Libya. The violent jihadi attacks in America, Europe, India, Israel, Lebanon, Ethiopia, Thailand, Russia, the Philippines, Indonesia, et al, constitute but one front in the global jihad. The propaganda is just as critical, if not more so, as we witness whole regions succumbing to the most radical and extreme ideology on the face of the earth.

Islam is the only religion with a propaganda arm, and its most powerful outlet for dissemination of disinformation, Islamic Jew-hatred, scrubbing of ethnic cleansing, gender apartheid, jihadist wars, land appropriations, and cultural annihilations is Al-Jazeera. Reasoned and rational free men have long known the pernicious influence of this jihadist news organization. But the recent legitimization and outrageous "lauding" of their coverage by mainstream news outlets is not only dangerous, it's civilizational suicide.

We must stop the expansion of the enemy propaganda in the United States.

Yet in May 2011, that expansion got a major boost when Columbia University announced that it was awarding its top journalism prize to Al-Jazeera English.[81] Just five and a half short years after Defense Secretary Donald Rumsfeld called the broadcaster's reporting "vicious, inaccurate and inexcusable" and President George W. Bush joked about bombing it, Columbia is bestowing upon Al-Jazeera its top journalism prize.[82] Al-Jazeera English, which refused to report that CBS newswoman Lara Logan had been brutally raped in Egypt's Tahrir Square the night Hosni Mubarak fell from power, was awarded the Columbia Journalism Award for "singular journalism in the public interest." The dean, Nicholas Lemann, said that "Al Jazeera English has performed a great service in bringing the English-speaking world in-depth coverage of the turmoil in the Middle East. We salute its determination to get to the heart of a complicated story unfolding in countries where news has historically been difficult to cover."[83]

Goebbels would be so pleased.

The failure of the King Hearings

Congressman Peter King (R-NY) took up the battle late in 2010, when he announced that he was going to hold hearings on the radicalization of Muslims in America. This was just what we needed, and it was long overdue. But in an indication of the power that the Muslim Brotherhood and its proxies hold in the information battlespace, King almost immediately began to fold under the pressure of the Islamic smear machine. In January 2011, he told Politico that he was "not planning to call as witnesses such Muslim community critics as the Investigative Project on Terrorism's Steve Emerson and Jihad Watch's Robert Spencer, who have large followings among conservatives but are viewed as antagonists by many Muslims."[84]

Based on that, his hearings took on the appearance of a show trial before they even began. Between Emerson and Spencer, the whole of the issue would have been covered. Emerson knows who all the players are and what groups and cells they are affiliated with. He knows who everyone is and what he's doing. For King to have acquiesced in his marginalization was almost criminal. In Spencer's case, it was just as bad. Why wouldn't King discuss the texts and teachings of Islam that jihadists use to justify violence and make recruits?

For King not to have availed himself of Emerson's knowledge and

Spencer's scholarship was an astounding case of willful blindness.

King did call as a witness Congressman Keith Ellison (D-MN), aka Hakim Mohammed, and the entire "enemedia" coverage was all about Hakim's bawling and crocodile tears over a fictitious tale. Hakim claimed that Mohammed Salman Hamdani, a Muslim paramedic killed on 9/11, was accused of terror ties when he went missing after that day, until his remains were found. In fact, the only mentions anywhere of his being accused of terror ties were in leftwing publications criticizing the right for these accusations—but there is no record of anyone on the right ever actually making the accusations.

Also, the media never reported that Congressman Hakim Mohammed Ellison's pilgrimage to Mecca was paid for with $13,350 by the Brotherhood, that Hakim was a vocal supporter of the vile Louis Farrakhan, or that Hakim has long time ties Muslim Brotherhood and is a vocal pro-Hamas supporter.

Shortly after his "performance," Steve Emerson's Investigative Project reported that two days after his weepy testimony, Ellison took a sharply different stance:

> But two days after a House committee hearing on Muslim radicalization, the Minnesota Democrat had a far more hostile tone. In a speech in Rochester Hills, Mich., Ellison made a series of personal attacks against three other witnesses who were on the opposite side of the issue.
>
> • He seemed to blame Melvin Bledsoe for the actions of his son Carlos, who stands accused of shooting and killing an Army private after converting to Islam and becoming radicalized.
> • A Somali-American who complained about interference from organized Islamist groups while trying to learn about a score of missing young men who turned up with a terrorist group in Somalia was there simply to "diss" the Muslim community in Minneapolis.
>
> His tearful tribute to Mohammed Salman Hamdani came before the House Homeland Security Committee and the national media drawn to the controversial hearing called by Rep. Peter King, R-NY Ellison's attacks on the other witnesses came before a friendlier and more partisan crowd, with sponsors that included the Muslim Students Association (MSA) at the University of Michigan-Dearborn.[85]

King's hearings should have been designed to expose stealth jihadists like Hakim, aka Ellison. But they fell far short of that. Ellison testified but Emerson and Spencer didn't. What could King have possibly hoped to achieve? *Investor's Business Daily* editorialized right after the hearings in March 2011 that King "blew it," and that he "didn't even come close to delivering what he advertised with his investigation." IBD criticized King for calling Ellison, who was, it pointed out, a "close ally" of Hamas-linked CAIR. Ellison, said the IBD editorial, "stole the show when he broke into tears while retelling the story of a Muslim paramedic who died in the World Trade Center. Ellison used the victim as an example of the 'witch hunt' against Muslims in America by claiming he was falsely accused of involvement in the 9/11 plot."[86]

All King really needed were Emerson, Spencer, and the great ex-Muslim scholar Ibn Warraq.

King also called Muslim reformer Zuhdi Jasser. Yet Jasser was anything but representative of the Muslim community in America. Jasser's Islam does not exist. He does not have a theological leg to stand on in Islam. Whatever he is practicing, it's not Islam, and he speaks for no one but himself and the two hundred Muslims who are members of his organization. And when I interviewed Jasser back in 2007, he referred to Israel as occupied territory in the last five minutes of the interview.[87] He blew his cover. Further, Jasser downplays the reality of Islamic anti-Semitism in the interview. He may be well-intentioned, but his approach and theology are just *plain un-Islamic*.

King probably thought, as do other conservatives, that Jasser was the voice of reason in our cause of educating Americans about the threat of Islamic supremacism and jihad.[88] But in this, Jasser fails miserably. First off, there is no "reason" in Islam. There is only Islam. You cannot question, reason, or go off the reservation in any way. Hence, Jasser cannot educate about the threat, because he obfuscates the truth and has invented the Islam he follows.

Methinks Representative King was a wee bit over his head. It was another lost opportunity. Didn't King know he was going to be smeared and defamed for these hearings no matter what? So why didn't he determine to achieve something anyway? Why not have the courage of your convictions?

Muslim groups were worried about these hearings with good reason. *"On the gonif brent a hittle"*—the Yiddish axiom translated means *"on the thief, the hat burns."* At Muslim Public Affairs Council Conference in December 2010, MPAC chief Salam Al Marayati asked a panel about King's hearings. One of the panelists, an attorney named Angela Oh, said that any person subpoenaed should hire an attorney and that the attorney should advise the committee that the person under subpoena would not appear. The other panelists agreed. They obviously knew that Muslims in America had something to hide.

One of the other panelists, an attorney named Reem Salahi, made a lot of noise about King and the IRA, clearly hoping that the media would exploit this connection—which they duly did. And so perhaps it was no surprise that Representative King conceded key points before his hearings even began. But why? *How could he in good conscience have squandered such an important, historic opportunity?*

Yet King, for all his failures, looks great compared to Barack Hussein Obama. As King began his hearings, the Obama Administration issued a statement saying, "We know there are many different reasons why individuals—from many different faiths—succumb to terrorist ideologies."

Many different faiths? Yet there have been over 15,000 Islamic jihad attacks around the world since 9/11, each one carried out with the imprimatur of a Muslim cleric. Just in the last few years, we have seen two Muslims in New Jersey found guilty of going jihad and plotting to kill Americans; the Christmas day underwear bomber on an airplane over Detroit, the Times Square jihad bomber, the Weapons of Mass Destruction bomber in Texas, the Fort Hood jihadist, the Christmas-tree lighting bomber in Portland, Oregon, jihadist pirates off the coast of Somalia, the jihad in Thailand, Hizballah's jihad in Lebanon, Islamic slaughter of Christians in Egypt, jihad murder in Ethiopia, Indonesia, Russia, and so many other places. Everywhere there are Muslims, there is a level of conflict.

How absurd, then, for the Obama Administration to claim that terrorists are "individuals" from "many different faiths." What other faiths? Where are the Christians or Jews committing acts of violence and justifying them by reference to their scriptures? This claim from the Obama Administration is deception to advance Islam; this is the same *taqiyya*, Islamic religiously-sanctioned deception, we hear from Muslim Brotherhood groups in the

United States on a daily basis. What does the mullah in the White House think he is going to achieve with this suicidal propaganda?

The Durbin counterattack

In the wake of King's largely toothless hearings, Senate Majority Whip Dick Durbin (D-IL) announced in March 2011 that he was scheduling Senate hearings on "Muslim rights" with the Orwellian title "Protecting the Civil Rights of American Muslims." According to the *Washington Times*, Durbin claimed that "there has been a spike in anti-Muslim bigotry in the last year that demands closer attention."

The *Times* also noted that "in 2009, the latest FBI statistics available, anti-Islamic hate crimes accounted for 9.3 percent of the 1,376 religiously motivated hate crimes recorded. That's far less than the 70.1 percent that were anti-Jewish."

That's just one reason why when Durbin announced his hearings, everyone thought it was a joke. No other group gets the extraordinary, unconstitutional special status that Muslims enjoy. Yet Durbin said, "Our Constitution protects the free exercise of religion for all Americans. During the course of our history, many religions have faced intolerance. It is important for our generation to renew our founding charter's commitment to religious diversity and to protect the liberties guaranteed by our Bill of Rights."

But all that was off the real point. Muslims are freer in this country than in any other country in the world, and frankly, no one gives a fig what they worship. The problem arose when thousands of Americans were slaughtered in the name of Allah and for the glory of jihad.

We are entitled to our lives, Mr. Durbin. We are entitled to our security, Mr. Durbin. We are entitled to keep our babies safe, Mr. Durbin.

Durbin's hearing, like King, showed the crying need for real hearings. Frankly, I might have agreed with a hearing on "Muslim rights" if it addressed the increasing surrender of secular law to Islamic law, and the assertion of Islamic supremacy over the rights of all others. We need hearings on the Florida circuit court judge who just ruled that a case be decided according to Sharia law. We need hearings on the special rights being afforded Muslims at the expense of everyone else. We need hearings on the Obama Justice Department's suing a school district for not allowing a Muslim woman to take nearly three weeks off during the school year to go on a pilgrimage to Mecca.

We need hearings on taxpayer dollars being used to fund Islamic finance (thereby funding jihad and prohibition on whole American business sectors). We need hearings on the violation of the separation of mosque and state in the public schools, in the workplace, in the court-room, and in foreign policy. We need hearings on the violation of the Constitution in regards to Muslims—no longer are equal rights sufficient, now it's special rights for a very extra special class, Muslims.

These would present a parade of reliable witnesses like the ex-Muslim human rights activists Wafa Sultan; Ayaan Hirsi Ali; Nonie Darwish, the former jihad slave; Sudanese Christian activist Simon Deng; witnesses to the Fort Hood jihad murders, witnesses to the Christmas Underwear Bomber jihad attack on a plane in Detroit, witnesses to the failed jihad bombing in Times Square, compatriots of jihad plotter Najibullah Zazi, and hundreds of victims of jihad attacks in the United States and elsewhere. These would finally educate the American people about abrogation and Islamic jihad.

But no. Durbin's hearings were shaping up to be an attack on free speech and the few, the brave who speak candidly about Islamic jihad and the hundreds of thousands who have been slaughtered in jihadist wars, land appropriations, cultural annihilations, and enslavements.

This useful idiot, Dick Durbin, wanted to use your taxpayer dollars to make sure that Osama bin Laden, Anwar al-Awlaki, Nihad Awad, Ibrahim Hooper, Sheik Qaradawi, and the hundreds of other Muslim Brotherhood individuals and groups achieve their goal unmolested, and that nothing stood in the way of that stated goal: "eliminating and destroying Western civilization from within and sabotaging its miserable house."

"Watch for this to be an orgy of Muslim claims of victimhood and demonization of freedom fighters trying to defend Constitutional free-doms against Islamic supremacism," said Robert Spencer.

Ironically, just as Durbin announced his hearings, Muslims bombed a bus in Jerusalem, killing at least one person and injuring dozens. And this followed on the heels of the heinous jihad murders of the Fogel family in Israel. I look forward to the day that Israel and America shed their shameful cloak of dhimmitude, the state of subservience that Islam prescribes for Jews and Christians in the Islamic state, and respond with robust defensive moves.

One could point to Alger Hiss or Benedict Arnold for like historical antecedents. The difference between then and now was that we didn't know that Hiss et al. were seditionists whose objective was to overthrow the government. We do know who and what the Muslim Brotherhood is, but the political elites, the chattering classes, and the media elites have taken up their considerable weapons against those who are exposing this century's Nazis.

Durbin was pulling out all the stops to ensure that the hearing was little more than a pathetic exercise in dhimmitude with only one viewpoint represented, that of the Islamic supremacists. Indeed, the four scheduled witnesses were (i) Muslim activist Farhana Khera, the President and Executive Director of Muslim Advocates in San Francisco; (ii) Catholic Cardinal Theodore McCarrick of Washington, D.C.; (iii) Tom Perez, the Justice Department's Assistant Attorney General for Civil Rights and resident militant leftist who has advocated openly for the non-enforcement of federal immigration laws; and (iv) Alex Acosta, the Bush Administration top civil rights official and current dean of fourth-tier Florida International University Law School, a notorious hotbed of left-wing academics.[89]

I'm surprised that Yusuf al-Qaradawi, the Muslim Brotherhood's ideological point-man on sharia law, didn't make the cut.

The presence of Khera, McCarrick, and Perez was no surprise. All are longstanding liberals who, for a variety of reasons, have exhibited a distressing willingness to cast aside any concern over the Islamic, Koran-based terrorism committed by a growing number of American Muslims. Think *Queers for Palestine*.

But why would Acosta be added? Apparently, Acosta, the Bush Administration's most outlandish stooge-in-chief, decided that he needed to further burnish his credentials with the left in an effort to remove any conservative taint. One would have thought that he achieved that goal years ago.

During his tenure in office, Acosta famously mugged for the camera while seeking justice for an Oklahoma girl who was prevented from wearing a headscarf to school.[90] He also arranged to meet monthly with every Muslim group in Washington—including Hamas-linked CAIR—thinking that these jihad supporters might facilitate some cushy presidential appointment. It wouldn't have been any surprise if this time around, we would see Acosta even embracing DOJ's crazy recent lawsuit against Berkeley, Illinois, for not allowing a first-year teacher to take a nineteen-day hajj to Mecca in the middle of final exam preparation, a lawsuit that former Attorney General Mukasey said reflected "dubious judgment" for which "the upper reaches of the Justice Department should be calling people to account."[91]

So desperate was Acosta for political advancement that he was willing to sacrifice any principle and his soul to get there. Perhaps he'll eventually strap one on for the cause.

For him, the ends completely justify the means. To paraphrase Sir Thomas More's epic line to Richard Rich in *A Man for All Seasons*: Alex, it profits a man nothing to give his soul for the whole world...but for the support of the Islamic Left? Desperately, Acosta sold his soul long ago. America is teeming with sold-out souls.

Clearly Acosta, Durbin, and their allies were determined to do the bidding of the Islamic leaders that he and Obama were determined to appease no matter what. What did the mullah in the White House and the stooge Durban think they were going to achieve with this suicidal propaganda? Likewise, what did Peter King hope to achieve by sugar-coating the problem we face? Wasn't there anyone on either side of the aisle who would do what was necessary to defend the American people from the jihad?

Shortly after Durbin's hearing, New York State Senator Greg Ball held a hearing of his own, focusing New York's preparedness for jihad terror attacks and featuring speakers who spoke honestly about the Islamic jihad threat in many of its forms. This hearing, too, became a flashpoint for the Muslim victimhood card and the smearing of Ball's witnesses—particularly former Muslim Nonie Darwish.

Darwish stated in her testimony that "the education of Arab children is to make killing of certain groups of people not only good, it's holy. It becomes holy in our culture." At that, Senator Eric Adams held up a Koran and accused Darwish of "bringing hate and poison" into the hearing.[92] Adams was accusing Darwish of originating the hate and poison that she was pointing out in the jihadists—a familiar diversionary tactic.

Even worse, shortly after the hearing, Senator Ball received a threatening package to his office containing a letter and a stuffed animal bearing the Star of David. Note the presence of the Jewish star. When it comes to Jew-hatred, Islamic jihadists can't help themselves. Forget the fact that neither Ball nor those who testified were Jewish. A local news report described the contents of the enclosed letter:

> The letter signed by Jameela Barnette with kind regards accused Ball, a Catholic, of being a Jew-worshipping, Muslim hater." Instead of bashing the intellectually superior Muslims, shouldn't a handsome, cannibalized crazy, Christian cracker like yourself be in church chomping on Jew-god corpse and washing it down with Jew-god blood under the pretense of 'Holy Communion,'" the letter stated.[93]

The threat and the Islamic Jew-hatred contained in it received little to no national media attention. The double standard is dangerous and disturbing. My colleagues and I receive threats on a regular basis, but it is the false flag of "anti-Muslim" bias spun by Islamic supremacists that the media advances.

Geert Wilders, Icon of Free Speech

There isn't a great truth-teller and defender of freedom comparable to Geert Wilders in America so far, although there are some promising upcoming voices. Where King faltered, Geert Wilders never has. The Dutch Parliamentarian and anti-jihad warrior Wilders is the modern-day icon in the war on free speech. In 2010, he was in court on specious "hate speech" charges filed by a corrupt, criminal court in the Netherlands that has, in effect, submitted itself to enforcing Islamic blasphemy laws.

How dare they subjugate their Western values to Islamic supremacism in this dangerous farce?

Geert Wilders was our proxy in this trial. He was representing us in this historic trial against free men, defending our basic unalienable right to free speech. This case was not about Wilders. It was a major battle in the clash of civilizations: free men vs. subjugation.

Wilders explained what was at really on trial in Holland in his case: "I am standing trial," he said, "because of my opinions on Islam...and because the Dutch establishment—most of them non-Muslims—wants to silence me. I have been dragged to court because in my country freedom can no longer be fully enjoyed. In Europe the national state, and increasingly the EU, prescribes how citizens—including democratically elected politicians such as myself—should think and what we are allowed to say."

It was, in fact, a heresy trial. In the eyes of Islam, Wilders was a blasphemer because of his criticism of Islam. Through the insidious and omnipresent machinations of the Organization of the Islamic Conference (OIC), what amount to prosecutions for blasphemy against Islam are taking place in the West, with the Wilders trial standing as the foremost example. The pioneering historian of dhimmitude and the Islamization of Europe, Bat Ye'or, explains that "the OIC's aim is to punish and suppress any alleged Islamophobia, around the world but particularly in Europe." The OIC is one of the most destructive and yet least-known organizations in the world. Bat Ye'or elucidates their nature and purpose:

> The OIC is one of the largest intergovernmental organizations in the world. It encompasses 56 Muslim states plus the Palestinian Authority. (Those are the 57 "states" that Barack Obama may have had in mind when he made his famous gaffe about 57 states in the Union.) Spread over four continents, it claims to speak in the name of the *ummah* (the universal Muslim community), which numbers about 1.3 billion. The OIC's mission is to unite all Muslims worldwide by rooting them in the Koran and the Sunnah—the core of traditional Islamic civilization and values. It aims at strengthening solidarity and cooperation among all its members, in order to protect the interests of Muslims everywhere and to galvanize the ummah into a unified body.

Bat Ye'or explains that the OIC has created an "Observatory of Islamophobia, which puts pressure on Western governments and international bodies to adopt laws punishing 'Islamophobia' and blasphemy." And "Geert Wilders is the latest victim of this enormous world machinery. His crime is maintaining that Europe's civilization is rooted in the values of Jerusalem, Athens, Rome, and the Enlightenment—and not in Mecca, Baghdad, Andalusia, and al-Kods. He fights for Europe's independence from the Caliphate and for its endangered freedoms. He had received serious death threats even before *Fitna* was released."[94]

For a moment, it looked as if the Dutch might come to their senses and stop harassing this warrior for freedom. In October 2010, just as his heresy trial was about to resume, Wilders said, "I am on trial, but on trial with me is the freedom of expression of many Dutch citizens. I can assure you, I will continue proclaiming it." Then, according to the notoriously leftist and morally bankrupt *Guardian,* he "asserted his right to remain silent for the rest of the trial, prompting a comment from the presiding judge, Jan Moors, which was challenged by Wilders's lawyer."

Moors said, according to the *Guardian,* that Wilders "was known for making bold statements but avoiding discussions," and concluded by saying, "It appears you're doing so again."

Wilders' lawyer Bram Moszkowicz then asked that the proceedings be halted and Moors removed. But a special panel refused to remove Moors, and the trial resumed again. That episode shows that a "fair" trial is not even remotely possible in this case. Wilders himself articulated what is at stake in his trial in January 2010:

> Freedom is the most precious of all our attainments and the most vulnerable. People have devoted their lives to it and given their lives for it.
>
> Our freedom in this country is the outcome of centuries. It is the consequence of a history that knows no equal and has brought us to where we are now.
>
> I believe with all my heart and soul that the freedom in the Netherlands is threatened. That what our heritage is, what generations could only dream about, that this freedom is no longer a given, no longer self-evident.
>
> I devote my life to the defence of our freedom. I know what the risks are and I pay a price for it every day. I do not complain about it; it is my own decision. I see that as my duty and it is why I am standing here....

You weren't going to hear from the mainstream media about the price Wilders was paying. They, too, have already submitted to a self-enforced Sharia. While they hold Christianity and Judaism in contempt, their respect for the Islamic blasphemy laws seems absolute. They refused to stand up for the freedom of speech by running the Danish cartoons of Muhammad that caused worldwide riots among Muslims in 2006, or to report on the worldwide jihad, the Islamic ethnic cleansing of non-Muslims, or related issues.

So let's take a step back and understand the price that Wilders and others really are paying. Former Muslim and author Wafa Sultan, former Muslim and Dutch MP Ayaan Hirsi Ali, scholar Robert Spencer, former Muslim and scholar Ibn Warraq, scholar Bat Ye'or, former Muslim Nonie Darwish, cartoonist Lars Vilks, cartoonist Kurt Westergaard, Danish newspaper publisher Flemming Rose, South Park producers Trey Parker and Matt Stone, Salman Rushdie and countless others, myself included, receive horrible threats all the time. Wafa Sultan was the first American to have to live in hiding because of Islamic jihad threats. Wilders himself lives under round-the-clock tight security because of the hundreds of death threats he receives every year.

These threats are not idle. Theo Van Gogh was murdered in cold blood in the streets of the Netherlands in 2004 because of a perceived insult to Islam. And in September 2010, Molly Norris, an unknown Seattle cartoonist, had to go into witness protection because she dared to initiate "Everyone Draw Muhammad Day," a response to the Muslim death threats against the producers of Comedy Central (they dared to utter the name "Muhammad," and put him in a huggy bear costume).[95] So Norris had to change her name, leave her job, her home, her life, *at her own expense,* because jihadists holding the world hostage were…offended.

Molly Norris should have been the top story of the day. Norris' story should have been splashed on the front pages of newspapers nationwide. Norris should have been the poster girl for media and free press everywhere. Instead, no one knew who she was.

Threats and abuse are the price we must be prepared to pay if we're going to stand up against the Islamization of America. The real hero of freedom is not Daisy Khan, but Geert Wilders and others who stand with him. During the Ground Zero mosque controversy, Daisy Khan claimed to have received a death threat; her claim made national news. Yet the mainstream media has never been interested in reporting about death threats that foes of jihad and Islamic supremacism receive on a regular basis—although the real ones under threat are not Daisy Khan and the Imam Rauf, but people who have spoken out, even accidentally like Molly Norris, and those who are opposing their Islamic supremacist plan to put a mosque at Ground Zero.

Geert Wilders is our proxy. We are all on trial. Our freedom of speech is on trial. The Organization of the Islamic Conference means to shut us all up. Wilders is us. If you value your freedom, stand with him.

As Ayn Rand said, "Truth is the recognition of reality." Even as we are marginalized, vilified, and defamed, we are being proven right by the events of every day. And the light of truth shines more brightly all the time.

The Dutch courts, the media, and the political elites have subdued themselves and voluntarily assumed the role of the dhimma in Islam. According to Islamic scholar Robert Spencer,

> Dhimmitude is the status that Islamic law, the Sharia, mandates for non-Muslims, primarily Jews and Christians. Dhimmis, 'protected people,' are free to practice their religion in a Sharia regime, but are made subject to a number of humiliating regulations designed to enforce the Koran's command that they 'feel themselves subdued' (9:29). This denial of equality of rights and dignity remains part of the Sharia, and, as such, are part of the legal superstructure that global jihadists are laboring to restore everywhere in the Islamic world, and wish ultimately to impose on the entire human race. If dhimmis complained about their inferior status, institutionalized humiliation, or poverty, their masters voided their contract and regarded them as enemies of Islam, fair game as objects of violence. Consequently, dhimmis were generally cowed into silence and worse. It was almost unheard-of to find dhimmis speaking out against their oppressors; to do so would have been suicide.[96]

Spencer notes that this attitude of subjugation can be found in the West today, among people in free societies who for some reason are yearning for slavery:

> For centuries dhimmi communities in the Islamic world learned to live in peace with their Muslim overlords by acquiescing to their sub-servience. Some even actively identified with the dominant class, and became strenuous advocates for it. Spearheaded by dhimmi academics and self-serving advocacy groups, that same attitude of chastened sub-servience has entered into Western academic study of Islam, and from there into journalism, school textbooks, and the popular discourse. One must not point out the depredations of jihad and dhimmitude; to do so would offend the multiculturalist ethos that prevails everywhere today. To do so would endanger chances for peace and rapprochement between civilizations all too ready to clash."

Islamophobia

For the enemies of freedom, telling the truth about the Islamization of America in all its various guises is stigmatized as "Islamophobia."

The very word "Islamophobia" is a fictional construct, as journalist Claire Berlinski explains,

> The neologism "Islamophobia" did not simply emerge *ex nihilo*. It was invented, deliberately, by a Muslim Brotherhood front organization, the International Institute for Islamic Thought, which is based in Northern Virginia....Abdur-Rahman Muhammad, a former member of the IIIT who has renounced the group in disgust, was an eyewitness to the creation of the word. "This loathsome term," he writes, "is nothing more than a thought-terminating cliche conceived in the bowels of Muslim think tanks for the purpose of beating down critics."[97]

The term "Islamophobia" was designed specifically for the Western mindset of liberal white guilt, stealing the "civil rights" narrative from black Americans and mining the "oppression" of Native Americans—even throwing in the specter of the Japanese internment camps during World War II. These are the clubs Islamic supremacists in the West use to beat down their opponents. Islamophobia is the knee-jerk smear thrown at anyone who dares to speak out or push back against the encroaching Sharia, the appeasement of Islamic supremacists demands on the secular marketplace, and the restriction of free speech.

In reality, "Islamophobia" is nothing more than a term that Islamic supremacists use to enforce what they can of Islamic blasphemy laws in the West: in Islamic law, to defame or insult Muhammad or Islam is blasphemy, and in many Muslim countries it's punishable by death. There are daily reports of death sentences handed down in Muslim countries for perceived insults to Muhammad or Islam. Recently a doctor was charged with blasphemy because he threw away the business card of a Muslim whose name was Muhammad.

Clearly, that sort of thing isn't going to fly in the West. Thus the term "Islamophobia" was invented as a variation on the Muslim playing of the "race card," which they also do frequently, despite the fact that Islam is a religion not a race. The trick is to portray 1.5 billion Muslims as victims—so that now anyone who speaks candidly or honestly about jihad, about Islamic misogyny, gender apartheid, or other human rights abuses that are sanctioned by Islamic law, is smeared with the nonsensical charge of "Islamophobia."

Defaming truth-tellers with charges of "Islamophobia" is a means to an end. The objective is to shut you up, because no one wants to be a racist–Islamophobic–anti-Muslim–bigot. Meanwhile, the Los Angeles City Council passed a resolution recently that decried "Islamophobia."

The term *"Islamophobia"* itself is an enforcement of Islamic blasphemy laws. Islamic law commands that there be no candor about Islam or criticism of Islam. Any truthful statements about Islamic supremacism and violence are considered blasphemy. That's why it is shocking that Los Angeles, which is just this side of Sodom and Gomorrah, is passing resolutions that accord with Islamic law. No one in America cares what and who you worship; just don't force it upon us. And stop telling us how many Muslims don't commit jihadi acts. Of course they don't. So what? I don't believe in rewarding people for doing the right thing. I don't believe in congratulating people for not committing acts of violence against people outside their religion.

Thus the Los Angeles City Council's passage of this resolution opposing "Islamophobia" and repudiating violence against Muslims is a step back centuries into the dark ages. Will heresy trials like the one that Dutch authorities are persecuting Geert Wilders with be far behind? According to the FBI, "hate crime" against Muslims is at its lowest in a decade, but acts of jihad are accelerating at warp speed. Yet the Los Angeles City Council passes no resolutions against jihad, honor killings, misogyny, gender apartheid, Islamic antisemitism, kuffarophobia (fear and hatred of unbelievers), etc.

It's not Islamophobia. It's blasphemy laws. It's truthophobia. It's Islamorealism.

Do not be cowed. Don't stop telling the truth. These attacks are part of their war on us. Do not shut up. Ever. Shout louder. Fight back. Be as free as you can be. The more they try to oppress you, be freer. The more they attempt to shackle you, the louder you must bellow from the hilltops.

The ongoing campaign not only to silence the truth tellers but to change the lexicon as well takes many forms. For example, the Obama

Administration has directed the Department of State and Department of Defense not to speak of jihad or Islamic terror. The crushing stupidity of such suicidal strategies was made plain in the aftermath of the worst post-9/11 jihad attack on U.S. soil, the Fort Hood massacre. The DOD and the Executive branch refused to address the motive of the jihad murderer, Nidal Malik Hassan. How can you address a threat if you refuse even to name it or recognize that it exists? How many people have to die?

When Barack Hussein Obama took office as president of the United States with a decidedly pro-Islamic agenda, one of the first things that the Hamas-linked Muslim Brotherhood front organization known as the Council on American-Islamic Relations (CAIR) did was give him a list of terms not to use in reference to Muslims. They were written by a dhimmi Christian, Chris Seiple, president of the Institute for Global Engagement, which the *Christian Science Monitor* (initial publisher of the advice) describes as "a 'think tank with legs' that promotes sustainable environments for religious freedom worldwide."

This would have been hysterical if it were theatre or *Saturday Night Live*. But it was deadly serious. CAIR, an unindicted co-conspirator in a Hamas jihad terror funding case, sent out this "advice" (warning?) to the President in its daily mailing shortly before Obama's celebrated trip to Turkey and Egypt in June 2009, during which he made his notorious address to the Islamic world from Cairo on June 4.

But the list was very revealing. It stood in sharp contrast to all of the previous deceptive propaganda that the Hamas-linked group CAIR had been peddling. Further, it showed that CAIR was confident that at last they had a pro-Islamic president in the White House, ready and willing to advance their supremacist agenda. And so they passed on Seiple's advice to him.

Seiple wrote that he was sharing "advice given to me from dear Muslim friends worldwide regarding words and concepts that are not useful in building relationships with them." Since when it comes to Muslims "building relationships" is a completely one-sided affair: if you are willing to accommodate Islamic practices, you can be friends with Muslims. Otherwise you'll be cast aside or worse. And so "building relationships" is properly translated as "submitting to Islam."

One of the terms to which Seiple objected was "the Clash of Civilizations." Yet if not in connection with the conflict of Islam vs. the West, I don't know where one would ever use such a phrase. It is an apt term for the attacks of September 11, July 7 in London, March 11 in Spain, Mumbai in November 2008, as well as for the jihad in Thailand, the jihad in the Philippines, the Khobar Towers bombing, the *U.S.S. Cole* attack, the Glasgow airport attack, the Beslan jihad massacre, the Fort Hood jihad massacre, the Christmas Tree lighting jihad in Portland, the Detroit airplane Christmas underwear bomber, all the incidents of lone jihad syndrome, the jihads in Somalia, Sudan, and elsewhere in Africa, the punk jihad in France, in which gangs of "youths" have terrorized non-Muslims and committed brutal murders, notably the horrific anti-Semitic murder of a young Jewish man, Ilan Halimi; the biker jihad in Australia, in which Muslim bikers have terrorized Australian non-Muslims; the 15,000-plus deadly Islamic attacks since 9/11, the meat jihad, the food jihad, the fecal jihad, in which Muslims have poisoned food with feces; the litigation jihad, the academic jihad, the social jihad, the economic jihad and Sharia finance, the papal jihad, the cartoon jihad, the war on the Jews...and the list goes on.

Seiple then complains about the word "secular," saying that "the Muslim ear tends to hear 'godless' with the pronunciation of this word. And a godless society is simply inconceivable to the vast majority of Muslims worldwide." Of course. There is no such thing as secular Islam. Only pious Islam. Secular Islam is the only shot Islam has to live in peace and harmony with the rest of the world, so don't even think of mentioning it. And the United States is a secular society. So the objective here, once again, is to place Islam above all other systems. And the mere mention of a "competing system" is an insult.

In a similar vein, Seiple decries the word "assimilation," complaining that "this word suggests that the minority Muslim groups in North America and Europe need to look like the majority, Christian culture."

Of course. Assimilation is punishable by death among Muslims in Western countries. In February 2011, Turkish Prime Minister Recep Tayyip Erdogan visited Turkish immigrants in Germany and warned them not to assimilate into German culture. Assimilation would allow Muslims to live in peace and harmony with their non-Muslim neighbors; yet Islam is a constant state of war until worldwide domination is complete.

Assimilation. Don't even think of mentioning it.

"Muslims know quite well," Seiple says, "and have an opinion about, the battle taking place within Islam and what it means to be an orthodox and devout Muslim." That means that non-Muslims must not speak about "reformation" of Islam: "They don't need to be insulted by suggesting they follow the Christian example of Martin Luther. Instead, ask how Muslims understand *ijtihad*, or reinterpretation, within their faith traditions and cultural communities."

Muslims "don't need to be insulted" by talk of reformation. And it's true: in the Koran, Islam is presented as perfect and complete (5:3); consequently, reformation and reinterpretation are crimes punishable by death. Don't even think of mentioning them.

Seiple reminds his sheep-like readers that "the jihad is an internal struggle first, a process of improving one's spiritual self-discipline and getting closer to God," and that therefore one should not use the word "jihadi" for terrorists: "The lesser jihad is external, validating 'just war' when necessary. By calling the groups we are fighting 'jihadis,' we confirm their own—and the worldwide Muslim public's—perception that they are religious. They are not. They are terrorists, *hirabists*, who consistently violate the most fundamental teachings of the Holy Koran and mainstream Islamic scholars and imams."[98]

How did the "worldwide Muslim public" get the idea that they were religious? Apparently from their own words and actions, and how those words and deeds match up with the "fundamental teachings of the Holy Koran"—not from what non-Muslims in the West are saying.

"Moderate" is also out the window. In Islam, there is no such thing as a moderate. Prime Minister of Turkey, Erdogan said, "There is no moderate or immoderate Islam. Islam is Islam and that's it." Indeed. Those who stray from that rigid path are considered apostates and hypocrites, both of which are punishable by death in Muslim countries.

"Interfaith" is out, too, and that is not unexpected for anyone who knows anything about Islam's unilateralism and intransigence. There's no such thing as "interfaith" cooperation because from the Islamic perspective there is only one valid religion. Interfaith dialogue for Muslims is generally a euphemism for proselytizing. Many non-Muslims in the West engage in dialogues with Muslims thinking they can effect some change, some negotiation, some element of compromise. But this is self-delusion. Interfaith dialogue for Muslims goes only one way and one way only—to Islam. Islam offers Jews and Christians the options of conversion, subjugation as dhimmis, or death. Muslims pursue interfaith dialogue in order to bring about the conversion of non-Muslims, or else their submission.

"Freedom" has to go, because "freedom can imply an unbound licentiousness." Yes: in Islam, *freedom as it is understood in the West is a dirty word.* The understanding of freedom in Islam is "perfect slavery" *to Allah.* "Religious Freedom" is out, because "sadly, this term too often conveys the perception that American foreign policy is only worried about the freedom of Protestant evangelicals to proselytize and convert, disrupting the local culture and indigenous Christians." Much more "sadly," in Islam *there is no such thing as "religious freedom." There is only Islam. And Seiple's exercise in moral equivalence is wrongheaded:* Protestant evangelicals do not go around chopping peoples' heads off if they do not convert. Evangelicals are not the problem.

"Tolerance," must go also, Seiple says, for it "is not enough." Yes. In Islam, only total submission will suffice.

This piece, published in the *Christian Science Monitor* and distributed by Hamas-linked CAIR, was but one in a long series of propaganda moves involving manipulations of the language and the lexicon. Their intention was to obfuscate and deceive.

Regarding the perversion and the twisting of the language epitomized by this *Monitor* piece, I want to strongly encourage people not to submit to the Orwellian war on words. This is yet another weapon of the Islamic supremacists, designed to try to gain control of the language in order to control the debate. Islamic supremacists manipulate the language so that every debate is tilted in their favor; it's hard to debate an opponent when he dictates the very words that may or may not be used. In this, as in everything, Islam demands concession. Submission. Concede nothing. Proceed with the battle and don't look back.

CHAPTER 5

LITIGATION JIHAD

One of the most effective weapons in the arsenal of the enemy within is, sadly, the very legal system that the jihadists hope ultimately to overthrow and replace with Sharia. It has become standard operating procedure for Islamic supremacists to sue freedom fighters and file lawsuits against anyone who exposes their true agenda, their funding, their links to jihad groups, and the like.

This is what the U.S. government ought to be doing: exposing the agenda and funding of Islamic supremacist groups. But instead, the Islamic supremacists have the Obama Justice Department in their pocket. It came to light in April 2011 that the Obama Justice Department quashed indictments that were about to be issued against Omar Ahmad, the co-founder and longtime Board Chairman of Hamas-linked CAIR, and many other prominent Muslim leaders in the U.S.[98]

The effects of this are far-reaching. In October 2010, the unindicted co-conspirator status of Hamas-linked CAIR in the Holy Land Foundation case, the largest Hamas terror funding trial in American history, was reaffirmed.[99] CAIR has since done its best to spin this decision, counting on the Obama Justice Department's dereliction of duty in not prosecuting the case against Muslim Brotherhood, Hamas-linked groups that are plotting on "eliminating and destroying Western civilization from within" (according to the internal, captured document entered into evidence in that trial).[100]

That's why you must support candidates who promise to follow through on prosecutions resulting from the evidence that was presented about Muslim Brotherhood proxies in the United States during the Holy Land Foundation jihad funding trial. This miscarriage of justice must not stand.

But in the meantime, Islamic supremacists are bolder than ever in resorting to our legal system to get what they want.

Silencing Freedom Fighters

The legal system is a powerful weapon in silencing those who are brave enough to speak candidly about Islam. While death threats and death fatwas are issued on our heads on a regular basis, that's just part of the campaign of the Islamic machine to silence us. Filing lawsuits alleging defamation or libel is a most potent weapon. Of course, these frivolous lawsuits always end in defeat for the Islamic supremacists, but they know that going in. The object is not to win. The objective is to tie up your time, money, and resources fighting a frivolous lawsuit. These legal actions are expensive and draining for their target.

Islamic supremacists are rich in donations from jihad-loving countries. They use our legal system to kill our legal system. They use freedom of speech to kill freedom of speech. They use our way of life to kill our way of life.

Writes Robert Spencer:

> Stealth jihadists will use—and are using—all available legal channels to silence criticism of their agenda, their activities, and of Islam in general. By turning to the courts, stealth jihadist organizations maintain their carefully constructed façade of moderation—after all, suing somebody these days is as American as apple pie. However, when combined with media assaults...on their critics, and working against a backdrop of violent threats against them, a broader campaign of intimidation emerges.[101]

One of the most obvious and high-profile cases was against Rachel Ehrenfeld, the investigative journalist who founded the American Center for Democracy. Ehrenfeld was sued by a Saudi billionaire, Khalid bin Mahfouz, for writing in her expose of terror financing, *Funding Evil,* that he had given money to Hamas and al Qaeda, which bin Mahfouz denied having done *knowingly.* However, bin Mahfouz was the "principal donor" to the Muwafaq Foundation, an Islamic charity that the Treasury Department stated was "an al-Qaida front that receives funding from wealthy Saudi businessmen."[102]

Nonetheless, making use of Britain's notorious plaintiff-favoring libel laws, bin Mahfouz brought suit against Ehrenfeld in that country, even though he didn't live there and *Funding Evil* wasn't even published there. But a few copies were sold there through Amazon.com, and for the British courts that was enough.

It was an attempt at legal intimidation—a courtroom jihad. And it worked: leftist British judge David Eady ruled in May 2005 that Ehrenfeld had to pay more than $225,000 to bin Mahfouz, and apologize to him as well. Ehrenfeld then countersued in New York, beginning a legal battle that went on for the better part of the next five years. Finally, in 2008, New York State adopted what came to be known as "Rachel's Law," protecting American citizens from libel judgments in foreign courts that do not respect the U.S. Constitution's protection of the freedom of speech. Several other states followed suit, and a similar bill is as of this writing being considered by the U.S. Congress.

When he signed "Rachel's Law," then-New York Governor David Paterson said, "New Yorkers must be able to speak out on issues of public concern without living in fear that they will be sued outside the United States, under legal standards inconsistent with our First Amendment rights. This legislation will help ensure the freedoms enjoyed by New York authors....We really need Congress and the President to work together and enact federal legislation that will protect authors throughout the country against the threat of foreign libel judgments."[103]

One would have thought that that would have discouraged such frivolous lawsuits in this country. But only to the uninitiated. The outcomes of these cases are irrelevant—as is, in the case of Rachel's Law, legislation enacted to combat such harassment. The objective of these legal attacks is to shut down free speech, despite the fact that you're telling the truth. Lawsuits cost money. Big money. Their side is well funded, as evidenced by the fifty million dollars the Saudis contributed to CAIR for these very acts of harassment and financial jihad. It costs tens of thousands of dollars, and at times hundreds of thousands, to fight the Wahhabi legal machine. Consequently, it is incumbent upon free men and lawyers of conscience to create a repository of legal aid to defend free speech and fight off the litigation jihad.

There is not one effective counterjihad fighter who has not been subjected to lawfare in one form or another. Two of the country's leading jurists, David Yerushalmi and Robert Muise of the Thomas More Law Center, have single-handedly defended numerous cases, including my own, against a ten-million-dollar lawsuit by an Islamic supremacist lawyer, and a number of free speech cases in Miami, Detroit, New York, and San Francisco.

The Detroit Freedom Bus Ads Lawsuit

In one notable assault on the freedom of speech, in the spring of 2010, Detroit's SMART public transportation system refused to run my religious liberty bus ads offering help to people wishing to leave Islam safely, without having to live in fear of their family or social circle. Despite the desperate need for resources for Muslims under threat for leaving Islam, the city of Detroit refused to run our freedom campaign on the Dearborn and Detroit buses. In May of that year, my group, the American Freedom Defense Initiative, sued the city of Detroit for refusing our ads—the same ads that were dropped and then allowed on free speech grounds in Miami, and which ran without legal challenge in New York City and San Francisco.

But in Detroit, they caved to Islamic supremacism and violated their own ad guidelines of freedom of speech. Here is SMART's first guideline for bus ads:

> As a governmental agency that receives state and federal funds, SMART is mandated to comply with federal and state laws. First Amendment free speech rights require that SMART not censor free speech and because of that, SMART is required to provide equal access to advertising on our vehicles.[104]

What's more, contrary to claims from Hamas-tied CAIR and other Islamic supremacists that the ads were "offensive," the need for them was obvious. According to the *Washington Times*, a teacher in Dearborn noted that there was "a climate of fear in the Detroit area's community." The educator explained, "The fear is palpable. I know there are things I am 'not allowed' to say. A discussion of religion with a Muslim person is often prefaced by the statement, 'Don't say anything about the Prophet [Muhammad].' In free society, open and honest conversation is not usually begun by a prohibition. Threats and intimidation are just part of life here."[105]

SMART was saying that our ads offering help to those threatened for leaving Islam were political. They were effectively admitting that Islam was political—an admission that had immense implications (far beyond, I'm sure, what Detroit imagined). If Islam is political, it ought to be subject to the restrictions and scrutiny to which all political entities in the United States are subject. This could open the door to a reevaluation of the unthinking assumption that Islam is simply a religion like Judaism or Christianity, and transform anti-terror efforts that are now hamstrung by the all-too-common idea that all that goes on in mosques is purely "religious."

In our AFDI motion to compel SMART to run our ads, we explained, "The fact that society may find speech offensive is not a sufficient reason for suppressing it. Indeed, if it is the speaker's opinion that gives offense, that consequence is a reason for according it constitutional protection."[106] I flew to Detroit to testify in the suit back in July 2010.[107] Robert Muise, who is with the Thomas More Law Center, and David Yerushalmi represented me. I was armed with hundreds of pictures of honor killing victims; the testimony of ex-Muslim teenager Rifqa Bary, whose life was threatened; screenshots of Facebook fatwas on apostates, and the actual death fatwa issued at Al-Azhar University in Cairo, the most important institution of Islamic law in the Sunni world and the authority that approved the revealing English-language guide to the Sharia (Islamic law) known as *Reliance of the Traveller*.[108]

Reliance of the Traveller is a one-volume manual of Sharia. (The title implies that this is a handy compendium of Islamic law so that when you're on the road, you know how to behave in unfamiliar situations.) It is a product of the Shafi'i school of Islamic jurisprudence, which is one of the four Sunni schools of Islamic law. It is all the more valuable because it often notes how the other schools, the Maliki, Hanbali, and Hanafi, differ from Shafi'i rulings where there is a difference. And on apostasy they all agree: those who leave Islam must be killed.

The judge in the case promised a decision the following week (July 2010), but didn't rule until late March 2011, when Judge Denise Hood finally ruled in our favor.

This was a huge win, not just for us, but for the First Amendment, and a defeat for all those who claim that I am a hater because I am willing to talk about what is wrong in Islam—including, as in this case, honor killings and fatwas for apostasy. Judge Hood protected free speech and did not take any swipes at my message, which she could have (such as saying, "While we might despise AFDI's message, we must protect it..."). She did not do that. Good for her.

I was thrilled, not just for the protection of free speech, but for those living in danger who will be helped by our freedom buses.

What To Do If You Get Sued

If you should get hit with a lawsuit by a Muslim Brotherhood proxy, or an Islamic supremacist, fight it. Contact me, Robert Spencer, the Thomas More Law Center, and other individuals and groups dedicated to fighting Islamic supremacist legal intimidation. And remember that one of the most important things that you can and must do is shine light on the tactics of the bullies: send news of the lawsuit to all the blogs that fight jihad, and to any other media contacts you may have.

Remember also that these lawsuits are a sword that cuts both ways. The Islamic supremacists will vigorously pursue the lawsuit until you vigorously pursue discovery: your opportunity to request documents pertinent to your case from your accusers. When CAIR sued the founder of the Web site Anti-CAIR, Andrew Whitehead, for pointing out that CAIR had numerous links to terrorist groups, the Islamic supremacist thugs backed off after Whitehead's lawyers asked questions about CAIR's funding that CAIR didn't want to answer.[109]

My Own Fight Against the Litigation Jihad

In July 2009, a teenage girl ran away from her home in Ohio after she reported that her father threatened to kill her upon discovering her conversion out of Islam. When she disappeared, many of her friends and those of us who had heard of her plight thought that she had met the worst of fates (as almost of these cases end the same horrible way). Imagine our joy when she emerged alive.

Who can forget the case of Rifqa Bary, which caught the attention of the entire nation and shone unprecedented light on Islam's death penalty for apostates? Reliable reports informed us that members of the Islamic supremacist Noor mosque in Columbus, Ohio, which Rifqa's parents had attended, spied on her and found out that she had converted out of Islam. This, plus the reported threat from her father, was the occasion of her fleeing from her home. Islamic supremacists, Rifqa's parents, and the Hamas-linked Islamic supremacist group the Council on American-Islamic Relations (CAIR) then subjected Rifqa to a shameful campaign of intimidation and persecution. Their objective was to shut her up and return her to the hellish home that she fought so desperately to escape.

The pressure on Rifqa Bary had been intense, the fatwas calling for her death numerous. Readers of my Web site AtlasShrugs.com fought hard for Rifqa. We rallied, covered her trials to return her home, sent her hundreds of Christmas cards in a holiday campaign (which her parents' lawyer, Omar Tarazi, tried to have seized and censored—unsuccessfully, I might add), and we contacted Florida and Ohio politicians and officials to keep Rifqa safe from her Islamic fundamentalist home and mosque.

And ultimately, the Islamic supremacists lost. The lovers of freedom and those who were determined to defend it were victorious: Rifqa was not forced to return home, and went free when she turned eighteen in August 2010. But no good deed goes unpunished. Much less well-known than Rifqa's plight and her fight for freedom of conscience was the campaign of intimidation that Tarazi, her parents' Islamic supremacist lawyer, continued to wage after her case was over. In September 2010, Tarazi filed a federal lawsuit against me and one of Rifqa's lawyers for defamation. Tarazi was enraged that I had identified him, using material readily available on the Internet, as having ties to Hamas-linked CAIR, and demanded ten million dollars in damages.

This little piggy cried all the way home. Boiled down to its essential oils, this was a ridiculous, frivolous lawsuit, designed to intimidate and silence foes of Islamic supremacism. *It's free speech, stupid.*

Tarazi had been a featured speaker at the Noor mosque that reportedly spied on Rifqa and publicly ridiculed her. His clients, the Barys, worked closely with the Muslim Brotherhood front, Hamas-linked CAIR, to return this poor tortured girl to her violent home. CAIR-Columbus executive director Babak Darvish was photographed in summer 2010 advising the Barys on how to compel Rifqa to return home. Tarazi claims that he has no association with CAIR at all, but at a January 2010 hearing, he was reportedly going out into the lobby and apparently colluding with the CAIR representative several times before and after the hearing. A Christian minister and ex-Muslim, Jamal Jivanjee, who was an eyewitness at the courtroom proceedings for Rifqa on December 22, 2009, reported that "the CAIR representative for central Ohio was present just outside the courtroom today. I observed Rifqa's parents attorney shaking hands with him and talking with him numerous times before the start of the hearing."[110] It is also worth noting that Tarazi admitted that his mother served as an officer of CAIR-Ohio in Columbus.

Tarazi's lawsuit against me was an embarrassment to the legal profession. Apart from being factually wrong, his emails and court filings were riddled with spelling and grammatical errors and evinced an ignorance of basic First Amendment law, Ohio defamation law, and the Federal Rules of Civil Procedure. One has to wonder how these incompetents pass the bar. Were those who had to pass on him afraid of being charged with "Islamophobia"?

All of us know what the real objective of this litigation jihad is. This lawsuit by Omar Tarazi is yet another attempt to impose the Sharia prohibition against blasphemy on the free marketplace of ideas. But I will not be silenced; nor will my colleagues. This is free speech. Period.

Flouting the Law

Yet another feature of litigation jihad springs from the First Amendment as well: the litigation and administrative legal initiatives that accompany all efforts to build mosques in American communities. In the case of the Ground Zero mosque, the mosque organizers had to overcome several legal hurdles—notably, they had to obtain the approval of the local Manhattan community board and face a challenge from the New York City Landmarks Commission, which had been considering designating the building they want to demolish to build the mosque as a landmark for two decades.

These hurdles were more pro-forma than anything else: At public hearings related to these legal challenges, Islamic supremacists skillfully exploited the leftist/liberal mindset by greasing the skids beforehand, sounding the usual notes of multiculturalism and accusing their opponents of bigotry, so that when they went in seeking approval for building in certain areas, the fix was already in.

This is happening around the country. Nonetheless, these hearings can provide a platform for a public airing of the opposition to the mosque, which might not otherwise have any forum in which it can be heard. Be informed, courteous, well prepared, and indefatigable. Make the most of whatever opportunity you get.

Pay attention also to any restrictions that local officials might place on the construction of the mosque, since the Islamic supremacists will often disregard them, and that will give you another avenue of resistance. This takes place in other areas of Islamization as well. In Hamtramck, Michigan, in July 2004, voters approved a change in the city's noise ordinance in order to allow for Islam's call to prayer to be broadcast over loudspeakers throughout the city. However, the secretary of the al-Islah mosque in Hamtramck, Masud Khan, said after the vote that it really didn't matter how the results had come out: the Muslims were going to broadcast the call to prayer anyway.[111]

Since the vote went his way, the point was moot; however, his disregard for the rule of law and for the wishes of the area non-Muslims were telling—and these Islamic supremacists' attitudes manifest themselves quite often in Islamization initiatives in the United States. And so we have witnessed time and time again the Muslim builders' flagrant disregard for zoning laws and city ordinances. Where naïve multiculturalist city officials don't rush to bend every rule to give them what they want, they do what they want anyway.

In 2010, the Muslim American Society (MAS), the Muslim Brotherhood's chief front in the United States, began building a mega-mosque on another quiet, tree-lined residential street in Sheepshead Bay in Brooklyn despite fierce opposition from the neighborhood and in violation of zoning ordinances and other regulations. Early in 2011, the leadership of Bay People, a local community group leading the fight against this mosque, contacted me asking for help in their fight. They had met a brick wall. The Islamic supremacists were violating building codes and ordinances in their voracious expansionist plans, while city officials and the Building Department turned the other way. Despite following the letter of the law, the Bay People were hopelessly abandoned. I met with leadership soon after and crafted a strategy to impede the unauthorized construction of this mosque.

The Islamic supremacists of the MAS are on a mission. Their consistent dishonesty serves a much larger, malevolent plot. Clearly they respect the Sharia (Islamic law). But American rule of law? Not so much. In Sheepshead Bay, they ignored procedure and flouted the law. They ignored inspectors from the Department of Buildings, complaints from neighbors and a stop work order, and began furiously building the massive structure in violation of code and certain requirements.

The Bay People consistently played by the rules; by contrast, the Islamic supremacists' contempt for American governance was made plain. Their obfuscation and misrepresentation of the project hardly instilled confidence that they were being straight about anything. When non-Muslims dared to try to film the construction, Muslims began yelling at them to stop filming. Why? What else were they hiding from the neighbors?

And more to the point, why there? Voorhies Avenue is a beautiful little street in Sheepshead Bay. Small, pretty, well-cared for homes line the street. There are no stores, churches, synagogues, or businesses there. So why did the Muslim Brotherhood want to build a beachhead there? There were no Muslims living on the street where the mosque was slated to be built, and not many in the neighborhood.

The Bay People wanted to keep the street residential and quiet. That was hardly unreasonable. The idea of a giant mosque, out of all proportion to the other homes on the street, was offensive. The traffic, congestion, and noise, as well as the call to prayer would forever change the landscape of this otherwise quiet street. And so the Bay People made this argument during the controversy over the mosque: don't neighborhoods have a say on what can or cannot be built? Don't neighborhoods have a right to preserve the sanctity of their streets and their homes? If it had been a Lowe's or Wal-Mart or a Limited Express that began construction in this residential area, it would have been voted down and decisively rejected out of hand by city authorities. But it was a mosque, so all bets were off. For mosques, every rule is broken, every ordinance tossed aside.

And it's not just for the mosques, but for the Islamic schools that are teaching jihad and incitement to violence all over the country. In October 2010, the Fairfax County, Virginia, Board of Supervisors voted to renew the Saudi government's lease of county-owned buildings for the notorious Islamic Saudi Academy (ISA) in Fairfax. The Islamic Saudi Academy is operated by the Royal Embassy of Saudi Arabia. The Saudis are well known for their promotion of the virulent and rigorist form of Islam known as Wahhabism, and they promote it at the ISA as well.

The results are clear: the ISA's class of 1999 valedictorian, Ahmed Omar Abu Ali, is serving life in prison for plotting to assassinate then-President Bush. This boy learned his lessons well: an investigation by the U.S. Commission on International Religious Freedom examined textbooks used at the school and found passages demonizing the Jews and saying that under certain circumstances Muslims could lawfully kill non-Muslims.[112]

Yet in 2008, State Department officials decided not to close the ISA, even though it had done nothing effective to change the content of its textbooks. And in 2010, the Board of Supervisors voted to extend the school's lease, despite heated protests from determined and well-informed freedom fighters. As we have seen, activist James Lafferty fought them every step of the way, commenting, "We were present at every hearing, no matter how small….We lost all of the recorded votes, but we won the war when the Saudis relented and dropped their plans to expand."

That they had to fight at all speaks volumes. Saudi money corrupts absolutely.

CHAPTER 6

CULTURAL JIHAD

The stealth jihadists' covert war takes many forms in every aspect of the culture, both obvious and subtle. We cannot point to one thing and say, "Aha! You see?" Instead, it is a chip-chip-chip away at cultural norms and secular mores. The norming of Islamization and Islamic law becomes part of the unraveling of the daily social fabric of our lives, and if you point to it and speak of it, you will be vilified—unlike the little boy who said that the Emperor had no clothes, and was cheered. You will not be cheered. You will be jeered. But do it anyway.

The Islamic/Leftist Alliance

I think it is important to point out that Islamic supremacism could never have advanced so far and so fast without its alliance with the left. And while it seems counterintuitive on its face that the left would be carrying water for the most extreme and radical ideology on the planet, it is not. The left traditionally aligns itself with the totalitarian ideology of the day, whether it was Stalinism, Communism in other parts of the world (i.e., Maoism, the Pol Pot regime, etc.), or National Socialism (Nazism), all of which resulted in the murder of hundreds of millions. The left is all about control. The Sharia is also all about control. The Sharia exerts total control over the people, which is the very thing that the left desires and demands.

Leftists are sympathetic and even positive toward Islam because of Islam's obvious ability to subdue people, compelling them to obey and even to practice self-censorship so as to avoid the threats and abuse that inevitably come to those who resist. So the left recognizes Islam's usefulness in advancing its authoritarian, totalitarian agenda. Islam's transnational, supranational quality also aids the left's desire to obliterate the sovereignty of individual nations and establish international rule that would destroy Constitutionally-protected American freedoms.

So while "Queers for Palestine" may sound insane and illogical considering the brutal treatment (and murder) of gays living in Muslim countries under the Sharia, it is consistent with leftism and statism.

We see the effects of the Islamic/leftist alliance in the advance of cultural jihad initiatives all over the country. The left has been joining forces with Islamic supremacists since 9/11 to protest the Bush Doctrine, operations in Iraq and Afghanistan, and the existence of Israel. Every anti-war and anti-Israel rally was hosted by a leftist/Islamic cabal including subversive groups such as Al-Awda; International Action Center (IAC); Code Pink; the ANSWER (Act Now to Stop War and End Racism) Coalition; American Muslims for Palestine; UIC Students for Justice in Palestine; the Mosque Foundation Community Center; the Muslim American Society; the Palestine Solidarity Group; the United States Palestinian Popular Conference Network; the International Solidarity Movement (ISM); and others.

In the summer of 2010, it came to light that the "humanitarian aid" flotilla that sailed from Turkey to Israel—whose passengers were actually jihadists who chanted a genocidal Muslim war cry dating back to the time of Muhammad while on the ship—was linked to radical left terrorist Bill Ayers, a longtime friend of Barack Obama, and even to John O. Brennan, Obama's deputy national security adviser for homeland security and counterterrorism. It was more evidence of the hard left tilt of the Obama Administration—and of the closeness of the Islamic/leftist alliance.[113]

In a similar vein, a September 2010 FBI raid in Minneapolis revealed extensive ties between American leftists and groups aiding the Islamic jihad against Israel. Marxist/Leninist agitator Mick Kelly, a chief target of the raid, was being investigated for his trips to, among other places,

Jordan, Syria, and the Palestinian territories, and for his links to the Popular Front for the Liberation of Palestine (PFLP) and the Arab American Action Network.[114]

In April 2011, the leftist/Islamic alliance made plans to descend upon the annual gathering of the American Israel Political Action Committee (AIPAC) in late May and to spew its poison and propaganda there. Code Pink announced that "Women for Peace (www.codepink.org), Global Exchange (www.globalexchange.org), and the U.S. Campaign to End the Israeli Occupation (www.endtheoccupation.org), together with over fifty peace and justice groups, were organizing a gathering in Washington D.C. from May 21–24, 2011, called 'Move Over AIPAC: Building a New US Middle East Policy.'"

The aim was to "learn about the extraordinary influence AIPAC has on U.S. policy and how to strengthen an alternative that respects the rights of all people in the region"—in other words, how to try to compel the United States to abandon Israel altogether: "AIPAC's unconditional support for Israel's illegal policies—separation walls, settlements, the siege of Gaza—has been devastating for Palestinians and the rest of the Middle East, but it also hurts Israel and the United States. While AIPAC is meeting at the D.C. Convention Center, we will be 'unpacking AIPAC'—educating the public about AIPAC's means, motives, and support for Israel's war crimes."[115]

Notice the use of the phrase "unpacking AIPAC." This mimics radical Imam Feisel Rauf (of Ground Zero mosque infamy). He, too, uses this phrase when talking about turning on Israel: "unpack Israel."[116] What they really wish to "unpack" is freedom, democracy, and the Jews.

Another example of the Islamic/left alliance was the American Library Association's joining up with Hamas-linked CAIR to oppose Peter King's hearings.[117] The ALA is the same craven organization that caved and cancelled an appearance by Robert Spencer in 2009 after Hamas-linked CAIR demanded adherence to Islamic law: Do not defame or insult Islam.[118] The ALA accommodates the Sharia.

Meanwhile, where are the feminists and women's rights groups fighting against clitorectomies, honor killings, gender apartheid, and the oppression and suppression of women in Islam? They are guilty of silence and complicity. Instead of standing for women's rights, radical feminist darlings like Naomi Wolf extol the cloth coffin of the burqa. Wolf insists that the Islamic chador is sexy, and supports its institutionalization throughout the Islamic world.[119]

Those are just a few examples of a large-scale and ongoing phenomenon. With leftist individuals and organizations of all kinds so anxious to subjugate themselves to Islam, it is no wonder that the cultural jihad is advancing so rapidly. And it is advancing on many fronts.

The Mosqueing of the Workplace

In the summer of 2010, a Muslim woman, Imane Boudlal, was turned away four times from her job as a restaurant hostess at the Storytellers' Cafe in the Disneyland Resort's Grand Californian Hotel. Boudlal was persistently violating the company's dress code by insisting on wearing a hijab to work. By sending her home, Disney was simply sticking to its own standards: the Orange County Register reported that "Disney is known for its strict dress code, called the Disney Look, which has been in place since 1957."[120]

Sue Brown, a Disney spokesperson, explained, "The company values diversity and has a long-standing policy against discrimination of any kind. Ms. Boudlal has worked for the company for more than two years and recently made the request to wear a hijab, and we have been working directly with her on accommodations. In the interim, we offered reasonable accommodations to allow her to work during her scheduled shifts, which she declined."

Boudlal refused to take any job that would remove her from public view: "I'm not going to accept to work in the back."

That made it clear that her insistence on wearing hijab was not just a matter of her personal piety; she wanted to make a political statement. Here was a woman who, after working for years at Disney, decided to challenge Disney's dress code and ultimately to sue Disney for the right to wear the hijab at work.

This case was not about the hijab, this was about Islamic supremacism and imposing Islam on the secular society. Cultural icons are a favored target of this tactic: that's almost certainly why Disney was chosen for this showdown.

The idea was to establish and enforce the principle that wherever Islamic law and American customs, practices, business policies, and laws conflict, the American side would have to give way. That's why Imane Boudlal insisted on working in public: she was showing that Islam was stronger than Disney's fifty-year-old dress code, and could make the richest, most powerful of corporations bend to its will.

This is the stealth, cultural jihad.

Challenges to institutional dress codes by hijab-wearing Muslims are growing increasingly common. In March 2011, a Muslim defendant sued Orange County, California, for being forced to remove her hijab while in jail.[121] In September 2009, a Muslim girl sued Abercrombie & Fitch, claiming that the edgy clothing manufacturer had denied her a job because she was wearing a hijab.[122] In November 2009, CareNow, a medical clinic in a Dallas suburb, apologized to a Muslim doctor and changed its no-headgear policy after initially telling her during a job interview that she couldn't wear her hijab. Initially, CareNow's President, Tim Miller, was unapologetic: "I would apologize for any misunderstanding, definitely...but I don't really feel like there is anything that we did that is wrong and our policy is wrong." But the following day, inexplicably, Miller had completely changed his tune: "We apologize to Dr. Zaki for the misunderstanding. We will clarify our policy, and will continue our ongoing sensitivity training."[123]

Obama's White House has come down on the side of the hijabs. When he gave his notorious address to the worldwide Islamic *umma* from Cairo on June 4, 2009, Obama made sure they knew which side he was on in the cultural jihad: "The U.S. government," he bragged, "has gone to court to protect the right of women and girls to wear the hijab, and to punish those who would deny it....I reject the view of some in the West that a woman who chooses to cover her hair is somehow less equal." He didn't say anything about the women who have been harassed, threatened with death, and killed for *not* wearing the hijab in Muslim countries, and even in the West: Aqsa Parvez was murdered in Ontario by her father and brother for refusing to wear the hijab. How many Muslim girls in the United States have been threatened by their fathers for not wearing the hijab? We will never know; no one speaks for them. And in Cairo, Barack Obama certainly wasn't interested in protecting *their* rights.

Obama in the Muslim capital of Cairo promised to punish infidels for not submitting. And so he did. Just five days after his Cairo speech, Obama and his Attorney General, Eric Holder, showed that he meant what he had said, and demonstrated their determination to go to court "to protect the right of women and girls to wear the hijab, and to punish those who would deny it." The Justice Department sued Essex County, New Jersey for discrimination in the case of Yvette Beshier, a Muslim corrections officer who insisted on wearing a khimar, an Islamic headscarf, to work.[124] The Essex County Department of Corrections (DOC) had first suspended and then fired Beshier for violating its dress code by wearing a Muslim headscarf.

The DOC was just sticking to its dress code. But Obama and Holder were determined to advance Islam. And they won. Obama's headscarf jihad took the New Jersey county to court, and the county caved. In November 2010, the county reached a "settlement" with Beshier, agreeing to pay her $25,000 and to adopt a "religious accommodation policy."[125] It was an historic event: the United States Justice Department had won a lawsuit meant to enforce Islamic law.

In March 2007, Target stores in Minneapolis shifted Muslim cashiers who refused to check out pork products to other jobs in the stores.[126] The J. B. Swift meat packing plant in Greeley, Colorado, in September 2008, fired Muslim workers who turned violent and walked off their jobs when denied special break periods to end the Ramadan fast at the appointed time.[127] The Equal Employment Opportunity Commission, however, sided with the Muslim workers and forced Swift to reinstate them.[128] Ultimately, Swift added footbaths and bidets to its plant for the Muslim workers.[129]

In November 2008, a federal judge ordered Gold'n Plump, Inc., a chicken processing plant, to pay $365,000 to Somali Muslim workers for firing them for walking off the job to pray, and for making new hires sign a form acknowledging that they may have to handle pork on the job.[130] And in February 2010, a group of Muslims in Colorado sued Wal-Mart, claiming that they were fired in order to provide jobs for local non-Muslims, and that they had been denied prayer breaks while on the job.[131] Mind you, it is not necessary for a Muslim to pray at a certain time if necessity makes it impossible to do so. These actions are merely devices in which to impose Islam on non-believers. Prayer is not absolutely required on a strict schedule, and Muslim prayers are commonly "made up" after work or school. This is true even in Muslim countries such as Iran.

When Campbell's Soup introduced a halal line—that is, a line adhering to the dietary requirements of Islamic law, for their soup division, a Muslim Brotherhood group with known ties to terror, the Islamic Society of North America (ISNA), was the organization that they affiliated with for halal certification. This is part of the cultural jihad: the mainstreaming of jihadist organizations. When this news was announced, I immediately called for a boycott on AtlasShrugs.com, as did other blogs. Campbell's, instead of being swayed by the voluminous incriminating data on the Islamic Society of North America, dug in its heels and refused to budge.

SIOA and others called for a boycott, and it went viral; the next quarter, Campbell's Soup's stock was down eight percent.

It is worth noting that the leftist media, dishonest as always, characterized our boycott as being called because we objected to Campbell's offering halal food. That was false, of course. What we objected to was their using a Muslim Brotherhood-linked group as their halal authority.

And in that case, we were able to send Campbell's a message. But they continued to consult with ISNA, and the cultural jihad also kept on advancing on other fronts.

Secret Halal Meat

It is not labeled or advertised as such, but the meat you buy at your local supermarket could be halal. In October 2010, the latest submission to Islam came to us from the meat industry in both Europe and the United States. There have been numerous explosive revelations recently about the little-reported fact that much of the meat in Europe is being processed as halal and yet sold without the halal label.

This is not the exception, but the rule. The people are being betrayed by their own elected officials, who should be on top of this.

Yes, folks, if you're in Europe, and in many areas in America as well, the meat you are eating is probably halal, unless you're keeping kosher. In a little-known strike against freedom, yet again, we are being forced into consuming meat slaughtered by means of a barbaric, torturous, and inhuman method: Islamic slaughter, the cutting of the animal's throat without stunning or any other form of mitigation for the animal's pain.

Where were the PETA clowns and the ridiculous celebs who pose naked on giant billboards for PETA and "animal rights"? They would rather see people die of cancer or AIDS than see animals used in drug testing, but torturous and painful Islamic slaughter is OK.

Many people have written to me saying that they simply won't eat halal meat, as they object to the slaughter methods. And I agree. The Sharia term for halal slaughter is dhakat. Dhakat is to slaughter an animal by cutting the trachea, the esophagus, and the jugular vein, letting the blood drain out while saying "Bismillah allahu akbar"—in the name of Allah the greatest.

Many Christians, Hindus or Sikhs, and Jews find it offensive to eat meat slaughtered according to Islamic ritual (although Jews are less likely to be exposed to such meat, because they eat kosher). The issue for many Christians is that in halal slaughter, an imam offers the animal up as a sacrifice to Allah, which makes it meat sacrificed to idols.

Shockingly, 70 percent of New Zealand lamb imported into the United Kingdom is halal. It is not labeled as such, so people are eating halal without even knowing it. But people there are fighting back: When halal food was imposed on public schools in the United Kingdom in 2007, parents were in an uproar. And in March 2010, Stop Islamization of Europe (SIOE), the sister organization to my group SIOA, called for the cessation of mandatory consumption of halal meat on the continent.

As halal slaughter becomes more common in the United States, the likelihood of non-Muslims who object to halal meat for whatever reason unknowingly buying it also increases.

I wanted to know if this Islamic supremacism in being imposed on U.S. meat processors as well. Imagine my surprise at many of the findings. After asking lots of questions of people inside the meat-packing industry, I discovered that only two plants in the United States that perform halal slaughter keep the halal meat separated from the non-halal meat, and they only do so because plant managers thought it was right to do so. At other meat-packing plants, animals are slaughtered following halal requirements, but then only a small bit of the meat is actually labeled halal.

This is because neither the United States nor Britain requires that halal meat be labeled as such. Nor do government regulations require that halal meat and non-halal meat be kept separate.

Yet there are existing labeling laws requiring that meat be labeled in a truthful and not misleading way. These labeling laws could be and should be used to make sure that all halal meat is clearly sold as such, so that those who want to avoid it for whatever reason can do so.

But the way it looks right now, most of the beef sold in the United States comes from meat-packing plants that engage in at least some halal slaughter—and don't always tell the public that they've slaughtered the animal according to halal rules. There's no easy way to tell exactly how much of this is occurring, but I am still investigating.

One thing appears clear now: some of this halal meat is going to public school lunch programs.

And the United States Department of Agriculture's Food Safety and Inspection Service (FSIS) stated that if free citizens wanted a labeling change to state clearly whether or not meat was halal, they'd have to file a petition, due to the extensive nature of the labeling changes needed.

SIOA will be filing that petition.

Meanwhile, why were meat-packing plants in the United States and Great Britain engaging in any halal slaughter at all? Because they export a great deal of meat to Muslim countries. That's fine. But non-Muslims in America and Europe don't deserve to have halal meat forced upon them in this way, without their knowledge or consent. It is Islamic supremacism on the march, yet again.

Freedom fighters should bring lawsuits against meat-packing plants that practice halal slaughter on the grounds of cruelty to animals.

The Islamization of the Schools

As every American knows, there must be a separation of church and state: "Congress shall make no law respecting the establishment of a religion." Yet the Tarek ibn Ziyad Academy (TIZA), a K–8 charter school in Inver Grove Heights, Minnesota, came under fire in 2009 for accepting public funds while teaching Islam and conducting Islamic prayer on school grounds. Charter schools are public schools, and by law must not endorse or promote religion. But TIZA is an Islamic school that is funded by Minnesota taxpayers.

TIZA is housed in a building also inhabited by the Muslim American Society of Minnesota, whose stated mission is "establishing Islam in Minnesota." There is a mosque inside the building also. TIZA's executive director, Asad Zaman, is an imam. Students pray every day, and the food that the school's cafeteria offers is halal. At the end of the school day students take "Islamic Studies." One TIZA teacher said, "Teachers led the kids into the gym, where a man dressed in white with a white cap, who had been at the school all day," led the students in Islamic prayer. Another man was "prostrating himself in prayer on a carpet as the students entered." This assembly was not voluntary for the students, virtually all of whom were Muslim.[132]

The Muslims in the Islamic public school were taking off the gloves. This is *unbelievable* and sanctioned by the state. Freedom fighters should bring lawsuits against all madrassas that receive public funds of any sort. Sue to enjoin the funding, and sue the public agencies and politicians personally who legislate such funding.

And it's not just Minnesota. This is happening all across America. In this case, the dhimmi media painted the case as Muslims "seeking to protect their rights"—as what? Muslims? Certainly it did not involve protecting their rights as Americans. It is against the law for my taxpayer dollars and your taxpayer dollars to be used to fund indoctrination into a supremacist ideology.

Look how they use our Constitution, our democracy to kill it. TIZA's case was so egregious that eventually even the ACLU got involved. I cheered when the ACLU finally filed a lawsuit in January 2009 against this publicly funded Islamic school. The suit argued that TIZA "violates the First Amendment by sharing space with the Muslim American Society of Minnesota, promoting prayer in school and endorsing Muslim clothing rules and dietary practices." It was a "when pigs fly" moment. I hadn't cheered the ACLU in decades. They are notorious for suing Christian organizations in the petty exploitation of the separation of church and state (i.e., suing to remove nativity scenes on public ground, removal of a cross that was first erected in 1934 by a group of veterans, opposing family festival day events and displays containing religious and nonreligious artifacts, including a menorah, a red sleigh, even Kwanza symbols—the list goes on and on) while remaining conspicuously silent on the egregious acts of advancement of Islamic supremacism in almost every aspect of American life.

So what did the Islamic school do? **Sued the ACLU, of course.** Litigation jihad. TIZA claimed that the ACLU defamed it and was trying to hurt "the good name of TIZA" among parents of prospective students, as well as teachers who might be considering applying to work there. With breathtaking audacity, the TIZA lawsuit even claimed that the ACLU action had resulted in threats being made against school employees.[133] In reality, it was TIZA employees who had threatened those who blew the whistle on the school.[134]

Watch for such schools in your area. If there are charter schools receiving public money that are attended almost exclusively by Muslim students, call for an evaluation of their curriculum and practices. If you don't do this, who will? School district authorities are generally ignorant of and indifferent to this problem.

And the problem was not just Islamized charter schools getting taxpayer money while teaching Islam to Muslim students. It's not just the charter schools we need to be concerned about; it's Arabic public schools. When I interviewed Mark Steyn, author of *America Alone*, he boiled the problem down. Speaking about the Khalil Gibran International Academy, New York's controversial Arabic public school, Steyn explained why free citizens should be wary of such public Arabic-language academies:

> It shows how we mischaracterized, we willfully misunderstand Islam. Yes, on the face of it, yes, Arabic is a language in a sense there is would be no difference between opening a foreign language school—a Spanish-language school or a French-language school—but in fact, Arabic is more than a language. It is explicated the language of Islam, so in that sense, it is part of the Islamic religious imperial project. Radical Islam advances through the Arabic language. And you go all kinds of places that aren't in the Arab world now, like Pakistan, Indonesia, Central Asia, the Balkans, the Netherlands, the United Kingdom and Canada and the United States, and you will hear those imams preaching in Arabic. Arabic is not just another language like French or Italian; it is the spearhead of an ideological project that is deeply opposed to the United States.[135]

The Khalil Gibran International Academy was beset by difficulties from the day that New York City officials announced that it was going to open in 2007. Even the name of the school was controversial—Eblan Farris of the Friends of Gibran Council, a founding member of the United States Chapter of the World Council of the Cedars Revolution, which has as its main goal the freedom, democracy and independence of Lebanon, has stated emphatically that the Lebanese writer Khalil Gibran's name not be used for this public madrassa. On the school's advisory board was the imam Talib Abdul-Rashid, the "resident imam" of the Mosque of Islamic Brotherhood, Harlem. On the Mosque of Islamic Brotherhood's Web site is the motto of the Muslim Brotherhood:

Allah is our goal
The Prophet Muhammad ibn 'Abdullah is our leader
The Qu'ran is our constitution
Jihad is our way
And death in the way of Allah is our promised end.

The school's hijab-wearing first principal, Dhabah Almontaser, was fired after a controversy arose over her approval of a t-shirt emblazoned "Intifada NYC." The Intifada, of course, is the Palestinian jihad against Israel. The indefatigable SIOA activist Pamela Hall took the picture that exposed Almontaser's militant ties, and ultimately forced her resignation. The NYC Intifada t-shirt was produced and distributed by AWAAM, a group closely affiliated with Almontaser. This shows what one determined activist can accomplish.

The school turned out ultimately to be an abject failure. At one point in 2010, the school had fully suspended a third of its student body for infractions ranging from hitting another student to bringing weapons to school. In a student body populated mostly by Muslims, this was a telling indication of the effects of the Religion of Peace.

And in March 2011, the Department of Education announced that it was closing the middle school because of low enrollment and perhaps the worst violence of any New York City school, and would attempt to reopen it as a high school. We will watch those developments carefully.

The problem extends to public schools attended largely by non-Muslims as well. In late May of 2010, Wellesley, Massachusetts, public middle school students took a field trip to the Islamic Society of Boston Cultural Center—a controversial Saudi-funded mega-mosque run by the Muslim American Society of Boston. There the students were separated by gender and the boys were asked to join the Muslim adults in their prayer. Several of the public school boys took part.

The implications of this cannot be understated. This is an outrage. Your taxpayer dollars were going to brainwash our children to Islam. It's bad enough that the history books have been whitewashed of the over a millennium of jihadi wars, land appropriations, cultural annihilations, and enslavements.

Whitewashing the Textbooks

Islamic supremacist groups have for quite some time consulted with public school textbook publishers and made sure that material presented on Islam was heavily slanted, even to the point of proselytizing. Combine that with the anti-Western multiculturalist bias of the publishers themselves, and the result is a large number of public school textbooks that denigrate Judeo-Christian Western civilization and portray Islam in a glowingly positive light.

The American Textbook Council, an independent national textbook monitoring organization, issued a report in 2008 that showed that many commonly used public school textbooks "present an incomplete and confected view of Islam that misrepresents its foundations and challenges to international security." For example, the popular middle school text *Across the Centuries* defines jihad as a struggle "to do one's best to resist temptation and overcome evil."[136] Another middle school text in common use, *History Alive! The Medieval World and Beyond*, is just as distorted: "Muslims should fulfill jihad with the heart, tongue, and hand. Muslims use the heart in their struggle to resist evil. The tongue may convince others to take up worthy causes, such as funding medical research. Hands may perform good works and correct wrongs." Not a word about war, conquest, or subjugation.[137]

Islam's history of conquering and Islamizing non-Muslim cultures is whitewashed as well. A high school textbook, *Medieval and Early Modern*

Times, calls medieval al-Andalus, Islam-ruled Spain, a "multicultural society." Likewise, *History Alive!* says that in medieval Spain "a unique culture flourished in cities like Cordoba and Toledo, where Muslims, Jews, and Christians lived together in peace."[138] But in reality, Jews and Christians in medieval Spain were subjugated as dhimmis and never had equal rights with Muslims. Even historian Maria Rosa Menocal, who has done a great deal to spread the myth of a tolerant medieval Muslim Spain, admits that in al-Andalus, Jews and Christians "were required to pay a special tax—no Muslims paid taxes—and to observe a number of restrictive regulations: Christians and Jews were prohibited from attempting to proselytize Muslims, from building new places of worship, from displaying crosses or ringing bells. In sum, they were forbidden most public displays of their religious rituals."[139]

Why are the textbooks this bad? The American Textbook Council report reveals that "Islamic organizations, willing to sow misinformation, are active in curriculum politics. These activists are eager to expunge any critical thought about Islam from textbooks and all public discourse. They are succeeding, assisted by partisan scholars and associations."[140]

It is very important that you monitor your children's textbooks, and the textbooks used in general at your local public school, for this bias. It is quite pervasive, and yet has received virtually no attention. In a singular incident, in September 2010, the state of Texas began to fight back. A resolution passed by the Texas State Board of Education detailed just how pervasive the "pro-Islamic/anti-Christian" bias was in history and social studies textbooks:

- In one instance, devoting 120 student text lines to Christian beliefs, practices, and holy writings but 248 (more than twice as many) to those of Islam; and dwelling for 27 student text lines on Crusaders' massacre of Muslims at Jerusalem in 1099 yet censoring Muslims' massacres of Christians there in 1244 and at Antioch in 1268, implying that Christian brutality and Muslim loss of life are significant but Islamic cruelty and Christian deaths are not...

- In another instance, allotting 82 student text lines to Christian beliefs, practices, and holy writings but 159 (almost twice as many) to those of Islam; describing Crusaders' massacres of European Jews yet ignoring the Muslim Tamerlane's massacre of perhaps 90,000 coreligionists at Baghdad in 1401, and of perhaps 100,000 Indian POWs at Delhi in 1398; thrice charging medieval Christians with sexism; and saying the Church "laid the foundations for anti-Semitism"...

• In a third instance, spending 139 student text lines on Christian beliefs, practices, and holy writings but 176 on those of Islam; claiming Islam "brought untold wealth to thousands and a better life to millions," while "because of [Europeans' Christian] religious zeal ... many peoples died and many civilizations were destroyed;" and contrasting "the Muslim concern for cleanliness" with Swedes in Russia who were "the filthiest of God's creatures"...

Patterns of pejoratives towards Christians and superlatives toward Muslims, calling Crusaders aggressors, "violent attackers," or "invaders" while euphemizing Muslim conquest of Christian lands as "migrations" by "empire builders"...

Politically-correct whitewashes of Islamic culture and stigmas on Christian civilization, indicting Christianity for the same practices (e.g., sexism, slavery, persecution of out-groups) that they treat non-judgmentally, minimize, sugarcoat, or censor in Islam...

Sanitized definitions of "jihad" that exclude religious intolerance or military aggression against non-Muslims—even though Islamic sources often include these among proper meanings of the term— which undergirds worldwide Muslim terrorism...

This resolution shows how people can affect change—how *you* can affect change. In a victory for freedom, the Texas State Board of Education approved the resolution by a narrow 7–6 vote.[141] In its report, the local news station KXAN stated the case succinctly: "The State Board of Education is sending a message to textbook publishers: Don't promote one religion at the expense of others."[142] Texas activist Randy Reeves, who drafted the resolution, understated his case when he commented, "I think our documentation clearly shows that the bias is there. And we feel that it was not done on accident."[143]

All this was happening according to the Islamic supremacists' predetermined plan. And even where Islamic supremacists are not employing such subterfuge, they're working to gain special accommodation for Muslims in public schools. They have a playbook for how to impose Islam in the public schools. In Islam, there is no separation of mosque and state—mosque is state in Islam.

In May 2010, the Islamic Web site Sound Vision published a six-step plan by the founding director of the Council on Islamic Education, Shabbir Mansuri, on how to pressure public school authorities into allowing special accommodation for Muslims. These included "knowing what laws and regulations govern the issue of religious accommodation"—Islamic groups make skillful use of government directives requiring reasonable accommodation of religious practices. Mansuri also directed Muslims to make friends with a teacher and enlist him or her as an ally, even inviting the teacher over for dinner; to "leave a paper trail, but first, be really nice" (at first!); and to repeat these steps as necessary with the school principal and even the district superintendent. The Muslim complainant is never to give up until the concessions are granted.

If this guide shows us anything, it's what idiots they take us for. This is, of course, an outrage. None of this should be introduced into the public school. If this is what Muslim parents want, they should send their children to madrassah.

This Islamic supremacist was directing Muslims to make friends with teachers and education officials in order to use them, and to take advantage of procedures and practices instituted by short-sighted American multiculturalists to gain yet another advantage for Islam.

The freedom fighter need not and should not resort to such subterfuges. But you can and should learn from the opposition. You should be no less informed, determined, and persistent.

The Buried Memorial

One obvious manifestation of the cultural jihad was the burying of the 9/11 memorial museum. When our new AFDI documentary, *The Ground Zero Mosque: The Second Wave of the 9/11 Attacks*, made its New York premiere in February 2011 to a fierce and energized packed house at the St. Luke's Theatre on West 46th Street in Manhattan, 9/11 family members Nelly Braginsky, Rosaleen Tallon, Sally Regenhard, Rosemary Cain, and Rosa Leonetti joined Robert Spencer and me for a spirited Q&A/strategy session after the screening. Sally and Rosaleen gave the astonished crowd the shocking details of the travesty that is the 9/11 victims memorial, which is planning to put the unidentified remains of 9/11 victims seven stories underground inside a museum that charges admission—and which will include lavish profiles (above ground, of course) of the 9/11 hijackers. Daisy Khan of the Ground Zero Mosque is on the Board of the commission putting together the memorial, charged with making sure the Muslim perspective is represented in every aspect of the memorial.

What about the kafir perspective?

CHAPTER 7

THE EROSION OF WOMEN'S
RIGHTS IN AMERICA

Another front in the cultural jihad opened in Spring 2010, when the American Academy of Pediatrics announced that it would be recommending that American doctors offer clitorectomies to Muslim women—in what can only be construed as a complete loss of any semblance of goodness and morality in the name of multiculturalist poison. The AAP issued a policy statement suggesting that doctors in the United States perform a mild form of this sick barbarity on girls in order to keep their families from sending them overseas for it.

It is unbelievable, but true: according to the *New York Times*, the American Academy of Pediatrics in May 2010 advocated that American doctors be allowed to stick girls' clitorises with a needle so as to satisfy Muslim and African families' demand for female genital mutilation: "It might be more effective if federal and state laws enabled pediatricians to reach out to families by offering a ritual nick as a possible compromise to avoid greater harm." This is sexual abuse.

Congressman Joseph Crowley (D-NY) commented on the danger of this: "I am sure the academy had only good intentions, but what their recommendation has done is only create confusion about whether F.G.M. [female genital mutilation] is acceptable in any form, and it is the wrong step forward on how best to protect young women and girls. F.G.M. serves no medical purpose, and it is rightfully banned in the U.S."

Georganne Chapin, executive director of Intact America, a group defending women from this practice, was "astonished that a group of intelligent people did not see the utter slippery slope" that the AAP had started on by allowing for the "ritual nick." Chapin asked, "How much blood will parents be satisfied with? There are countries in the world that allow wife beating, slavery, and child abuse, but we don't allow people to practice those customs in this country. We don't let people have slavery a little bit because they're going to do it anyway, or beat their wives a little bit because they're going to do it anyway."

Chapin was right. What next? Wife-beating seminars and its unintended benefits? Or a strip in Vegas for child marriages so they won't go overseas for the nuptials? Allowing for this "ritual nick" would not have the effect these nudnik do-gooders imagine. It would have just the opposite effect. Islamic misogyny would be given the seal of approval by the American Academy of Pediatrics.

Also, this was not the first time that the *New York Times* gave clitorectomies its tacit approval. In January 2008, it painted a rosy picture of the ritual in a piece that never mentioned the pain, bleeding, and infections that often result from it.

Female genital mutilation is not the only horrific Islamic custom that is coming West; the number of honor killings is skyrocketing in Europe and America. But genital mutilation is spreading at an alarming rate. It has been reported that thousands of girls in the United Kingdom have been mutilated and the authorities can't (or won't) stop it. To the credit of the U.K. media, at least they have been having a public discussion about it. It's happening here, but to speak of it publicly would insult CAIR.

The AAP recommendation was another example of the cultural jihad, of raging Sharia in the U.S. Despite the taqiyya that is always spread by Muslim leaders in the West about the practice, Islam sanctions female genital mutilation, and sometimes even encourages it. Muhammad Al-Mussayar, an Islamic scholar at Al-Azhar University, the most prestigious and influential institution in the Islamic world, said that Islam doesn't forbid female genital mutilation:

All the jurisprudents, since the advent of Islam and for 14 centuries or more, are in consensus that female circumcision is permitted by Islam. But they were divided with regard to its status in shari'a. Some said that female circumcision is required by shari'a, just like male circumcision. Some said this is the mainstream practice, while others said it is a noble act. But throughout the history of Islam, nobody has ever said that performing female circumcision is a crime. There has been a religious ruling on this for 14 centuries.[144]

And now it effectively had the approval of the American Academy of Pediatrics.

By G-d, these are our daughters. This is our culture that these clueless dhimmi buffoons are throwing away with both hands. No matter how you couch this argument, and the *New York Times* is the master of velvet-tongued barbarity, what the American Academy of Pediatrics did was grotesque—and it would lead to more approval for Sharia teachings on women.

Amina and Sarah: Honor Killing

Our daughters and granddaughters would be the ones who would suffer for this approval of barbarism.

We can see that coming in the honor killing of Amina and Sarah Said. It is worth examining this case in detail, for it is emblematic of the government and media establishment's indifference to the plight of all too many Muslim women and girls in the United States today.

When Amina and Sarah Said were brutally murdered by their father on New Year's Day 2008, I thought, *this is it.* This is going to break the dam wide open. America would not, could not possibly, ignore this horror caused by and sanctioned by Islamic beliefs, assumptions, and attitudes.

We love our seventeen-year-old cell-phone-toting, tiny T-shirt wearing, boy-crazy, diva-girl teens in this nation. They are our (baby boom) daughters. They are our icons: think Miley Cyrus, Britney Spears, and Lindsey Lohan (once upon a sober time). They are our ideal: so many forty-year-old American women try to look seventeen—think *Desperate Housewives.* We have a soft spot for such girls, which is why America is so obsessed with little girls lost like Britney and Lindsey. The Said girls were so cute—and they were both American model-beautiful, epitomizing both blue-eyed, light-skinned, and brown-eyed, café au lait beauty.

The Said sisters, Amina, eighteen, and Sarah, seventeen, were shot to death by their father as New Year's Day 2008 dawned. Their father, Yaser Said, is still at large. Friends of Amina and Sarah remember that he was proudly Egyptian and critical of popular American lifestyles. "He was really strict about guy relationships and talking to guys, as well as the things she wears," said Kathleen Wong, a friend of the dead teenagers. "I'm definitely 100% sure that it was her dad that killed her."

Why didn't Oprah run a series on the treatment of these girls? The average Oprah-watching American woman would have cared. Deeply. At present, people don't care about Islamic honor killings overseas, because they take place in another country and culture and "we can't tell them what to do"—but this is America. These girls were killed for being typical American teens, and this should have been a huge story.

Clinging

To all outward appearances, Amina Said, eighteen, and her sister Sarah, seventeen, projected an appearance of naïve, innocent sweetness in their hundreds of photos together. Smiling. Wrestling. Hugging. Playing.

In every photo, Amina and Sarah are close. Very close. But look closer and you can see that they are, in fact, clinging to each other—clinging for dear life, putting on a brave face against a home life of violence and terror that most Americans would find unimaginable. It almost seems as if they are posing for their posthumous photos that would inevitably hit the net and the press.

They were cell phone-toting, t-shirt wearing, soccer playing American girls.

In one widely circulating photo, Amina is wearing what looks like a sweatshirt bearing the name "AMERICAN." It was a legend that proved bitterly ironic.

Amina and Sarah were brutally murdered in Irving, Texas, on New Year's Day 2008. Both were shot to death.

But their murders were only the last act of an unremitting tragedy—what was for both girls a lifetime of terror, beatings, and oppression. They weren't Muslim enough.

Reliance of the Traveller: A Classic Manual of Islamic Sacred Law, one of the most important English-language sources for the content of Islamic law, specifies that in murder cases, "the following are not subject to retaliation," and then lists—after the lovely, egalitarian "Muslim for killing a non-Muslim" and "Jewish or Christian subject … for killing an apostate"—"a father or mother (or their fathers or mothers) for killing their offspring, or offspring's offspring."

In other words, a father faces no punishment, according to Islamic law, for killing his daughter.

Tissy

The stage was set when a shy, pudgy Texas teenager, Patricia Owens, who was known to everyone as "Tissy," met an Egyptian immigrant named Yaser and his brother Yassein. Both were working at a 7-Eleven. According to Tissy's aunt, Gail Gartrell, Tissy and her family lived in an apartment complex very close to this store. When Tissy and her siblings went to the store, Yassein flirted with Tissy, giving her gifts and making the awkward girl feel special. Soon Yassein asked Tissy to marry him, and she enthusiastically accepted.

But then the very same week, Yassein inexplicably and abruptly broke off the engagement. Tissy's aunt recalls what happened next: "Then, up steps Yaser! He began the same process and told my brother-in-law that he was a college student, self sufficient and Tissy would be well cared for. They became engaged and the gifting process continued. *Tissy was fifteen.* He said he was in school, but I never heard what his major was! I am not sure he was actually in school!"[145]

And there was another, potentially larger problem: "Yaser was Muslim, and I warned my niece and begged her to please read and UNDERSTAND Yaser's religion and culture. She promised me she would. She did not…I later found out."[146]

It didn't take very long. Tissy's aunt Gail recalls hair-raising details:

"Yaser's need to control was implemented immediately! Tissy took a photo album to my sister's house and showed them pictures of Yaser holding a knife to her throat! Yaser always carried a machine gun, in his car! My sister was terrified of him! She would tell me that she was afraid that he would kill those children and her daughter, Tissy!"

Another hint of the terrors that lay in the future came in October 1998, when Amina was eight and Sarah was seven, Tissy reported Yaser to a Hill County Sheriff's deputy: Amina and Sarah, she said, were telling their grandmother that he was sexually abusing them and had done so for several years. Tissy appeared to believe the girls; she left Yasir, and not for the first time. She had initially left Yaser in October 1997, after getting fed up with his not working—which forced her to find jobs to bring some money into the house. But Yaser struck back hard: he picked up Islam, the brother of Amina and Sarah, and the girls at school and went to Virginia. According to Tissy's sister, Connie Moggio, he told Tissy that "he was going to take the kids to the Middle East where he is from and she would never see them again." Tissy and Yaser soon got back together.[147]

The Sheriff's report makes for harrowing reading: "The girls were staying with [the grandmother] and were afraid to go with their father and told [the grandmother] that their father had put his finger in their vagina and rectum and he had put his penis in Amina's vagina one time."

It continued: "Complainant [Tissy] advised that Sarah told her that her father had stuck his finger inside of her and that Amina told her that her father had stuck his finger inside of her, touched her bottom and her top." The report stated that Yaser had most recently abused the girls as recently as two weeks before Tissy called the Sheriff's office.

Amina told sheriff's deputies that Yaser had "put his front part in her front part" and that she was "afraid of her father...afraid he will hit her." Sarah said that she also was afraid of "her dad and his brothers...scared they will take her."

Tissy was afraid too—as the sheriff's report shows. "The complainant," it noted, "was very nervous about anyone questioning her husband, Yaser Said...The complainant advised she would like to file charges against her husband so she could get a court order to keep him and his family away from her kids."

But no such court order was ever issued. According to journalist

Glenna Whitley, "Yaser adamantly denied the charge and said he was willing to take a polygraph test. He blamed Tissy for not providing for the children. Yaser never took the polygraph. In Dallas County, he was charged with felony 'retaliation' after Tissy filed a complaint alleging he threatened to kill her and take the children after being indicted on December 17, 1998, for 'sexual penetration' of both girls."[148]

But less than a month after that, the girls recanted, and a judge dismissed their charges against Yaser. It wasn't until two years later, in March 2001, that he was finally arrested on the "retaliation" charge—and that charge was then also dropped when, according to Whitley, "Tissy refused to cooperate with prosecutors and Yaser agreed to take an anger-management course."[149] Tissy moved in again with Yaser.

This judge doesn't seem to have made any attempt to determine whether or not the girls were coerced into recanting their charges. According to Gail Gartrell, Amina said that she was no more than four years old when Yasser first started sexually abusing her.[150] This matched what the girls' grandmother had told Tissy: that Yaser's abuse had been going on for two or three years. Did the judge hear of this? Did he take it into account? Did he consider the possibility that a father who would rape his daughters might also threaten them into keeping silent about the rapes? The judge should have been disbarred. Any rapist child beater who would rape his seven- and eight-year-old daughters would subject them to threats and violence, so of course the girls were sure to recant.

Years later, Amina told her boyfriend, Eddie, about the abuse. Just a few weeks before she was murdered, she wrote him in a text message: "You're probably going to think I'm dirty and won't look at me the same way. My dad had sex with me and my sister Sarah." Eddie reassured her, telling her, "We're in this together" and recalling later that Amina spoke of Yaser "with so much hatred. She wanted him to die." She told Eddie: "My father is really psycho."[151] Gail recalls that Amina "was very honest with Eddie about her dad's secret life. She spoke of how evil her dad was and how he was capable of all manner of evils!"[152]

Threats

Yaser Abel Said physically and emotionally abused his children. "Yaser was cruel to the girls," said Tissy's aunt. He was kind to his son Islam, "but these girls were scared to death of him. Yaser beat Amina and Sarah... not Islam!" He ruled the Said household with an iron fist, and exuded an atmosphere of menace even as he did little to provide for his family. Tissy's aunt recalled: "He was a sharp dresser...even if the children and Tissy had little, he always dressed very nicely. Tissy was the primary money-maker in the home. He did not work most of the time. He smoked cigarettes even if it meant there would be little to no food on the table." And when he did work, what he earned from driving a cab was his alone, "never to be touched by anyone!"

Yaser, according to the aunt, "had Tissy doing much of the dirty stuff! She lied to get government subsidies, telling them Yaser had left her and the children. Not true! They learned of this, and my niece was arrested for fraud." Tissy was hiding Yaser so that they could get government money to which they were not entitled. Amina told her boyfriend Eddie that Yaser ran money for Al Qaeda, and so he did not need to hold down a conventional job. She also told Eddie that Yaser, the girls' brother Islam, and Yaser's father celebrated and prayed on 9/11.[153]

Gail also recalled that "Yaser owned many weapons! Knives, guns and such"—and that he always claimed to have a weapon on him, even if he didn't. Once Tissy's sister, Connie Moggio, came to visit the Saids. As she was leaving, she recalled later, Yaser "blocked me in." He told her, "I can hurt you right now, and nobody would ever know it."[154] Gail says that "there is a storage place in Euless, Texas, where Tissy stored many tapes and pictures. Why? Because the pictures are of the girls, Islam, Tissy and Yasser all dressed in jihadist wear with weapons which are illegal to own! Joyce saw these as Islam showed them to her!"[155]

With a similar tone of menace, Yaser told Amina and Sarah from the time they were young that they were to never have American boyfriends— ever. One of Amina's school friends recalled Amina telling her of Yaser's threat; he said that if she did get an American boyfriend, he would take her to Egypt and kill her there. "I remember her telling me that her dad told her he would take her back to Egypt and have her killed. He said it's

OK to do that over there if you dishonor your family."[156]

Yaser was openly hostile to Americans, according to Tissy's aunt Gail: "Yaser took my niece, whom he raped, to a firing range and asked her, 'You see that target?'" When she replied that she did, Yaser replied: "Every time I shoot this, I am shooting an American!"

Yaser and the girls' brother, Islam Said, kept strict watch over both of the girls. When Amina became old enough to drive, Yaser gave her a car—but fixed it with a hidden microphone, over which he heard Amina talking to her non-Muslim boyfriend on her cell phone. Yaser was enraged. According to Whitley, he "hit and kicked Amina in the face, shredding her lips on her braces." A schoolmate of Amina recalls: "Her lips were pretty much attached to her braces, but they wouldn't take her to the doctor because her family feared her father would be taken to jail."[157]

Yaser even chose a husband for Amina—an Egyptian who was much older than the girl. Yaser told her that she would marry him after she received her high school diploma. He was planning to take the family to Egypt for Islam's wedding, and threatened to leave Amina in Cairo if she refused to get engaged while there. "Yaser went to Egypt at least once a year," Tissy's aunt remembered. He "bought property in Egypt, on the Mediterranean, and had Islam and Amina a flat built...from ground up! He had intended to build one for Sarah as well."

It may seem odd that Yaser Said was so intent on making sure his girls married Muslims, when he himself was hardly the picture of a devout believer. After all, his sexual abuse of the girls directly violates a Koranic prohibition (4:23) forbidding men sexual contact with their daughters, mothers, and other female relatives. But at the same time, Islamic culture relegates women to a second class status that renders them virtual possessions of their fathers and then their husbands; the culture of honor killing, including the stipulation that a parent who kills a child incurs no penalty, arises from attitudes and assumptions that are constantly reinforced by the institutionalized and theologically justified marginalization of women that is intrinsic to Islamic texts and teachings. The murders of Amina and Sarah arose directly out of Yaser Said's bedrock assumption, inculcated by his Islamic upbringing, that his daughters were his possessions who must accept his will—and had no right to live if they did not do so.

Dreams

But they did not do so. Amina had no desire to become a secluded and obedient Muslim housewife. She wanted to be a doctor. Such a dream was not at all out of reach. Allison Villarreal, a student at Lewisville High, which the sister attended, recalled that "they were extremely smart—like geniuses." Another Lewisville student, Liz Marines, remembered that "Amina was very nice with everybody. She helped me in [Advanced Placement English] class."[158]

On Christmas Eve 2007, Yaser Said drew a gun on Amina and told he would murder her. What had she done to be treated this way by her own father? She had a non-Muslim boyfriend: a college student named Eddie. And the Christmas Eve threat came as no surprise. Amina's friend Justin Finn recalled that Amina had once told him that if Yaser discovered that she was dating Eddie, "he would kill them, no doubt." She was, after all, supposed to marry the Egyptian, many years her senior, to whom Yaser had promised her. To make matters even worse, Amina's brother Islam told Yaser that Sarah also had a non-Muslim boyfriend—whereupon Yaser threatened to kill her as well.

Flight

Tissy knew these were no idle threats. She took the girls, along with both boyfriends, and fled to Kansas, to the home of her aunt. Soon they went to Oklahoma, where they planned to settle. "We were going to get engaged and get married," says Eddie. But Tissy actually had other plans. She lied to Amina and Sarah, telling them that she wanted to return to Lewisville for her late mother's birthday—New Year's Eve—in order to lay flowers on her mother's grave. Sarah agreed to go; Amina didn't, and spent New Year's Eve with Eddie. Ultimately Tissy showed up at Eddie's house, pleading with Amina to come home. Eddie recalled, "She said he just wanted to talk to Amina and that everything was going to be OK. Amina was crying and didn't want to go, but her mom made her. I trusted her mom to take care of her."[159]

Amina was not so sure. "You're letting me down," she said to Eddie.

"It's over. He won't let me see you again." Eddie never saw Amina alive again. Her father murdered her and Sarah just a few hours later.

Torture

I went through the autopsy reports on Amina and Sarah with a former prosecutor, John Jay, who has seen a fair number of autopsies in his time. These reports paint a gruesome picture. Yaser Said was a beast who inflicted a brutal death upon his daughters.

This was abundantly clear even though the autopsies appear to have been done on the cheap, fast, and dirty, with no intention on the part of the authorities to do anything other than a very cursory and superficial death investigation. Jay said that he had never, in twenty-five years of viewing autopsies in rural counties in Washington state, ever seen anything so superficial: "Not even the most inexperienced pathologist report I ever saw was so superficial." And when something about the deaths was discovered that was out of the ordinary even for such brutal murders as these, nothing was done to elicit confessions, find eyewitnesses, or examine weapons. No pathologists were flown in from the state crime lab and pathologist's offices to perform competent examinations. Both girls should also have been administered a pelvic exam, to search for semen—their father's or someone else's. That wasn't done either. Remarks Jay: "Again, this goes to the motive of the sadistic dad. I am not saying that he raped them before he killed them; the negative general findings of the condition of the bodies upon post mortem seems to indicate otherwise. But from an evidentiary standpoint, it would have been highly relevant."[160]

Yaser shot his girls at close range. The wounds and the placement of the gun against the skin were point blank.

Amina was killed very "efficiently," with two rounds to the central chest area that would appear to have been intended to kill her quickly. It may seem odd given all that we know about Yaser Said, but it would appear that he had no intention of making her suffer, or to torture her with a prolonged death. He wanted her dead quickly.

Sarah, however, was different. She died a long, painful death. Yaser appears deliberately to have shot her in a way that would not kill her immediately, but would prolong her suffering. None of the wounds appear to have been administered in a way that would have proven instantly fatal. The wounds to her chest were administered up close, with evidence of much more trauma than in Amina's case. The wounds that killed her can be clearly distinguished from wounds to her outer extremities, but clearly the wounds to the outer extremities came first. What would have been the point of administering the killing wounds first, and then the wounds to the outer extremities?

Three shots (arbitrarily labeled numbers one, two, and three in the autopsy report) are particularly interesting for their peculiarities. They were fired point blank, perhaps even with the gun next to the skin. The entrance wounds are described as elongated and eccentric. This suggests distortion by the gun barrel and perhaps by the blast of the powder. One of the wounds has soot along the path of the wound. Propellant gas was blown through her body. Some shots—to Sarah's arms and shoulders—indicate that she was moving around, trying to defend herself. Most entered her body at a slightly downward angle, as if she was hunched over as her father shot at her.

The upper chest area contains what is known as the aortic bundle. Yaser shot Sarah at such close range, with the gun pressed against her chest, yet he wounded her upper lung area without touching her heart or the aortic bundle. He had to be consciously avoiding shooting her in the heart or implicating the aortic bundle. Says Jay: "This is not easily done. You would think that he would have hit it by accident. This man received professional training, or was a very sadistic and talented amateur. You cannot shoot a person multiple times in this area, a little girl like this, without stumbling onto some kind of major artery, and he tiptoed his way around all of it. There are more arteries flowing around in there than you can shake a stick at, and he avoided all of them. Then, when he finally shot the extremities, it was just time to have fun. He must have thought her nearly dead by then."[161]

And he shot her nine times, with, in all likelihood, the gun held pressed directly to her torso. If he had wanted to end it all quickly by shooting her in the heart, he could have done it in an instant. But he did not. This could not have been accidental.

Sarah, in short, was tortured quite skillfully and deliberately. Yaser

Said tortured his daughter Sarah as surely as if he had put her on the rack and drawn and quartered her.

Yet Sarah was tough. She lived long enough for a bruise to form, even after being shot point blank in the chest. Indeed, she lived long enough to call the police (Yaser did not know she had a phone with her) and gasp out, "I'm dying, I'm dying, I'm dying..."[162]

How can a person go from being a cold-blooded, competent executioner, relatively efficient in terms of target and shooting, as was Yaser Said in Amina's case, to being unable to kill her sister with the same dispatch? Jay declares, "We have absolutely no reason to believe it was because the act of shooting somehow traumatized him, and rendered him so distracted that he could not have killed the girls in the same manner. He could have killed Sarah with the same dispatch with which he killed Amina."[163]

Perhaps Yaser Said killed Amina relatively quickly because she was the willful one, and Yaser suspected that she would be more likely to put up a spirited resistance than would Sarah. Amina wanted out. She had a mind of her own. She had the boyfriend that her Muslim father detested because he was not Muslim or even Egyptian. Sarah, on the other hand, was the dutiful child. She had tried to be a good little Muslim girl. Perhaps Yaser enjoyed torturing his submissive child and getting sordid details out of her before she died—after all, this was a man who raped his daughters when they were just seven and eight years old.

Islam

Other than the Fox show, the mainstream media never took much interest in these horrific murders. Yet the story is ongoing. Family members who might speak out have been threatened, while law enforcement efforts are hampered by a politically correct hands-off policy stemming from fear of offending Muslims in the community. One only had to watch the defensive and hostile posturing of law enforcement officials in Irving when they were questioned about the lack of energy in their pursuit of double murderer Yaser Said—and they still refuse to call it an honor killing.

Another lead they have let grow cold has been the involvement of the girls' brother. It has become increasingly clear that Islam Said, older brother to Sarah and Amina, had some involvement in their murders. Connie Moggio noted that Islam had long held a privileged position in the Said household—consistent with the strong preference in Islamic culture for boys over girls and men over women. Thus Islam's influence in the house was second only to that of Yaser himself, and greater than Tissy's—and the little emperor was not blithely crossed: "He'd cuss you out," recalled Moggio.[164] Yaser used Islam to help him keep a close eye on Amina and Sarah.

Gail recounts that when Yaser lured the girls back from Oklahoma after they had run away from their brutal and violent home life, he forced them into the back of his cab and yelled to Islam, "Get me my gun." Which he did. Islam later told his Aunt Joyce that "the girls got what was coming to them….The girls got what they deserved because they knew the rules."[165]

Why hasn't Islam Said been indicted as an accessory to the murders? Why has he been allowed to threaten and intimidate the aunts, the girls' boyfriends, and anyone else who speaks out about the heinous crime?

Islam Said is apparently now in Egypt, from which he threatens Gail Gartrell relentlessly. "Now," she recounted in an email to me, "the terror has been turned on me. No, not by Yaser but by Yaser Jr.: Islam, his stepford son! He has sent me phone threats, which I have recorded, blogged threats and hopes to send me to hell so I can say hello to Amina and Sarah! GRRrrrr! See, he can't even threaten me without being nasty towards his dead sisters!! What a loving brother, NOT! Islam has sent threats through the girls' site, which was set up for the sake of advertising the reward fund for Yaser's capture. This boy is one tacky, angry and militant thinker. It is sad that he has so much hatred instilled within him but, he is Yaser's clone!"[166]

Here is just one of the many threats to Gail Gartrell (whom he refers to as "Gall") that Islam Said has posted on a Web site:

F--- YOU!!! AND THE FBI YASER DID NOT KILL HIS KIDS HE LOVE AMINA AND SARAH I DO NOT SEE YASER KILLING THEM SO THE FBI CAN GO TO HELL IF YOU THINK YOU CAN STEP ON US YOU ARE SO F--- UP!!! WE WILL SHOW ALL OF YOU TO PLAY THIS GAME I HAVE YOUR NAME GET IT B--- I LIKE YOUR KIDS LETS HOPE GOD GET TO THEM BEFOR I DO LOLLOL

Elsewhere Islam has written:

we all love yaser and we will fight for him to the dealth f--- americans
all of them ربك الله [Allahu akbar]

And just before a memorial service that Gail held for the girls on
Saturday, March 21, 2009, Islam Said sent these messages:

will shot you gall like a dog your time is coming it may take years but
you will diey by my hands we will show you a honor killing so smok
your weed if you can i will get you all
    i will show you a honor killing gall will be shot frst i am in dallas
going too a gun show i am buying gun and boms to get you all no one
is going to step on us you think you can run but cant your time is come
we will fight for yaser . all i can say f--- the u.s.a and kill them all this
sunday you will see i will kill one of you god is god good. do not play
games all the time[167]

Approval

Relatives say that the girls' mother, Tissy, after dragging her daughters
back to their father to be murdered, has gotten on with her life. She has a
new boyfriend—another Muslim man who has, according to family members, already threatened one of her relatives. She speaks to mosques about
honor killing, although which side of the issue she is on remains unclear.

Why would Tissy take up with another Muslim, and effectively choose
to walk this road again? Why would she get involved with another man
like Yaser, who murdered her girls? Unless, of course, she is of the same
mindset, either from agreement with the Islamic principles of honor
killing, or the battered-wife syndrome, or both. There are several indications that she is: Tissy would not talk to FOX News for its August 2008
special, "Murder in the Family: Honor Killing in America." Indeed, no
one from the Said family was willing to speak on camera to the FOX news
team except for Yaser's brother Yassein, who screamed at the FOX crew:
"Get out of here, mothererf---ers! I hate FOX news. You're racist!"[168]

Tissy Said lured Amina and Sarah back to Texas after they had safely flown out of Yaser's grasp. Good old Ma went to live with Yaser's brother, Mohsen, the day after the girls were buried. *That's right: the mother of two murdered girls went to live with the brother of the murderer, a day after they were buried.*

And she even called herself "Yaser's girl" on her Myspace page as late as April 2008, three months after the murders.

Yet the only time the police questioned Tissy was on the night of the murders. Why hasn't she been questioned further? *Yaser's girl.*

Hiding

Yaser Said could still be in this country, hiding in plain sight with the aid of the Muslim support network in America. After he killed the girls, he moved their bodies to a deserted area in a hotel parking lot. He must have been covered with blood—and was too far away from the main area of the city to walk anywhere. Someone must have come and picked him up. Who helped Yaser that night? Did Yaser Said call someone on his cell phone after the murders? Have police even checked his cell phone records? Gail Gartrell says that Tissy named Yaser's brother Mohsen "as the getaway person! He owns a limo service and did receive a phone call minutes after the girls were killed. Verified by police! Even so, they NEVER brought this man in for questioning!"[169]

Yaser's brothers could be taking care of him. They are very close and have many connections in Muslim communities in the United States. The brothers are partners in real estate, owning properties together in Indiana and New York, as well as Texas.

Denial

The girls were memorialized twice—at a Christian funeral and a Muslim funeral. At the Christian funeral, aunt Gail said to a Muslim imam: "This is an honor killing. Don't deny it."[170] She told others that Yaser had long abused the girls, and after discovering that they had boyfriends, had threatened to kill them—whereupon their mother fled with them. "She ran with them," said Gartrell, "because she knew he would carry out the threat."

Still, the denials started almost immediately. Islam Said denied that the murders had anything to do with Islam at all. "It's not religion," he insisted. "It's something else. Religion has nothing to do with it." Yaser's brother complained to the *Dallas Observer*: "Only when it's Muslim do they call it an honor killing. They don't call it a Christian killing. They just say they went nuts."[171]

However, as columnist Rod Dreher reported in the *Dallas Morning News*, it was clear that there was more to this than a father who happened to be a Muslim killing his children. At the Muslim funeral, Dreher noted, "One imam talked about the primary importance of the family in Islam and of the responsibility parents have to keep their families strong. These are arguments used to justify honor killing. But if a word against honor killing—or violence against women—was spoken in English at that service, no one heard it."[172]

Perhaps this was why the girls had spoken of not wanting an Islamic burial.[173] They had always regarded Islam with reserve. Justin Finn stated that "her father wanted the Muslim way of life. She was Muslim because her family was, but she wasn't sure about it. She wanted to go her own way." Eddie agreed: "Amina didn't want to be a Muslim. She felt cursed, like it was something she was born into." Amina told him: "I don't believe any of it, because I see how their women are treated. They have to walk behind the men. They beat up their wives."[174]

Silence

Surely if Natalee Holloway and Stacey Peterson could evoke such a visceral response in America, then Amina and Sarah would light fires in the American soul. But this was not to be.

The media has subjugated itself to Islamic supremacism and would not say what these murders really were. And so as the West failed them in life, we, too, failed them in death. If any American girl had been born into a situation like that of Amina and Sarah Said, she would have behaved the same way, embraced the same things, fought back the same way—and been murdered with the same savagery. Yet American women are not rising up against this savagery.

And where were the moderate Muslims taking to the streets protesting against these heinous acts of Islamic misogyny? They never materialized. Not then, and not for Noor Alamaleki of Arizona, nor for Aasiya Hassan in New York. No calls for reform. No calls for the end of gender apartheid. The silence of Islamic supremacist groups like CAIR, ISNA, ICNA, MAS, MSA, etc., was the sanctioning of such savagery in the name of Islam.

These girls were Americans. They trusted America. They trusted the West. They believed the West would save them. They believed that education would save them. They believed that soccer would save them, that AP classes would make a difference, that a teacher would intervene. And so they poured themselves into their studies. They played soccer hard and tennis too. They got scholarships. They were preparing to live as free American women, but this was not to be.

In the end, no one helped them.

What Can We Do?

The first thing we need to do about this barbaric practice is raise awareness of it among Americans who have no idea that it is happening. The Aqsa Parvez memorial was the very first occasion on which non-Muslims began to take note of the victims of Islamic honor killing, and to serve notice to their killers that the victims would not be forgotten or their murders ignored. Memorials to Aqsa Parvez were planned in the Canadian town of Pelham, Ontario, and in Jerusalem.

Aqsa Parvez was brutally murdered by her father and brother in December 2007 for refusing to wear the Islamic headscarf. But that was only the beginning; the abuse of this girl continued. She was buried in an unmarked grave. Her family refused to acknowledge her life, as she had "dishonored" them. In defiance of her devout father and brother, she had refused to live under the suffocating dictates of Islamic law. The eleventh grade student began taking off her hijab, a traditional Islamic headscarf, when she went to school, and would put it back on when she returned home. Her dad would go to her school during school hours and walk around trying to find her, trying to catch her not wearing Islamic garb, talking to boys, or hanging out with "non-muslims." "She wanted to dress like us," said one friend of Aqsa. "To be normal." For this, her family prefers that she be forgotten—unknown, unloved, unmourned.

In December 2008, when I read that Aqsa lay in an unmarked grave, I felt sick. I started a memorial fund to get her a headstone. But I had no idea how difficult and ugly it would be simply to honor a teenage girl in Canada who just wanted to live free—and how eagerly Western non-Muslims would aid and abet the family's efforts to dishonor her in death as they did in life.

Readers of my weblog, AtlasShrugs.com, opened their hearts and their wallets, and contributed $5,000 for a headstone for Aqsa. Not a political statement, not a brouhaha, just a headstone that read, "In loving memory of Aqsa Parvez, Apr. 22, 1991—Dec. 10, 2007—Beloved, remembered, and free." All was going according to plan until, after much silence, Meadowvale Cemetery in Brampton, Ontario, where Aqsa is buried, advised me that the family (yes, the family that murdered her) had refused to "sign off" on the headstone. The director of the cemetery said, "The family wants changes and is planning on coming in to see me. They did not book an appointment yet but I hope to see them soon."

Of course, the family never came, and when we inquired as to purchasing a plot near Aqsa's body, we could not. Not a tree. Not a rock. Not a bench. All the plots were owned by the Islamic Society of North America. I tried to contact the family at that time, but they would not take my calls—I spoke to them once, but they pretended not to speak English. And they were adamant; the family refused to allow the headstone to be put on Aqsa's grave, and according to the cemetery, could remove it if it were placed there by others.

But those of us who had contributed to the Aqsa Memorial Fund were determined to make sure that Aqsa would be memorialized. We checked into other locations and made plans, only to see them canceled at the last minute out of...fear. We checked into the arboretum at the University of Guelph in Ontario, but a university official wrote me to say that "no matter how worthy, a memorial to Aqsa Parvez would draw much public attention and would thus be inconsistent with current use of The Arboretum."

But not everyone was ready to cower before Islamic anti-woman violence. The town of Pelham, Ontario, responded to the outcry at Atlas Shrugs and Jihad Watch and passed a resolution honoring Aqsa, and the Aqsa Parvez Memorial was erected in Pelham in the summer of 2009, featuring a granite bench inscribed, "In loving memory of Aqsa Parvez, Beloved, Remembered, and Free." This was placed in the Aqsa Parvez Peace Park.

Internationally, we took the monies raised, and are planting the Aqsa Parvez Grove in American Independence Park in Jerusalem, Israel, where the plaque will read, "In Loving Memory of Aqsa Parvez and All Victims of Honor Killings Worldwide."

The memorials in Pelham and Jerusalem are the first indication that we are not going to stand by silently in the Free World while the Islamic world brutalizes women and treats them as worthless trash. These are two small steps toward widespread resistance against honor killing in the West and elsewhere.

The Honor Killing Ad Campaign

In the summer of 2010, SIOA began a campaign to reach and educate the American people about the phenomenon of Islamic honor killings, hitting the streets of Chicago with the first rollout in what became a nationwide campaign of taxitops. This was especially timely in light of the fact that in July 2010, a beautiful young Muslim actress, *Harry Potter* star Afshan Azad, was badly beaten, but thankfully escaped death when her father and brother attempted to honor murder her. She was dating a non-Muslim.

It is important to note that both of Azad's parents were born and grew up in Britain. They were not unassimilated immigrants, which the media and the apologists always associate with honor killings in the West.

Instead of featuring the usual ads for strip clubs, shows, etc., our taxi ads featured pictures of several beautiful young women who were murdered for Islamic honor by their families. One ad featured Amina and Sarah; another depicted Noor Almalaki who was run over in an honor killing in November 2009, in Arizona, by her father for being "too Westernized" and not Muslim enough.[175] She hung on to dear life for three days before succumbing to her wounds.[176] A third featured Gülsüm Semin, who was scared to death of her family (and rightly so), and ultimately brutally beaten beyond recognition and "honor" murdered because she refused a forced Islamic marriage in Turkey.[177] The fourth ad showed Banaz Mahmood who was killed in her apartment in London by her father, Mahmood, and his brother Ali because they didn't approve of her boyfriend. She had dishonored her Muslim family by falling in love with the "wrong" man. So they stomped on her and then strangled her to death. Then they buried her in a suitcase in a garden behind a house. Banaz had reported to the police four times that her family was trying to kill her.[178]

In the case of Tulay Goren, police sent her home to die at the hands of her violent father. Tulay Goren, a Muslim schoolgirl, was murdered by her father in another honor killing. She repeatedly told police in the days before her death how she was being threatened and assaulted.[179]

The stories are endless and these girls have nowhere to go.

I thought that taxitops were a perfect medium to get our message to the people who are hungry, tired of the lies, and starving for information that the media is too afraid to provide. The taxis pulled the curtain back on the obfuscation and deception on honor killings.

The purpose of this pro-freedom ad campaign was twofold. Primarily it was to help girls in trouble, but it was also meant to raise awareness of the rise of honor killings in the West. Young Muslim girls must know that there is an escape from their homemade concentration camps.

The response from the media and the Islamic supremacist groups revealed their true agenda. Instead of supporting a message of help for victims of Islamic abuse, the campaign was derided as "anti-Islamic." When I appeared on television (when given brief opportunities to do so), I had to defend the ads from supposedly objective media spokesmen, as if saving a life were a bad thing. Yet those who came out against these honor-killing ads were in support of the death penalty for apostates or for young Muslim girls who refused to live under the boot of Islamic gender apartheid.

The idea that these ads were "anti-Muslim" was just another supremacist restriction of free speech, another enforcement of Islamic blasphemy laws that command non-Muslims not to tell the truth about Islam. I do not believe that we in America have so lost our moral compass that it is preferable for a girl to live in abject terror, and to suffer beatings and abuse, and perhaps become a victim to an honor killing, so as not to insult Islam.

There was a difficulty in keeping the ads on the taxis. They would disappear off the taxi tops. Residents in many of the cities where the campaign ran reported never seeing them. News organizations calling for comment could not find them. Were Muslim cab drivers removing them? In one instance, the word *Leave* was cut off one of the posters, so that it said IslamSafely.com instead of LeaveIslamSafely.com. Not to be deterred, I bought that URL as well.

Studies have shown that 91 percent of honor killings worldwide, as well as 84 percent of honor killings in the United States, are done by Muslims. Such misogyny was unheard of in this country thirty years ago—and now the appeasement of Islam and the Sharia will only serve to advance this grotesque ideology. According to one expert, honor killings are on the rise.[180]

These girls must not have died in vain. These girls are not invisible. Their terrible, miserable existences must be made known, and their stories will save the lives of other girls and boys in trouble.

There are Muslim girls in your communities who need your help.

You can run similar ads in your area. And if local taxi or bus companies refuse them, you can make it into a freedom of speech issue. Make the transit authority explain why it is carrying water for Islamic supremacists.

CHAPTER 8

OUTLAWING THE BARBARIC
AND UNSPEAKABLE

Oklahoma Leads the Way

In November 2010, after many years of Islamic supremacists flouting American law across the country, Oklahoma became the first state to stand up for and protect the Constitution by passing a proposition that Sharia-based court decisions and foreign law should be banned—an idea that our Founding Fathers and any patriot could love. But just days after the vote, a federal judge, Vicki Miles-LaGrange, issued a temporary restraining order blocking Oklahoma's new state constitutional amendment which forbade courts to decide cases using Islamic law (Sharia)—against the will of the people, the brave people of Oklahoma, who had just approved the law by 70 percent of the vote. Subversive Muslim Brotherhood groups, such as the Hamas-linked Council on American-Islamic Relations (CAIR), tried hard to block the law and ultimately succeeded. On November 29, 2010, Miles-LaGrange issued a permanent injunction blocking the law.

Despite the many missteps in the approval of the Oklahoma law and its aftermath, this was a supremely teaching moment. When you have 70 percent of voters approving a ban on Islamic law, the will of the people should not be subverted by a technicality. Oklahoma's experience provided activists around the country with an opportunity to improve the wording of their proposed anti-Sharia laws, so that they would not be subject to the whims of misinformed, politically correct judges.

Miles-LaGrange's decision showed that her CAIR advisers had misled her about the nature of Sharia. She wrote in her decision that the plaintiff in the request to block the law—that is, Hamas-linked CAIR—had "presented testimony that 'Sharia Law' is not actually 'law', but is religious traditions that provide guidance to plaintiff and other Muslims regarding the exercise of their faith." She accepted CAIR's false claim that "the obligations that 'Sharia Law' imposes are not legal obligations but are obligations of a personal and private nature dictated by faith."[181]

The confused judge further noted that "plaintiff also testified that 'Sharia Law' differs depending on the country in which the individual Muslim resides. For example, the plaintiff stated that marrying more than one wife is permissible in Islam but in the United States, where that is illegal, Muslims do not marry more than one wife because Sharia in the United States mandates Muslims to abide by the law of the land and respect the law of their land."

This was bitterly ironic in light of the fact that in August 2007, when asked how common polygamy was among Muslims in the United States, CAIR's Ibrahim Hooper said that a "minority" of Muslims here were polygamous, and added, "Islamic scholars would differ on whether one could do so while living in the United States."[182] He didn't say anything about Muslims in the United States being given pause by the fact that the practice remains illegal in the United States. Miles-LaGrange's bland confidence that Muslims in the United States do now and will always abide by the laws of the United States was also given the lie a few years ago by an imam in Canada, Aly Hindy, who stated just the opposite view about the relationship between Islamic law and American law: "This is in our religion and nobody can force us to do anything against our religion. If the laws of the country conflict with Islamic law, if one goes against the other, then I am going to follow Islamic law, simple as that."[183]

Apparently many Muslims in America as well as Canada think the same way. A May 2008 estimate found between 50,000 and 100,000 Muslims living in polygamous arrangements in the U.S., in defiance of American law.[184]

Nevertheless, Miles-LaGrange found that "'Sharia Law' lacks a legal character, and, thus, plaintiff's religious traditions and faith are the only non-legal content subject to the judicial exclusion set forth in the amendment. As a result, the Court finds plaintiff has made a strong showing that the amendment conveys a message of disapproval of plaintiff's faith and, consequently, has the effect of inhibiting plaintiff's religion."[185]

Legal expert David Yerushalmi, a pioneering legal authority in the drafting of state laws banning Sharia, conceded that Oklahoma's anti-Sharia law was "poorly drafted and, as such, criticism directed at the legal professionals who had a hand in the drafting is entirely legitimate."[186] The Oklahoma law forbade recourse to foreign law in Oklahoma courtrooms, but, said Yerushalmi, "there are perfectly legitimate applications of foreign law in state courts that no one in their right mind would oppose." What's more, "two parties who agree to be bound by the law of a foreign jurisdiction when those foreign laws do not infringe upon any fundamental liberty or important public policy of the state of Oklahoma is as innocuous and conducive to the 'freedom to contract' and the liberty inherent in private property as it sounds."

Yerushalmi emphasized the need to define, in such laws, precisely what was meant by Sharia—a need made more acute by Miles-LaGrange's manifest ignorance of the political and supremacist aspects of Sharia: "Does 'sharia' mean some vague or subjective interpretation of religious practice as the current federal court challenge intimates or is it the sharia that occupies the place of secular law and political-military doctrine at the level of normative praxis in many countries, in a variety of political and military regimes, and as the guiding threat doctrine for terrorist organizations around the world?"

Against those who insist that Oklahoma and other states are in no danger from those who would wish to impose Sharia anyway, and thus such laws are unnecessary, Yerushalmi points out that:

> The global jihad leadership against which we have aligned most of our military and intelligence resources since 9/11 informs us in Arabic, Pashtu, Urdu, Persian, and even in English that the global jihad against the West is fundamentally directed and determined by Islamic law, or sharia. The jihad leaders further tell us that their ultimate goal, in addition to that of the "defensive jihad" incumbent on every Muslim to rid the Islamic world of an occupying infidel presence (including,

but only parenthetically so, those nasty Zionists residing in the midst of dar al-Islam), is the implementation of sharia law as the law of the land in any place Muslims step foot."[187]

He points out also that "surveys in the Muslim world consistently evidence that somewhere between 50% to 70% of the global Muslim community desires to create a unified Caliphate for all Muslims and to order that political hegemony according to a strict al Qaeda-like sharia."

And to the argument that "sharia is unknowable as an objective reality because Muslims can understand it in an infinite number of ways," Yerushalmi responds that laws proposing a ban on Sharia should specify that it is "the objectively knowable legal doctrine and system which operates effectively as the law of the land in several Muslim countries and which operates as the 'law of a sector' such as family law in almost all Muslim countries." And further:

> If sharia were in fact simply a matter of individual interpretation to all Muslims, it would not be the subject of entire university departments, it would not be reducible to a code of law as in the text Reliance of the Traveler endorsed by Al Azhar University, the citadel of Sunni jurisprudence, it would not be the basis for family laws of most Muslim countries, and it would not be the basis for the ultimate desiderata for 50-70% of the Muslims living in Muslim countries who desire an al Qaeda-like strict sharia.

He drives home the illogic of the pro-Sharia arguments:

> In other words, the slippery slope argument most certainly cannot rest on the argument that outlawing sharia would be like outlawing 'humanism'—that is, humanism can mean anything to anyone. To be sure, humanism is unknowable to the law precisely because there is no code or authoritative corpus juris that defines humanism. But sharia is, at least for the 600-840 million Muslims represented by the World Public Opinion survey, something quite knowable and as such quite subject to critical analysis and to the law's reach. To argue that sharia is akin to humanism is fatuous at best; purposefully deceptive at worst.

Being purposefully deceptive is what CAIR is all about—witness their inclusion of faked hate crimes in their reports about incidents of anti-Muslim bias. And when Vicki Miles-LaGrange issued her ruling, they had won. At least for the moment. In January and February 2011, Yerushalmi worked with Oklahoma lawmakers to draft a new law that is more pointed and doesn't mention Sharia, but accomplishes the intended purpose. Its salient section:

> SECTION 1 (C) Any court, arbitration, tribunal, or administrative agency ruling or decision shall violate the public policy of this state and be void and unenforceable if the court, arbitration, tribunal, or administrative agency bases its rulings or decisions in the matter at issue in whole or in part on any law, rule, legal code or system that would not grant the parties affected by the ruling or decision the same fundamental liberties.[188]

Every Victory for CAIR is a Defeat for CAIR

Whatever temporary successes Muslim supremacists attain or appear to attain, I believe that the suit against the Oklahoma anti-Sharia law and other actions like it were a good thing. The Islamic supremacists are showing their hand and revealing their agenda, and Americans know it. Within four months of the Oklahoma ruling, fourteen other states were considering bans on Sharia. The Ground Zero mosque revealed the true face of Islamic supremacists to the American people and *unmosqued* their real goals, and then so, too, did the lawsuit brought by the Hamas-linked, Muslim-Brotherhood front CAIR against the good people of Oklahoma.

CAIR's agitation for Sharia revealed its attachment to it, as Robert Spencer asked about the Oklahoma Sharia law hearings, "Will Sakineh Mohammadi Ashtiani be available to testify?" Sakineh Mohammadi Ashtiani was at the time of Judge Miles-LaGrange's ruling awaiting death by stoning in Iran after being falsely convicted of adultery. That was the true face of Sharia.[189]

Oklahoma's CAIR leader, Muneer Awad, claimed, "Sharia law has never been used in Oklahoma before this amendment came about," and so the law was unnecessary.[190] But then why sue to block it?

Thanks to the Islamic supremacist attitude that Islam must dominate, Americans across the great country are waking up to the enemy in our midst. Hamas-linked CAIR sued Oklahoma, but why wasn't CAIR as aggressive against jihad, the slaughter of non-Muslims? Hamas-linked Muslim Brotherhood CAIR was also suing Ohio to block anti-Sharia legislation. Why wasn't CAIR fighting against the jihadists with hate and determination? Why weren't they fighting the devout violent Muslims with such venom? Why were they instead suing Oklahoma to pave the way for the Sharia law? And who was funding them?

We are talking about millions of dollars here. Where did this money come from, funding our destruction from within? While the slaves at the leftist Web site *Politico et al.* were feverishly tracking down my $18 and $25 donations, they remained silent, complicit in the massive subversive funding of the supremacist groups whose stated goal, in the words of a captured internal Muslim Brotherhood document, was "eliminating and destroying Western civilization from within." These lawsuits cost a bloody fortune.

We have seen Sharia law in New Jersey. Back in July 2010, a Muslim husband raped his wife, and the judge determined that no sexual assault occurred because Islam forbids wives to refuse sex on demand from their husbands. Luckily, the appellate court overturned this decision, and a Sharia ruling by an American court was not allowed to stand—this time.[191]

The CAIR legal initiatives against anti-Sharia laws must be fought by the best Western minds, and won, and used as the template for all fifty states.

And Hamas-linked CAIR made a stunning admission in its press release about the lawsuit against Oklahoma. It called the Oklahoma amendment "anti-Islam," admitting that the brutal, oppressive, and radical Sharia, with its stonings and amputations and oppression of women, is Islam. Why call the amendment "anti-Islam"? It was anti-Sharia. Oklahoma meant to ban stonings, amputations for theft, death for apostates, and the other elements of Sharia that contradict the rights and freedoms guaranteed to American citizens by the U.S. Constitution. And now CAIR was admitting that all such practices go back to Islam itself.

By their fruits we shall know them, and so once again, we knew Islamic supremacist CAIR.

The ABA defends Sharia

As more and more states move to ban Sharia, the leftist establishment, in league with the Islamic supremacists, has swung into action. In February 2011, I broke the story on my Web site AtlasShrugs.com: the American Bar Association (ABA) had decided to undertake the fight for Sharia law. The ABA's Executive Council "organized a Task Force to review the legislation of 14 states—Alaska, Arizona, Arkansas, Georgia, Indiana, Louisiana, Mississippi, Nebraska, South Carolina, South Dakota, Tennessee, Texas, Utah and Wyoming—in which anti-Sharia legislation has been introduced."[192]

The goal of the ABA's Task Force was to fight against these legislative initiatives by free people, and to develop "an informal set of 'talking points' that local opponents of these initiatives could use to make their case in each of these states."

Here's the relevant extract from the ABA's International Policies 2010:

Oklahoma referendum related Rule of Law initiatives.
The Section's Executive Counsel [sic] has organized a Task Force to review the legislation of 14 states—Alaska, Arizona, Arkansas, Georgia, Indiana, Louisiana, Mississippi, Nebraska, South Carolina, South Dakota, Tennessee, Texas, Utah and Wyoming—in which anti-Sharia legislation has been introduced. The goal of the Task Force is to have a Report and Recommendation against such legislation as well as an informal set of "talking points" that local opponents of these initiatives could use to make their case in each of these states. We received a lot of interest from members and have forwarded your interest. At this point, the task force is in the planning and organizing stage. We will keep you updated as to the progress and we may call upon some of you who expressed their interest in this matter to volunteer.

In reality, Islamic law is the most radical and intolerant system of governance on the face of the earth. It denies the freedom of speech, the freedom of conscience, and legal equality for women and non-Muslims. That's why so many states are trying to ban it. The ABA should have been on the forefront of this battle. The Oklahoma ban was brilliant but poorly worded (which is why a liberal judge found it so easy to overrule the will of the people) and had 70 percent of voters approving of it—it was clear that American people understood the Islamic threat to our constitutional republic.

Instead, our cultural warlords in the mainstream media, academia, and entertainment strictly enforce the blasphemy laws of Islam, which command that one must not insult or slander Islam. In Muslim countries, blasphemy is punishable by death; in the West, it is your character that is assassinated if you dare to speak out against the Islamic supremacist agenda. Our last line of defense was always the rule of law. So it was particularly jarring and deeply disturbing to come upon this latest initiative from the ABA, one of America's last lines of defense against the litigation jihad and creeping Sharia in this country.

Furthermore, the ABA's "Middle East Law committee" has promoted Sharia finance, the implementation of Islamic laws regarding financial transactions (including its prohibition of interest-based transactions) for some time with the same warmly positive slant. Sharia is being imposed across state lines, across the country, by way of these varying initiatives. We must push back.

And the ABA has nothing to say about any of this; it is too busy fighting against anti-Sharia, pro-freedom laws. It is yet another terrible sign of a morally inverted world. When I wrote about their pro-Sharia initiatives in an article called "The ABA's Jihad" in *The American Thinker*, the ABA on the same day issued a statement in response to my article, claiming that "the American Bar Association has taken no action in support of, or in opposition to, judges considering Islamic law or Sharia."[168]

How dishonest and disingenuous.

The ABA statement said that the organization has nearly 400,000 members, many of whom volunteer with any of the ABA's 2,200 entities. One of those 2,200 entities is the Section on International Law, which has elected to assemble a taskforce of several individuals to examine this issue." The statement makes it sound as if this examination is completely neutral: "These individuals are examining whether the proposed changes to the law impact important constitutional questions. They are also considering implications for international commerce.[194]

Above all, the ABA claims that this taskforce has nothing to do with the organization itself: "The actions of a few interested members within one section are not and cannot be interpreted to be those of the entire

American Bar Association. Claims to the contrary are erroneous."

This was spin and damage control. The ABA did not address my quote from their own documents, stating that the ABA's Executive Counsel "has organized a Task Force to review the legislation of 14 states—Alaska, Arizona, Arkansas, Georgia, Indiana, Louisiana, Mississippi, Nebraska, South Carolina, South Dakota, Tennessee, Texas, Utah and Wyoming—in which anti-Sharia legislation has been introduced."

There was no way this Task Force could be understood as neutral. Clearly it was dedicated to working against anti-Sharia legal initiatives. It said that the Executive Council had "organized a Task Force to review the legislation" of states "in which anti-Sharia legislation has been introduced," so as to provide "a Report and Recommendation against such legislation as well as an informal set of 'talking points' that local opponents of these initiatives could use."

This should have incited justifiable public outrage, and increased support for and awareness of the legislation among the grassroots electorate.

A source knowledgeable about the ABA has also informed me that the organization's Middle East Law committee recently began a lobbying campaign, which the ABA's international law chair endorsed. It was a political act, not a neutral study. This source sent me ABA policy guidelines that made it clear that policies that are formulated by small committees or "entities" can and do become official ABA policy under certain circumstances, and those circumstances are present in the case of this pro-Sharia Task Force.

This puts the ABA on the spot: either its policy mechanism on Middle East law has been taken over by Middle East-based lawyer(s) with Islamic supremacist sympathies, or it hasn't, and the Middle East law committee did indeed represent the ABA's actual positions.

Further, was there any ABA group or task force assigned to helping those who oppose Sharia to craft legislation to ban it? No. There was only an initiative to oppose those fighting the Sharia.

Particularly troubling was the non-democratic way in which the ABA made the decision to oppose the anti-Sharia initiatives of various states. A tiny minority of the ABA's total membership steers its policies, which almost always are developed from the top down. The pro-Sharia initiative seems to have been pushed forward through what the ABA calls a "blanket approval" or even more rapid "technical comment" procedure, and seems to go beyond issuing mere statements to actively organizing lobbying to influence state legislation—a practice that is generally forbidden for tax-exempt organizations.

All this makes it obvious that the ABA's statement disclaiming any support for Sharia was completely false and dishonest.

There is one way the ABA could make at least partial amends now: it's time the ABA created a task force to help those of us who are fighting the introduction of Islamic law in America.

We're waiting.

In the meantime, let's encourage our friends and family members who are lawyers to follow the lead of the courageous counter-jihad legal experts David Yerushalmi and Robert Muise, and to volunteer for a Litigation Jihad Defense Pool, so that free Americans do not have to undertake this enormous burden alone.

We are all soldiers in this war. The enemy didn't target those in uniform on 9/11 or 7/7 or 11/26 or 3/11. They targeted moms and dads, doctors and lawyers, stockbrokers, food merchants, waiters, secretaries, firemen, policemen—you and me.

We are the soldiers. Lawyers, man up.

What you can do

1. Ask your state, local, and municipal representatives to introduce anti-Sharia laws in their respective legislative bodies.

2. Identify particular legislators who may be receptive to advocating such laws, and provide them with the necessary resources—especially the template for anti-Sharia laws found in the Appendix to this book.

3. Organize phone banks to call legislative committees to urge them to support anti-Sharia laws.

4. Publicize Web sites and spokesmen who answer common objections to anti-Sharia laws—particularly the claim that they limit religious freedom.

CHAPTER 9

THE MUSLIM BROTHERHOOD
PROJECT IN AMERICA

"War is deceit," said Muhammad, the prophet of Islam.[195] And his followers have taken this to heart.

The global jihad that Islamic supremacists are waging from Indonesia to Nigeria, from London to Moscow, from Bali to Portland, Oregon, proceeds not just by means of terror attacks, but through anything the jihadists can use to advance their cause of imposing Islamic law around the world and subjugating non-Muslims under its rule. This is happening in America, too: There are numerous ways in which the Muslim Brotherhood and its American proxies are working today to establish Islamic law (Sharia) in the United States, with willing help from Barack Obama and others among the America-hating left.

Why is all this happening? This is no accident. This is not a coincidental confluence of events. This is very deliberate. And the strategy was designed and outlined as far back as 1982. Everything that is happening, from the mainstream media pro-Islamic narrative to "Islamic community centers" popping up in small towns across America as well as in lower Manhattan at Ground Zero, is part of a grand design.

The Muslim Brotherhood's overall strategy

The Muslim Brotherhood revealed the overall strategy that underlies all these initiatives in an internal document that Swiss investigators discovered in November 2001. At the request of the Bush White House, the Swiss authorities searched the home of a Muslim banker, Yusuf Nada of the Al Taqwa bank, which had been accused of funding al-Qaeda. There they found the Brotherhood document entitled simply "The Project."

This document was dated December 1, 1982. Bush-era White House counterterrorism czar Juan Zarate says that "The Project" sums up the Brotherhood's strategy for "spreading their political ideology"—that is, imposing Islamic law over not only the Islamic world, but the West as well. The plan doesn't proceed through terror attacks, but through a sophisticated initiative involving propaganda and subversion.

For Muslims in Western countries, according to the Swiss investigative reporter Sylvain Besson in a French-language book about "The Project" that anti-terror investigator Olivier Guitta discussed in a 2006 *Weekly Standard* article, the plan involves establishing "a parallel society where the group is above the individual, godly authority above human liberty, and the holy scripture above the laws."

We see that happening now with initiatives such as the Muslim Students Association's Muslim Accommodations Task Force. This involves strategies for demanding and receiving for Muslims on campus separate gym facilities, dorm facilities, cafeteria facilities, and worship spaces.

Islamic scholar Robert Spencer, in his pioneering 2008 book *Stealth Jihad*, was the first to examine in detail the Muslim Brotherhood's strategic goals in the United States and the many ways their stealth jihad is advancing here. Spencer's book reveals the Brotherhood's activities in depth. Spencer explains that "when Muslim students present these demands to school administrators, they do so in language that those administrators find difficult to refuse. The MSA directs Muslim students to present its demands in the context of multiculturalism and civil rights."[196]

The MSA also tells Muslim students to invoke incidents of anti-Muslim bias when presenting these demands, which indicates why Muslims have on so many occasions faked hate crimes against themselves and then tried to use them to gain another advantage over unwitting infidels.

These demands for special accommodations proceed under the guise of civil rights, which is an insult to the real civil rights movement. The civil rights movement in America was waged by people who were committed to the principle that people should be treated fairly and equitably, should be equal before the law, and should have equal access to services. The Muslim Students Association's demands for separate living, eating, worship, and exercise facilities are the polar opposite of a movement toward integration. Yet no one seems to call them on the contradiction: they're claiming the mantle of a drive for equality in order to establish inequality. They're claiming the mantle of a movement dedicated to integration in order to establish segregation. They're claiming to be the heirs of a movement that taught that all people should be treated equally while demanding that they be treated unequally.

Will they get away with this? Will Islamic supremacist groups in the United States continue to win special accommodations that amount essentially to discrimination on the basis of religion? Or will Americans as a society remember what the civil rights movement was all about and not allow these segregationists and supremacists to steal it?

The answers to those questions are up to you.

More details about the Muslim Brotherhood's project were revealed in a Brotherhood document that came to light during the Holy Land Foundation jihad charity trial in 2007, "An Explanatory Memorandum on the General Strategic Goal for the Group in North America" by the Brotherhood's Mohamed Akram's. This document, dated May 22, 1991, reminded Brotherhood operatives in the United States that they "must understand that their work in America is a kind of grand jihad in eliminating and destroying the Western civilization from within and 'sabotaging' its miserable house by their hands and the hands of the believers so that it is eliminated and God's religion [that is, Islam] is made victorious over all other religions."[197]

The Brotherhood is working energetically now to make Islam victorious in the United States One of the main ways it is doing so, according to this "Explanatory Memorandum," is by establishing Islamic centers throughout the nation. Since the media and the leaders of the Ground Zero mosque initiative worked so hard to convince the American people that the Ground Zero mosque was not a mosque, but a "community center," it is enlightening to look at what this document has to say about what kind of centers that Brotherhood operatives ought to be establishing in the United States.

The Islamic center, Akram explains, must become "a seed 'for a small Islamic society' which is a reflection and a mirror to our central organizations." So if the Brotherhood itself is dedicated to "eliminating and destroying Western civilization from within," these Islamic centers must mirror that in their local areas. But they must do so, the document says, "in action not in words." That means that "the center ought to turn into a 'beehive' which produces sweet honey."

When seen from that perspective, the soothing words of the Imam Feisal Abdul Rauf and his wife Daisy Khan, when they were reassuring the leftist media that the mosque was just a benign community center designed to foster peace, harmony, and understanding between Muslims and Jews and Christians take on a whole new light.

The "Explanatory Memorandum" also says that the Islamic center would be "a place for study, family, battalion, course, seminar, visit, sport, school, social club, women gathering, kindergarten for male and female youngsters, the office of the domestic political resolution, and the center for distributing our newspapers, magazines, books and our audio and visual tapes." *Battalion.*

The Islamic center would also:

> become "The House of Dawa"—that is, Islamic proselytizing. Many different religious groups proselytize, but the document goes on to explain that the center's 'role should be the same as the "mosque's" role during the time of God's prophet, God's prayers and peace be upon him, when he marched to "settle" the Dawa" in its first generation in Madina. From the mosque, he drew the Islamic life and provided to the world the most magnificent and fabulous civilization humanity knew.[198]

It was in Medina that Muhammad, the prophet of Islam, became for the first time a political and military leader as well as a spiritual one. That's when he started waging war against non-Muslims, and he explained to his followers that they should offer those non-Muslims three choices:

Fight in the name of Allah and in the way of Allah. Fight against those who disbelieve in Allah. Make a holy war....When you meet your enemies who are polytheists, invite them to three courses of action. If they respond to any one of these, you also accept it and withhold yourself from doing them any harm. Invite them to accept Islam; if they respond to you, accept it from them and desist from fighting against them.... If they refuse to accept Islam, demand from them the Jizya [poll-tax on non-Muslims]. If they agree to pay, accept it from them and hold off your hands. If they refuse to pay the tax, seek Allah's help and fight them.[199]

The choices for unbelievers are thus to convert to Islam; or submit as inferiors to Islamic rule, paying the tax and accepting the discrimination that Islamic law mandates for non-Muslims in the Islamic state; or die. Those are the only choices offered. Islamic law doesn't envision a situation in which Muslims live together as equals with non-Muslims without any plan to impose Sharia upon them now or in the future.

Thus the ultimate goal of the Brotherhood project is the conversion, subjugation, or death of the Infidels, and the transformation of the United States into an Islamic state. They may never attain this goal, or even come close to doing so. But they can certainly erode many of our freedoms and the distinctive joys of being an American in their attempts to do so.

We must stop them. And we can. Once you are aware of who the Muslim Brotherhood is, and the goal of the Muslim Brotherhood project, you are activated. Clearly not every Muslim shares the goals of the Muslim Brotherhood, and I salute them all. I expect they will fight this scourge along with us. I don't believe all Germans were Nazis, either.

It won't be hard to discern if the Muslim Brotherhood has decided to target your town, your school, or any governmental apparatus in your area of influence. If, for example, you see a mega-mosque going up in a completely inappropriate location, start investigating the players. Are they tied to the Brotherhood—the Muslim American Society, ICNA, ISNA, CAIR, et al. Assemble a dossier. Get it to the local newspapers and your local politicians. It may very well fall on deaf ears, but all you need is one. Certainly send it to the counter-jihad blogs, such as AtlasShrugs.com, JihadWatch.org, Loganswarning.com, and Creeping Sharia. Start making noise. From there, develop a team of trusted colleagues. Confer with counter-jihad leaders and devise a strategy.

Be informed. Be determined. Never give up. Never give in.

CHAPTER 10

INFILTRATION

Will Assimilation Stop Jihad and Islamization?

Many Americans assume that Islamization is not a problem because, they say, Muslims will eventually assimilate into American culture and adopt Western values. Yet there are telling indications that many Muslims in America are doing anything but assimilating. Cell phone video emerged in December 2010 of Mohamed Osman Mohamud, the Muslim in Oregon who attempted to bomb Pioneer Courthouse Square at a point when 25,000 infidels had gathered there during a Christmas tree lighting ceremony. The video, captured in a dorm room, was very revealing.[200]

This was clearly an American Muslim, steeped in American culture, who wanted to destroy America. And the motive? Islam.

In the video, Mohamud says, "You know what the whole West thing is? They want to insult our religion. They want to take our lands. They want to rape our women while we're bowing down to them. This is what they want. This country and Europe and all those countries, that's all they want."

Mohamud also shows his violent streak, saying of someone unknown: "If I met him, I would get five, six Muslims, beat the (expletive) out of him." Why? Because apparently this person insulted Muhammad the Islamic prophet. Mohamud goes on: "That's something I have zero tolerance for. When it comes to our prophet, nobody can say anything. They're calling it freedom of speech. It's not freedom of speech."

Look at the bigger picture here. Mohamed Osman Mohamud acts in this video like any other nineteen-year-old in America today. He walks the American walk. He talks the American talk. He could be any American young man in any American town. He is the personification of assimilation, yes? And yet what is he talking? Jihad. What is he trashing? The West.

This is a very important video with a very important point. America pins all her hopes on assimilation and crows that Muslims in the United States assimilate better here than anywhere else in the world. We pop with pride that we won't suffer the same fate as Europe, because we don't have Muslim enclaves or no-go zones, as do an increasing number of European cities.

But this video blows that theory right up. No pun intended.

Meanwhile, the would-be bomber's mosque, which almost immediately claimed that arson had destroyed records in their office, should have been questioned. The media propagandists and apologists for Islam are using this arson claim to make the story of Mohamud's attempted jihad bombing in Portland all about the fictional "backlash" that Hamas-linked CAIR always claims after jihad plots in the United States They're whitewashing the fact that hundreds of Christians would have been massacred in this WMD attack.

But as for the mosque arson, color me skeptical. We have seen this time after time. It is an Islamic pattern to vandalize, set fire to and/or graffiti their own mosques in order to fabricate a "backlash" narrative while advancing Islamic supremacism on the backs of the kuffar, using the media shield as a human shield. Muslims vandalized their own mosque in Dayton, Ohio, in 2008, and in July 2010, a Muslim was arrested in the case of an "Islamophobic" arson attack against his own mosque in Marietta, Georgia.[201] And meanwhile, the perpetrators of the vandalism of the controversial mosque in Murfreesboro, Tennessee, are still…at large. Hmm.

The fire in the mosque in Portland was contained to one room only, burning the Islamic Center's office. Reports said that the worship areas, which one would expect an "Islamophobe" to target, were left completely untouched. That, too, is consistent with the pattern of faked crimes. No real damage is ever done.

If this really was an act of revenge or backlash, I fiercely condemn it.

But until we know, I am not buying.

The arson attack against the Portland mosque was, in my opinion, an attempt to deflect attention away from the blame that the mosque deserves for giving the world Mohamed Mohamud. Who is putting these ideas into the heads of young Muslims? Where is this anti-West, genocidal ideology coming from?

Remember that there have been over 15,000 Islamic jihad attacks around the world since 9/11. Every Islamic attack has the imprimatur of a Muslim cleric. This is the heart of the problem. The mosques must be monitored.

And American authorities need to stop putting all their hopes on the "assimilation" of young Muslims like Mohamed Osman Mohamud. To keep on doing so is just to play games with the safety of Americans, like the ones who gathered for the Christmas tree lighting ceremony that this barbarian targeted.

Infiltration at High Levels

Meanwhile, the Muslim Brotherhood and other Islamic supremacist organizations have infiltrated deeply into our government. I received some startling information about the full extent of that infiltration in the Department of Justice and their brazen pro-Muslim activities. Their "Monthly Outreach Meetings" with Muslim and Arab groups at the Civil Rights Division include a veritable who's who of Islamic supremacists, who were invited to the inner hallways of the DOJ every month. The Attorney General would often come to the meetings: Alberto R. Gonzales, George W. Bush's Attorney General, attended several of these meetings, as did his successor, Eric Holder.

The mastermind behind these meetings and epicenter of this activity was Eric Treene, special counsel for religious discrimination in the Civil Rights Division of the Justice Department. He organized the meetings, brought in the outsiders, and arranged for Muslim groups to get entrance badges for the DOJ headquarters; in fact, he likely got these groups green badges, which allowed them into the Justice Department unescorted, rather than red badges, which would have required them to be accompanied by an escort.

But I am most interested in DOJ actions to extend certain civil rights laws to Muslims in voting, particularly insofar as they involve the DOJ's Lema Bashir. Essentially, they wanted to convert a religious class into a racial one, to create majority-Muslim legislative districts.

Lema Bashir was at the center of Virginia's failing to mail military ballots in time in 2008. The same mistakes were repeated in 2010 and United States military voters were heavily disenfranchised because of in-actions by Bashir and the DOJ throughout 2010. Disenfranchising the military vote is policy. You could make a case that bad mistakes were made in 2008, but when those same mistakes were made and made worse in 2010 by a devout Muslim who calls Israel "northern Palestine," I submit that it is no accident but deliberate policy.

Before her seditious career at the Department of Justice, Lema Bashir was a legal adviser with the American-Arab Anti-Discrimination Committee (ADC) in Washington, D.C. The ADC opposes all American aid to Israel, as well as any anti-terror measure that would involve profiling of Arabs. It even supports Palestinian "martyrdom" operations—that is, suicide bombings—in Israel.

There seemed to be no way they could withhold the documents I have unearthed, so I made a Freedom of Information Act request:

February 28, 2011

CERTIFIED MAIL
Nelson Hermilla, Chief
FOIA/PA Branch
Civil Rights Division
NALC, Room 311
950 Pennsylvania Avenue, N.W.
Washington, DC 20530

Re: Request under the Freedom of Information Act

Dear Mr. Hermilla:

Enclosed is a request for government documents under the Freedom of Information Act ("FOIA") and the Electronic Freedom of Information

Act,5 U.S.C. § 552, and is submitted to the Department of Justice's Civil Rights Division on behalf of Atlas Shrugs, an Internet-based information source, the American Freedom Defense Initiative and Pamela Geller. This request therefore falls under 5 U.S.C. § 552(a)(4)(A)(ii) and 28 C.F.R. § 16.11(b)(6). I am seeking the following documents:

1. All communications between any employee of the Civil Rights Division and the Islamic Society of North America, the Council on American-Islamic Relations, the American-Arab Anti-Discrimination Committee, the Muslim Students Association or any affiliated student group. In particular, but not limited to, the request includes all communications related to appearances at or sponsorships of conventions or meetings of this organizations by the Department of Justice including conferences in 2006, 2007, 2008, 2009 and 2010.

2. Transcripts of speeches delivered by Civil Rights Division political appointees or section managers at any meeting of the Islamic Society of North America, the Council on American-Islamic Relations, the American-Arab Anti-Discrimination Committee, the Muslim Students Association or any affiliated student group. If transcripts of such appearances do not exist, please provide a list of such appearances instead.

3. Resumes of all attorney and intern hires in the Civil Rights Division in which the resumes list prior employment at the Islamic Society of North America, the Council on American-Islamic Relations, the American-Arab Anti-Discrimination Committee, or the Muslim Students Association.

4. All travel authorization forms, expense submissions and records of payment for any Department employee to attend any convention, conference or meeting with or at the Islamic Society of North America, the Council on American-Islamic Relations, or the American-Arab Anti-Discrimination Committee.

5. Any memorandum, document, email, telephone conference record or proposal discussing the use of civil rights laws in the Housing Section, Voting Section, and Education Section to use laws enforced by these sections to bring cases or potential cases on behalf of a protected class defined as Arab or Muslim or Islamic. Include any documents which discuss the applicability of civil rights laws to these classes from these three sections.

6.   Records relating to the meeting of the "Monthly Out-reach Meeting" (or a regular occurring meeting organized by the Civil Rights Division with substantially the same purpose even if it is referred to with a different name inside the Department) with Muslim and Arab groups at the Civil Rights Division. Specifically, include lists of attendees at each monthly meeting, the agenda of each meeting and any min-utes or summary prepared subsequent to each meeting. Please also specifically note the meetings at which the Attorney General of the United States attended.

All six requests seek documents from January 1, 2006 to the present day.

Because the information provided will be published at Atlas Shrugs, and will inform various appearances of the requestor during national cable television appearances, the request is exempted from costs associated with this Freedom of Information Act/EFIA request. The requestor disseminates news in text and interview form via 5 U.S.C. § 552(a)(4)(A)(ii) and 28 C.F.R. § 16.11(d)(1). The right to waive costs is triggered because the "disclosure of the requested information is likely to contribute to public understanding of the operations or activities of the government."

The information requested will be used to disseminate information and news and will not be used for commercial purposes per 28 C.F.R. § 16.11(k)(i) and (ii).

I request expedited processing of this request pursuant to 28 C.F.R. § 16.5(d)(1) on the grounds that this is an issue of significant public interest and immediate needs to obtain this information exist. Firstly, any association between the Department of Justice and various groups once designated as unindicted co-conspirators in the Holy Land Foundation Trial are of critical public importance. Secondly, any effort to expand the reach of the civil rights laws to include classes not based on constitutionally defined classes would be of enormous public impor-tance. And lastly, the extent of outreach the Department is making to one particular religion when compared with similar outreach efforts to other religious groups is of enormous public importance to the members of religious groups who do not enjoy such aggressive outreach.

You can reach me by Email at writeatlas@aol.com or by telephone at xxx-xxx-xxxx.

Respectfully,
Pamela Geller
Editor, Publisher Atlas Shrugs
Executive Director, FDI/SIOA

I knew these documents existed, indicating broad collaboration between the Justice Department and Muslim Brotherhood groups—just as was recommended in *Changing Course* and *The Doha Compact*. This was confirmed on April 29, 2011, when the Justice Department's Civil Rights Division finally responded to my request. Nelson Hermilla wrote me that "clearly your request encompasses thousands of records. The total located on a preliminary search totals 14,100 documents. Each document likely contains numerous pages." Hermilla also complained that "it is not clear in what manner the collection of all five-year's records might contribute to the general public understanding." He explained that these documents would only be made available to me if I paid $1,400.

This is astounding. I made a fairly narrow request, narrowed down to specific groups and carefully defined activity that the Civil Rights Division doesn't even have direct jurisdiction over—"Muslim Outreach"—and they come up with 14,100 matching documents. A knowledgeable Justice Department insider told me: "You couldn't generate 14,000 pages of documents if you asked for communications with lenders or apartment or hotels as part of the Housing Section enforcement activities. There are very few things in Civil Rights that would generate 14,000 pages of anything. It has got to be a treasure trove of information."

Indeed. And it reveals that the "Muslim Outreach" efforts inside the Justice Department are far more extensive than anyone has realized.

It is also remarkable that the Justice Department would deny that these records would advance "the general public understanding." Given the increasing number of cases in which Sharia is used in American courts, and the Obama Justice Department's assistance of stealth jihad, Islamic supremacist legal initiatives, this claim is extremely flimsy.

I intend to pursue this matter until the shameful records of this infiltration are made available to the American people.

Meanwhile, there are numerous indications of the Muslim Brotherhood's influence in our government. But in the age of Obama, we are not merely infiltrated, no...that is so five years ago. *They are running the show.* Yes, the enemy is in control.

Congressman Keith Ellison (D-MN) took $13,350 from the Muslim American Society, the Muslim Brotherhood's chief organization in the United States, to go on the pilgrimage to Mecca.

Rashad Hussain, Obama's envoy to the Organization of the Islamic Conference, characterized the Bush Administration's prosecution of Islamic Jihad leader Sami al-Arian as a witch-hunt.

Arif Alikhan, Assistant Secretary for Policy Development at the Department of Homeland Security, is affiliated with the Brotherhood-linked Muslim Public Affairs Council, and as deputy mayor of Los Angeles, quashed as "Islamophobic" an LAPD initiative simply to survey the demographics of area mosques.

On March 6, 2011, Obama's Deputy National Security Adviser, Denis McDonough, gave a speech at the ADAMS Center, a mosque in Sterling, Virginia. WND reported in February 2008: "Another D.C.-area mosque, the ADAMS Center, was founded and financed by members of the Muslim Brotherhood, and has been one of the top distributors of Wahhabist anti-Semitic and anti-Christian dogma."[202]

Also, Imam Mohamed Magid is the President of the Islamic Society of North America. ISNA has admitted ties to the Muslim Brotherhood and Hamas, and is an unindicted co-conspirator in a Hamas terror funding case.[203]

Ignorant of or indifferent to all this, McDonough said at the ADAMS Center that Islamic jihadists "falsely claim to be fighting in the name of Islam," and that "we're exposing the lie that America and Islam are somehow in conflict. That is why President Obama has stated time and again that the United States is not and never will be at war with Islam." McDonough also said, "We also undermine al Qaeda's ideology by exposing the lie that it is somehow defending Islamic traditions when, in fact, al Qaeda violates the basic tenets of Islam."

This started before Obama. Islamic supremacists have infiltrated at the highest levels, placing Muslim Brotherhood operatives in government agencies, where they hinder anti-terror efforts, as when Islamic law expert Steve Coughlin was fired from his job in the Pentagon at the instigation of Hesham Islam, a Brotherhood-linked operative who was an assistant to Bush's Deputy Defense Secretary Gordon England. They are now also running candidates for office, like Esam Omeish of Virginia, positioning them as "moderate" when they're anything but.

But during Obama's presidency the pace of Islamization has quickened. It was revealed in February 2011 that the Obama Administration had spent $770 million to renovate mosques in the Islamic world. When contacted about this by CBS News, hardly a bastion of anti-Islamic sentiment or an unsympathetic observer of the Obama Administration, the State Department refused a request for an interview. When asked why they were spending millions on mosques, the State Department said in an email that it was "fighting Islamic extremism by building relationships with Islamic leaders."

Ex-Muslim human rights activist Nonie Darwish commented, "Trying to buy respect in the Middle East just shows US weakness.... America is not showing its power, it is showing appeasement....They're laughing all the way to the bank."[204]

This, too, has been going on for quite some time. The State Department announced in August 2009 that "the Bureau of International Information Programs (IIP) has assembled a range of innovative and traditional tools to support Posts' outreach activities during the Islamic holy month of Ramadan."[205]

The State envisioned a broad range of Ramadan activities. "On August 10," the cable says, "America.gov will publish a 'Multicultural Ramadan' feature. American Muslims trace their ancestry to more than 80 countries and the feature will highlight the richness of these various cultural traditions through the lens of Ramadan and Eid. Content will include essays by young Muslims who are part of Eboo Patel's Interfaith Youth Core (IYC). Contact: Alexandra Abboud (AbboudAM@state.gov)."

The IIP was, said the cable, preparing to "publish three articles for Ramadan 2009 addressing the concept of an Islam in America 'brand'; advocacy (civic and political) of the Muslim American community; and community innovation/community building. The writer will contact Muslim American experts in each of these fields. These articles will be available on America.gov in English, Arabic, and Persian."

The main publication would be *Being Muslim in America*: "Conceived as IIP's flagship print publication on the rich and varied experiences of the nation's growing Muslim population, this lavishly illustrated new book links the Muslim-American experience to those of other American racial, religious, and immigrant groups as they moved into the American 'mainstream.'"[206]

Can you imagine the State Department's Bureau of International

Information Programs assembling a "range of innovative and traditional tools to support "the "outreach activities" of State Department posts in various countries to Jews during Passover?

Can you imagine the State Department assembling a "range of innovative and traditional tools to support Posts' outreach activities" to Christians around Easter or Christmastime?

Can you imagine rabbis or priests and pastors or Buddhist monks speaking about their faith at U.S. embassies and outposts around the world?

Only Islam warranted such unconstitutional treatment from the Obama Administration's State Department.

In June 2009, Ekmeleddin Ihsanoglu, Secretary-General of the Organization of the Islamic Conference (OIC), visited Barack Obama at the White House. At the OIC chief's urging, Obama created a new State Department Office for Muslim Outreach, appointing a Muslim woman, Farah Pandith, as U.S. Special Representative for Muslim Outreach.

As he pursues that outreach, Obama is heedless of its risks for our national security. After a series of successful and unsuccessful jihad attacks across this great nation, on Christmas Day 2010, the crotch-bomber attempted to explode a bomb hidden in his underwear while landing in Detroit on Northwest Flight 253. And so after months of ignoring the jihad against America and pretending that nothing was happening, Barack Obama could ignore it no longer. But given his well-established and often reinforced affinity for Islam and unstinting desire to reach out to Muslims, it was virtually inconceivable that he would do anything genuinely effective regarding the jihad threat. But he did spring into action—with useless, toothless reform of the government's criteria for determining if a potential entrant into the U.S. was a terrorist and should thus be kept out.

That's right: in the wake of the Christmas Day bomber's attempted attack, the Obama Administration did nothing to address the doctrine of jihad that inspired the bomber, Umar Farouk Abdulmutallab. He made no attempt to determine whether or not these doctrines were being taught in mosques in the United States, or to challenge the Muslim community in America to institute programs to teach against these doctrines. He made no attempt to challenge the multicultural, politically correct ethos that prevents sensible profiling of airline passengers, such that might have kept Abdulmutallab off the plane in the first place.

Instead of doing any of that or anything else effective against jihad activity, he took a step that was emblematic of how impotent and compromised he has allowed the U.S. Government to become in the face of the jihad threat: he took purely symbolic steps to broaden the U.S. Visas Viper terrorist reporting program criteria.

The Visas Viper program is used by the Department of State and other national agencies to place on "watch lists" known or suspected international terrorists in both unclassified and classified government lookout systems such as CLASS (Consular Lookout and Support Systems).

So it was a good thing that Obama is broadening the criteria for reporting terrorists in this program, wasn't it? Actually, no. Obama's "tough" new criteria didn't allow American officials to filter out potential terrorists using even minimal profiling criteria.

The vast number of bureaucracies involved had already rendered the "watch list" process a tangled inter-agency web. And it was simply ridiculous how Visas Viper, the main system that we were using to try to prevent terrorists from obtaining visas, used such vague and toothless criteria—even after Obama's "reform."

How vague? How toothless? Under the present system, people who express anti-American sentiments can fly. People who contribute money to identified terror organizations can fly, no problem. People who associate with known terrorists, but have done nothing further to support terrorism, can also fly. Even people who claim to be members of a terrorist organization but have done nothing to further support terrorism can fly.

This is insane. Isn't membership in a terror organization the support of terror?

All of this is consistent for Barack Obama. He has blamed Gitmo for Islamic expansionism, appearing to believe that if we bow to our mortal enemy, he will become a friend. Don't upset the Nazis, and they will love us!

Obama has long ignored the onslaught of jihad attacks in America. Close to 40 percent of the planned and actual Islamic attacks on America post-9/11 took place in Obama's first year.

Back in September 2009, in a breathtaking act of *audacity*, Obama stood at the podium of the U.N. in New York City, talking about what he thought was the greatest threat to Americans and to future generations: global warming. As he spoke, bomb-sniffing dogs were out in force in New York City. Ray Kelly, the New York City police commissioner, was giving a press conference on the situation. A cell of Islamic jihadis targeting New York City was planning to blow up the transit system, as well as sports stadiums and the sites used for Fashion Week. Self-storage lockers in Queens were being searched for bomb-making materials.

The president spoke of the global warming hoax like a snake oil salesman. He said that "we understand the gravity" of the threat. "We are determined to act. And we will meet our responsibility to future genera-tions." He said that a failure to address the threat could lead to an "irrevers-ible catastrophe." Time, he said, is "running out," but "we can reverse" the problem. "If things go business-as-usual, we will not live, we will die," he said. "Our country will not exist." He told us that it wouldn't be easy, but "I am here today to say that difficulty is no excuse for complacency. Unease is no excuse for inaction." Imagine: He said this while the city was in the throes of jihad terror—what would have been the worst attack on New York since 9/11.

Yet when Senator Jack Reed said on *FOX News Sunday* that the Obama Administration was better on terrorism than the Bush administra-tion, he wasn't joking.

Only the left can massacre and rape language, render words meaning-less, and have their egregious actions left unchallenged.

But they will not forever go unchallenged. The jihad will only get worse. And I predict that when a Muslim gets one off in a mall or an airport, and limbs are flying and babies are dying, that Tea Partiers and Town Hallers will be joined by counter-jihad protests. People will begin to wake up to the need to stop the Islamization of America.

They will be protesting the Obama Administration's hopeless inaction and impotence in the face of the jihad against our nation.

And the time for that protest, the time for that action, is now. The immense extent of the infiltration and compromise of our government means that the resistance to the jihad is up to us. To all of us. Without exception. It is up to you.

The U.S.-Muslim Engagement Project: Charter for Islamization

Why is the Islamization of America proceeding? Why are Brotherhood operatives operating at the highest reaches of our government, silencing honest discussion of jihad and Islamic law? Why is America doing nothing to address this cultural, societal jihad? Why is the mainstream media intent on whitewashing the activities and goals of jihadists and Islamic supremacists? Why is this all happening so rapidly, with mega-mosques going up all over the country in the last few years, and Muslims advancing the stealth jihad in large and small ways everywhere?

Much of the Islamization of America at high levels is taking place in accord with the directives of the U.S.-Muslim Engagement Project, a large-scale endeavor dedicated in its own words to devising "recommendations to improve relations between the U.S. and the Muslim world," as well as to advancing "this strategy in ways that shift U.S. public opinion and contribute to changes in U.S. policies, and public and private action."[207]

What is happening in America today was all laid out in two influential documents: the Report of the Leadership Group on U.S.-Muslim Engagement: *Changing Course: A New Direction for U.S. Relations with the Muslim World*, which was funded by George Soros, and *The Doha Compact: New Directions: America and the Muslim World*, from the Saban Center of the Brookings Institution's Project on U.S. Relations with the Islamic World. Both were published in Fall 2008.

A clear indication of the influence of these documents is the fact that Obama's chief Muslim adviser, the Islamic supremacist Sharia advocate Dalia Mogahed, signed *The Doha Compact* and is a member of the U.S.-Muslim Engagement Project's "Leadership Group." Mogahed has praised Sharia law on British television, on a show run by the Islamic supremacist group Hizb ut-Tahrir, which is banned in many countries. With her in the Leadership Group was Ingrid Mattson of the Muslim Brotherhood-linked Islamic Society of North America (ISNA). Former Secretary of State Madeleine Albright promoted *Changing Course* to the Senate Foreign Relations Committee.[208]

Changing Course made a series of recommendations for the President of the United States who would be elected in 2008 (and who turned out to be Barack Obama, who followed these recommendations to the letter, even down to "speak to the critical importance of improving relations with the global Muslim community in his 2009 inaugural address."[209]) Anticipating Obama's oft-repeated exact words, *Changing Course* declared that the President should "improve mutual respect and understanding between Americans and Muslims around the world."[210] *The Doha Compact* said essentially the same thing: "Repairing the rift between the United States and the Muslim world must begin with respect. Lack of mutual respect has been an important driver behind the deterioration of relations between the United States and the Muslim world since 9/11."[211]

Changing Course directed the President to "elevate diplomacy as the primary tool for resolving key conflicts involving Muslim countries, engaging both allies and adversaries in dialogue"—in other words, to de-emphasize military anti-terror efforts in the Islamic world. It recommended that "within the first three months of the Administration," the new President should "initiate a major and sustained diplomatic effort to resolve regional conflicts and promote security cooperation in the Middle East, giving top priority to engagement with Iran and permanent resolution of the Israeli-Palestinian conflict."[212]

It also called upon the President to "engage with Iran to explore the potential for agreements that could increase regional security, while seeking Iran's full compliance with its nuclear nonproliferation commitments," and to "work intensively for immediate de-escalation of the Israeli-Palestinian conflict and a viable path to a two-state solution, while ensuring the security of Israelis and Palestinians." Unsurprisingly, the document made no mention of the fact that a Palestinian State would, like Gaza after the Israeli withdrawal in 2005, become simply another base for jihad attacks against Israel.

Changing Course also called for efforts to "deepen mutual understanding and challenge stereotypes"—which we see the mainstream media doing every day with its whitewashed accounts of Islamic jihad activity.[213] It called for "engagement with groups that have clearly demonstrated a commitment to nonviolent participation in politics"—echoing many Washington policymakers who have called for engagement with the Muslim Brotherhood.[214] Likewise *The Doha Compact* shares that "the United States should be more willing to reach out to Islamist parties that genuinely demonstrate their readiness to embrace the democratic rules of the game and reject violence."[215] This, too, referred to the Muslim Brotherhood.

Turning to the information battlespace, *Changing Course* says that policymakers should not give "ammunition to extremists by linking the term 'Islam' or key tenets of the religion of Islam with the actions of extremist or terrorist groups."[216] *The Doha Compact* says much the same thing: "Ill-considered terms like 'Islamofascism,' 'Islamic terrorism,' and 'Islamic jihadist' tend to alienate potential friends, while implicitly endorsing the worldview of extremists like bin Laden by suggesting they are true Muslims."[217]

CHAPTER 11

THE REAL THREATS
TO FREEDOM

Fight on no matter how hard they're hitting you. As the old adage goes, when you're getting flak, you know you're over the target. An illuminating demonstration of how truth is the new hate speech, and just telling the truth is a radical act, came in February 2011, when the subversive uber-leftwing fringe group, the Southern Poverty Law Center (SPLC), slandered our human rights organization, SIOA, with the designation as a "hate group."[218] The designation came one day after another Islamic supremacist plot was thwarted in Texas (with the intention of "killing infidel Americans" with "weapons of mass destruction"[219]).

The haters and deceivers accuse us of what they themselves are guilty of.

Before the collapse of the Soviet Union, the SPLC was designated as a Communist front. It was essentially run by a couple, Anne and Carl Braden, who were Communist Party USA members. They had been identified in sworn testimony, and they made no attempt to deny the allegations. They would be proud that their legacy remains intact today: their "heirs"—destroyers and America-haters—continue their work to subvert and destroy America.

A slam from the SPLC is a badge of honor. In reality, it has no substance except as propaganda for far-left journalists. Jerry Woodruff, a keen analyst of SPLC activity, summed it up this way:

American journalists refer frequently and casually to SPLC and its minions as "experts" on hate groups, even though there is no college or university that awards degrees in the study of hate groups, nor is there any professional association for the study of hate groups that confers "expert" status on applicants after some rigorous apprenticeship. The designation of SPLC spokesmen as experts is simply a flimsy journalistic contrivance to justify quoting them. SPLC enjoys the masquerade, allowing it to conceal a history of publishing writers who praise communists, promoting people who endorse revolution against the U.S., recommending groups that defend cop-killers, and disseminating ideas and attitudes that provoke suspicion, division, and hatred based on race and class. Referring to SPLC and its minions as "experts" on hate is like calling Typhoid Mary an "expert" in epidemiology. If SPLC and its minions really are experts in hate, it is only because they have so much experience promoting it.[220]

And the "hate group" designation was not their first salvo. The Southern Poverty Law Center's ironically named "Intelligence Report" for Winter 2010 contained a hit piece entitled "Geller, Jones Amp Up Anti-Muslim Hate Rhetoric."

More disinformation and outright lying from leftist propagandists.

Their skullduggery was apparent in their presentation of a false narrative. Their report conflated me and my work with the cartoonish Terry Jones, the Florida pastor who gained international fame by threatening to burn the Koran—and then backing down (before finally, belatedly, carrying through with his threat in March 2011, long after his fifteen minutes of fame had passed). The SPLC was retailing Goebbels-style propaganda. Jones was a media creation, a fringe pastor who tweeted something stupid—that he was going to burn the Koran—whereupon the media descended on him like locusts. The Ground Zero mosque story, which first attracted the SPLC's attention to my work, unfolded in just the opposite way: it became national news in spite of the media's silence, and the American people stood against the mosque despite the media's relentless cheerleading for the Islamic supremacist slumlord Imam Feisal Abdul Rauf and other shady organizers.

The Ground Zero mosque was the people's story, the people's outrage, a cry against the disrespect and insult.

In lumping me in with Jones, the SPLC's "Intelligence Report" didn't bother to mention that I criticized Jones's plan to burn the Koran back on September 9, before Terry Jones backed off his threat to burn the book. I said it was a

> stupid idea, of course, but protected under the laws of free speech. The burning of books is wrong in principle: the antidote to bad speech is not censorship or book-burning, but more speech. Open discussion. Give-and-take. And the truth will out. There is no justification for burning books. If Americans are free and not under Sharia, then the church can do this if it wants, and their freedom and rights should be protected. Islamic supremacists should not be allowed a victory for their violent intimidation—if these people want to burn a book, they're free to do so.[221]

The SPLC "Intelligence Report" was just as unintelligent in what it did notice about my work: "Earlier this year, Geller—who also has questioned whether President Obama was born in America—bought anti-Muslim ads that were displayed on New York City buses for a month."

Actually, in the past, like many Americans, I simply pointed out that the president had never produced the long-form birth certificate that would definitively put to rest the questions about his place of birth. The new governor of Hawaii, Neil Abercrombie, promised to produce this proof when he took office late in 2010, but quickly backed off, saying that to produce Obama's birth certificate would have "political implications," ones "that we simply cannot have." When Obama finally did produce a long-form birth certificate, the document he produced raised more questions than it answered.

The very idea that merely questioning such things in a free society would get you preeminent status in the SPLC "Intelligence Report" speaks volumes about how much less free we really are, as the left tightens its chokehold on the culture, the media, and politics.

As for my bus ads, they were not "anti-Muslim." They merely offered help to those threatened with death in America for leaving Islam, under Islam's traditional death penalty for apostasy—like Rifqa Bary, the Ohio convert from Islam to Christianity who says she was threatened by her father and was certainly threatened by other Muslims on Facebook. Was the SPLC saying that people who receive such threats didn't deserve protection? Are we not all equal under the law? Are the lives of Muslims trying to escape the Sharia worth less than the Islamic supremacists imposing the Sharia in America?

The SPLC report also said that I warned that Muslims will "turn to further intimidation, murder, and terrorism" if they couldn't achieve a political takeover.

As the SPLC wrote this, there were Islamic terror plots uncovered in Portland, Oregon; Baltimore, Maryland; Stockholm, Sweden; Copenhagen, Denmark; Great Britain; and elsewhere. Islamic jihadists murdered sixty-eight Christians in a church in Baghdad. Each of these plots had the imprimatur of an Islamic cleric and was plotted in the name of Islam.

How much "intimidation, murder, and terrorism" from Muslims is the SPLC going to ignore before it speaks out for the victims of these attacks?

The charges the SPLC made against my work were illuminating, because all people who take up the fight for freedom will face similar smears.

The SPLC claimed also that my "comments were so incendiary, in fact, that several neo-Nazi organizations even ignored the fact that she is Jewish and published her diatribes."

Even if neo-Nazis published anything I wrote, it doesn't matter, since they did it without my knowledge or consent. In reality, neo-Nazi and white supremacist organizations are generally pro-Islam and pro-jihad, because they hate Jews above all. SPLC is engaging in more Goebbels-style smear tactics by trying to connect me to neo-Nazis.

This was an obvious ploy to keep politicians away from opposing the Ground Zero mega-mosque and taking a firm stand on any jihad-related issue. Trust me: the folks at Stormfront, whom I've monitored for years (they were the very first hate site to hit the web back in 1994), can't stand Jews or Israel or me, and it would be obvious to *anyone* that *if* there are posts there supporting my work, then this is a manifestation of Sun Tzu's strategy from *The Art of War* (deliberately planting misinformation from the "other side"). The idea of neo-Nazis who love Israel and hate Islamic jihad is a figment of the left's imagination.

The SPLC also outright twisted and misrepresented things I actually said. This, too, is illuminating, because it is common practice among leftist and Islamic supremacist groups. Another charge from the SPLC was that I "commented favorably on the South African, apartheid-defending terrorist Eugene Terre'Blanche after he was murdered, blaming his death on 'black supremacism.'"[222]

I never commented favorably on Terre'Blanche. I know little about him. But he was murdered, hacked to death at his home, and that's what I wrote deploring. I do not sanction cold-blooded murder.

In reality, I wrote this about Terre'Blanche: "Insofar as my sanctioning of white supremacists in South Africa—that is a blatant libel....I vehemently disagree with Terre'blanche's ideas...."[223]

The SPLC also pointed out that a Leftist/Islamic supremacist counter-demo held during our 9/11 Freedom Rally against the Ground Zero mosque featured a sign saying, "The attack on Islam is racism." What race is Islam? The Islamic supremacist ideology is at war against freedom of speech, freedom of conscience, and equal rights for women. People of all races hold to this ideology.

And the SPLC, instead of standing for those freedoms, was carrying water for the real haters, the real neo-Nazi Jew-haters: the forces of Islamic supremacism and jihad.

A still earlier SPLC attack on me was entitled "Hatewatch." Actually, I consider my work more like *"Lovewatch!* Keeping the world safe for lovers and other strangers."

I equate the Southern Poverty Law Center coming out for Islamic supremacists with the same organization coming out for Nazis. What's the difference, and why doesn't the SPLC even have not a single category for Islamic jihadi groups? The greatest threat facing our nation, our people, our world, and the SPLC is shilling for them.

Here is proof: around the time that the SPLC began attacking my freedom initiatives, a reader sent me an exchange he had with the SPLC's Mark Potok. Reader Bob wrote, "I started out by looking on their Web site for a definition of the term 'hate group' fully expecting that Islam would fit any reasonable definition. When I couldn't find such a definition (still can't today) I inquired." In the course of the exchange, Potok wrote back, "With regard to monitoring radical jihadists, we have made a pragmatic decision to leave that mainly to the major Jewish NGOs, which do a good job and have some real expertise that would likely take us years to develop." In other words, the real hate just doesn't matter to the SPLC. "Still," Potok continued, "we do cover black Muslim extremists and have written about such matters as the connections between radical Muslims and neo-Nazis."[224]

Except when they're pretending that the neo-Nazis are connected to me, that is.

But consider what they have admitted to here. They refuse to cover, evaluate, or report on the single greatest threat to free men here and across the world. The jihad is exempt from the prying, dishonest leadership of the SLPC, but those standing up against these tremendous odds are being smeared, defamed, and destroyed.

And the SPLC is getting well-paid to do this. According to the SPLC's 990 Form for 2008, the SPLC's Chief Trial Counsel Morris Dees made a generous $348,420 that year. SPLC President and CEO Richard Cohen was right behind him at $344,490. General Counsel Joseph Levin made $189,166. Legal director Rhonda Brownstein brought in $179,806; CFO Teenie Hutchinson, $155,414. Potok pulled in $143,099. Former Chief Operating Officer Jeff Blancett made $159,301—that's right, the *former* COO.

Who is funding this subversive and dangerous organization?

But the SPLC is hardly alone in this. Leading left-wing organizations traffic in this filth daily. There is no better example of this than Media Matters and the *Huffington Post*, et al. Their unabashed mission is to destroy any and all effective rational voices on the right. It is a machine of destruction, and all that we hold dear and our founding fathers fought and died for will be decimated in their wake.

The AFDI Threats to Freedom Index

Who appointed the Media Matters, the SPLC, or the mainstream media the judge and arbiter of what constitutes a hate group? My own group, the American Freedom Defense Initiative (AFDI), of which SIOA is a program, is much better equipped to identify such groups, since we are much more realistic about the real threats facing America today. The standard we use is objective reality. And so we have begun tracking the activities of numerous active groups that are threats to freedom in the United States today.

This year we began a preliminary list of groups that are Threats to Freedom; we call it the "Threats to Freedom Index." We plan to augment it periodically and publish it annually.

All Threat to Freedom groups have beliefs or practices that attack or malign American Constitutional freedoms and/or lawful initiatives for American self-defense.

We compiled the list from records of Threat to Freedom group statements and activities as they appear in their own publications and Web sites, as well as from reports from concerned citizens and mainstream media reports.

Threat to Freedom group activities can include misrepresentation of anti-terror and other law enforcement initiatives, attempts to restrict the freedom of speech regarding Islamic jihad or other threats to freedom, defamation of freedom fighters, disinformation campaigns in the mainstream media regarding attempts by the United States and Israel to defend themselves, and more.

Listing as a Threat to Freedom group does not in itself imply that a listed group calls for or participates in violence or criminal activities, although it does not rule out their doing so.

Threats to Freedom Index, preliminary listing:

Al-Awda, The Palestine Right to Return Coalition retails jihadist propaganda against Israel, distorting the facts of the conflict and attempting to delegitimize Israel's right to exist.

Code Pink: Far-Left organization aligned with Communists and Islamic jihadists, masquerading as a "peace" organization dedicated to stopping what it characterizes as unjust wars.

Cordoba Initiative: Stealth jihad organization aligned with anti-Israel jihad organizations and dedicated to building the triumphal Islamic supremacist mosque at Ground Zero.

Council on American-Islamic Relations (CAIR): Muslim Brotherhood, Hamas-linked organization spreading disinformation about Islam and terror, opposing anti-terror activity, and defaming freedom fighters. CAIR was one of the many Islamic groups that was named an unindicted co-conspirator in the Holy Land Foundation Hamas jihad funding trial.

Friends of Sabeel-North America (FOSNA): Palestinian Christians aiding the jihad against Israel and retailing jihadist propaganda against the Jewish state.

If Americans Knew (IAK) spreads disinformation about the Palestinian jihad against Israel and Israel's efforts to defend itself.

International ANSWER: a far-Left organization that opposes U.S. attempts to defend itself from jihad aggression.

International Institute of Islamic Thought (IIIT): Muslim Brotherhood organization with numerous documented links to Saudi Wahhabi organizations and jihad terror activity.

International Solidarity Movement enlists Leftist Americans to aid the Palestinian jihad against Israel and impede the defensive actions of the Israeli Defense Force (IDF).

Islamic Circle of North America: Muslim Brotherhood organization preaching a global Caliphate and Islamic law (Sharia) over the U.S. ISNA was another Islamic group that was named an unindicted co-conspirator in the Holy Land Foundation Hamas jihad funding trial.

Islamic Society of North America: Muslim Brotherhood organization named an unindicted co-conspirator in a Hamas jihad terror funding case.

Muslim American Society: chief arm of the Muslim Brotherhood in the U.S., which is dedicated in its own words to "eliminating and destroying Western civilization from within."

Muslim Public Affairs Council: Muslim Brotherhood-linked organization that has spread disinformation about the extent of Muslim cooperation with anti-terror efforts, and has encouraged Muslims not to cooperate with law enforcement.

Muslim Students Association: Muslim Brotherhood organization creating an atmosphere of intimidation for Jewish students on campuses nationwide, and bringing in speakers who preach jihad and hatred.

In one victory for the forces of freedom, the Muslim Student Union (another name for the MSA) at the University of California-Irvine was suspended, and several of its leading members arrested and brought up on charges, after they disrupted a talk on campus by Israeli Ambassador Michael Oren in February 2010. The magnitude of this victory is incalculable: it is a giant stop sign to the Islamic supremacism and jackbootery increasingly found on college campuses all over the country today. America is waking up to the enemy in our midst; yet the MSA still operates on campuses all over the country, trafficking freely in intimidation, thuggery, disinformation, and hate.

The New Black Panther Party (NBPP): a black militant group that relentlessly promotes violence against white people, and Jews in particular. During the 2008 election, New Black Panther party members openly intimidated voters at polling places in Philadelphia, threatening them with weapons. A witness wrote in an affidavit: "I watched the two uniformed men confront voters and attempt to intimidate voters. They were positioned in a location that forced every voter to pass in close proximity to them. The weapon was openly displayed and brandished in plain sight of voters."[225] They were duly arrested and charged, but like so many Islamic supremacist groups, the New Black Panther party has friends in high places: Obama's gang of thugs in the increasingly inaptly-named *Justice* Department dropped the charges. In July 2010, J. Christian Adams, a Justice Department lawyer who resigned over the DOJ's refusal to pursue this case, testified before the U.S. Civil Rights Commission, according to the pro-freedom watchdog Web site Discover the Networks, "that the DOJ had instructed attorneys in its civil rights division to ignore cases involving black defendants and white victims."[226]

North American Islamic Trust (NAIT): Muslim Brotherhood organization and subsidiary of the ISNA, holder of titles of hundreds of Islamic properties in the U.S. It funds mosques and Islamic schools nationwide, and safeguards and pools the assets of the Muslim community in America. In doing so, NAIT promotes the concept of *waqf,* the eternal Islamic ownership of land—which is certain to cause trouble in the United States in the future. It also is tied to Saudi Wahhabi groups that are aggressively pushing, all over the world, the most virulent, violent form of Islam on the planet. Further, it's the financial arm of the Muslim Students Association. NAIT was yet another Islamic group that was named an unindicted co-conspirator in the Holy Land Foundation Hamas jihad funding trial.

Organization of the Islamic Conference: International organization dedicated to destroying free speech about Islam and jihad in America and Europe. The great historian Bat Ye'or explains that the OIC is "close to the Muslim World League of the Muslim Brotherhood," and that "it shares the Brotherhood's strategic and cultural vision: that of a universal religious community, the Ummah, based upon the Koran, the Sunna, and the canonical orthodoxy of *shari'a*." The OIC's reach is immense: it "represents," says Bat Ye'or, "56 countries and the Palestinian Authority (considered a state), the whole constituting the universal Ummah with a community of more than one billion three to six hundred million Muslims."[227]

Bat Ye'or notes that in the OIC's 2008 Charter, all states that are OIC members "confirm that their union and solidarity are inspired by Islamic values. They affirm their aim to reinforce within the international arena their shared interests and the promotion of Islamic values. They commit themselves to revitalizing the pioneering role of Islam in the world, increasing the prosperity of the member states, and—in contrast to the European states—to ensure the defense of their national sovereignty and territorial integrity. They proclaim their support for Palestine with al-Quds Al Sharif, the Arabized name for Jerusalem, as its capital, and exhort each other to promote human rights, basic freedoms, the state of law (*shari'a*), and democracy according to their constitutional and legal system—in other words, compliance with *shari'a*."

The OIC is also committed, she observes, to "the universal propagation of Islam (*da'wa*)."[228] Essential to this propagation is an all-out campaign to restrict the West's freedom of speech regarding Islam, jihad, and Islamic supremacism, and to brand all honest discussion of such matters as "Islamophobia." In 2008, OIC Secretary General Ekmeleddin Ihsanoglu warned that the OIC had "sent a clear message to the West regarding the red lines that should not be crossed" when speaking about Islam and jihad. Ihsanoglu was happy with the results: "The official West and its public opinion are all now well-aware of the sensitivities of these issues. They have also started to look seriously into the question of freedom of expression from the perspective of its inherent responsibility, which should not be overlooked."[229]

Prince Alwaleed Bin Talal Center for Muslim-Christian Understanding: Saudi-funded center at Georgetown University spreading disinformation about Islam and jihad. It underwrites material by the deceptive pro-Sharia academic John Esposito, such as the 2011 book

Islamophobia: The Challenge of Pluralism in the 21st Century, a book-length barrage of Muslim victimhood propaganda, designed to deflect attention away from Islamic jihad activity and Islamic supremacism. The book carries this note in the Acknowledgments: "We thank the Organization of the Islamic Conference and its Secretary General, Prof. Ekmeleddin Ihsanoglu, who *provided financial support* for a conference at Georgetown and the development of a manuscript" (emphasis added).[230]

George Soros: The only individual to make the "Threats to Freedom" list, Soros is, according to Discover the Networks, "one of the most powerful men on earth," with personal assets of an estimated $13 billion. Soros' Open Society Institute (OSI) donates millions of dollars to far-Left, pro-Sharia, anti-freedom groups.

George Soros is the source of the dirty money behind the far-Left front group to destroy Israel, J Street—as J Street executive director Jeremy Ben Ami has finally admitted to the media, after lying about it since the group's founding: "I accept responsibility personally," said Ben Ami, "for being less than clear about Mr. Soros' support once he did become a donor."

Of course it was Soros. George Soros vowed years ago to start an anti-Jewish organization under the nefarious guise of a Jewish organization, in order to counter the influence of the American Israel Political Action Committee (AIPAC). He knew full well that there would be lowlife Jews who would be only too happy to serve as *funktionshäftling*—Jews who betray their own and side with their killers.

As a young man in Hungary he assisted the Nazis, so is it any wonder he wants to destroy the Jew?[231] *If at first you don't succeed...* If you are unfamiliar with Soros's actual past, remember that, as *60 Minutes* reported in 2006, "While hundreds of thousands of Hungarian Jews were being shipped off to the death camps, George Soros accompanied his phony godfather on his appointed rounds, confiscating property from the Jews."[232]

Since then, Soros—who has been convicted in France for insider trading—has had his black hand in every evil thing: the legalization of drugs and prostitution; betting against America and making millions by making what he called "a good call against the dollar"; violating the U.N.'s neutrality by funneling money through its Development Program to Georgia's President.[233] He was financier of guilty terror lawyer Lynne Stewart's defense fund; and was involved via his stooges at America Coming Together in election fraud and via his investment in WellCare, in Medicare irregularities.[234]

And Soros gave $750,000 to J Street. Another $811,697 came from a mysterious woman in Hong Kong named Consolacion Esdicul, who has apparently acted as a representative for Black Rock, a New York hedge fund with close ties to…George Soros.[235]

What galled me was the tragic gullibility of leading American Jewish organizations that insisted Soros was not funding J Street. I spoke to numerous heads of various organizations after J Street had been established, and they were parroting the leftist/Islamic narrative that Soros wasn't financing it.

It was a brazen deception. James Besser, the Washington correspondent for *New York Jewish Week*, says that when he had asked whether J Street was getting money from Soros, they lied to him outright: "I was one of the many journalists who asked the question and received in return something significantly less than the truth. Okay, it was a lie."[236]

But it also took extraordinary delusion for anyone to buy the idea that there was no connection between Soros and J Street. Back in October 2006 (before there was a J Street), I reported on how Soros was pairing with "the dovish pro-Israel community" to consider establishing an alternative to AIPAC in order to, at the very least, undermine it, and eventually destroy it.[237]

There were other connections between Soros and J Street as well. When Obama appointed anti-Israel Senator Chuck Hagel co-chair of his Intelligence Advisory Board in October 2009, the appointment was announced at J Street's first annual conference—by Steve Clemons of George Soros's New America Foundation.

Of course, it was common knowledge that J Street was an anti-Israel, anti-Semitic, fringe organization that no one took seriously. Isi Liebler, former chairman of the Governing Board of the World Jewish Congress, challenged J Street's "duplicity in trying to masquerade as a Jewish mainstream 'pro-Israel' organisation while consistently campaigning against the Jewish state."[238]

Philip Klein, *The American Spectator*'s Washington correspondent, says that "while the group bills itself as the 'pro Israel' and 'pro peace' alternative to the American Israel Public Affairs Committee, in reality it is a liberal organization actively campaigning against Israel's right to defend itself."[239]

Just how extreme and anti-Israel was J Street? According to Liebler, as of October 2009 "Arab and pro-Iranian elements were providing approximately 10% of J Street funding, a somewhat bizarre situation for a genuinely 'pro-Israel' organisation." That is, until Barack Obama became president. Obama is a longtime Soros toy, so it was no surprise when White House visitor logs listed Ben-Ami as a frequent visitor.[240]

Yet despite Obama's tacit support of this dangerous group and his manifest preference for the company of Jew-haters, the vile anti-Jewish J Street was shunned by K street [Washington's lobbying center], Congress, and anyone with an ounce of basic human decency.[241] Only Barack Obama sanctioned this Soros-funded stain on humanity.

Southern Poverty Law Center (SPLC) defames and attempts to marginalize conservative, pro-freedom organizations as "hate groups." It uses its listing of "hate groups" to try to stigmatize, and ultimately criminalize, love of country and patriotism. It works to systematically destroy voices that are speaking out against oppression and persecution. Further, they are notoriously well known in civil rights circles as doing little to nothing and raising enormous amounts of money, which are squandered.

Students for Justice in Palestine (SJP) spreads jihadist propaganda and disinformation about Israeli self-defense on U.S. university campuses.

EPILOGUE

ONWARD KAFIR SOLDIERS

Everything we believe in has to be defended. Everything we are. Everything we have must be defended with all our heart, and with all our soul, and with all our might. Our freedom, our constitutional republic, and our civilization are at stake.

You cannot depend upon anyone else to do this. No one is going to save you. It must be you. You must get involved. There is an enormous amount of work to be done. The Muslim Brotherhood project in America has been in play for six decades. The jihad against the non-Muslim world is 1,400 years old.

One only has to look at a fellow like Rich Davis to see that the individual can make an enormous difference. Rich, a twenty-year Navy veteran, was a longtime reader of my Web site, AtlasShrugs.com, who himself was so inspired by what one individual could do that in 2007 he started his own citizen activist group in Philadelphia to stand up against a weekly motley crew of anti-American, anti-Iraq war demonstrators comprised of seditionists, traitors, and your regular weak, run-of-the-mill group of hippie leftists. Rich wanted to make sure that the public and the troops knew that there were proud Americans who supported them.

Well, the anti-war cowards don't like to be challenged or questioned, or called out on their lies, especially by proud patriots. So they cry and whine and stomp and wail and summon the police, but to no avail. Rich's wonderful group of patriots grows and grows, so the leftists have been defanged, their group largely diminished after being unmasked. Despite vile name-calling and weekly agitation and harassment, Rich and his group were unintimidated and undaunted, and did not give an inch. They continue to soldier on, and have taken on other pro-freedom causes as they've grown to a vibrant pro-freedom activist group in the Philadelphia area. And Rich now sits on the board of the American Freedom Defense Initiative/SIOA. Rich Davis is living proof of the difference one individual can make.

That individual is you.

Each person comes to this battle differently. Your awakening may differ from mine. It's true that 9/11 shook me to my core. Up until that moment, I had assumed my freedom—taken it for granted. I had a post-historical perspective—the good guys won the big one and the good cop was on the beat.

It was 9/11 that jolted me into reality. Science and technology and modernity progress, but human nature never changes. The battle between good and evil is eternal.

Before jihad had come to America, I was the Associate Publisher of the *New York Observer*, a fashionista, and a mom. I loved my life. I loved my world. I loved my country. If Billie Holiday wasn't on the Bose, then full frontal fashion was on the Metro channel.

On September 11 2001, I felt guilty that I didn't know who had attacked this great nation. And when I found out, I felt guiltier still that I didn't understand who had attacked this great nation or why. I heard a name, but it didn't mean anything to me; I didn't grasp who and what it meant. I felt guilty that I didn't know who that person was.

And so I set out to learn everything about the enemy who vowed to destroy America.

And this is my advice to you. First, learn everything.

One of the first people I went to hear speak after I began studying Islam was Bat Ye'or. This tiny woman with a smaller voice made the most powerful presentation I had ever heard. After her remarks I asked her what I could do and she said, "First, learn everything."

And this was the best advice I got or could give. Read Bat Ye'or and Ibn Warraq, the world's leading scholar on Islam (and former Muslim). Read Mark Durie and Robert Spencer, Sir Martin Gilbert and Wafa Sultan.

Take no one's word for it. Do your homework.

The idea of a "moderate" Islam does not exist, not because I say so, but because the Koran says so and Muhammad said so. The Koran is the word of Allah, given directly to Muhammad, uncreated (unlike the Old or New Testament). Who can "reinterpret" or "reform" the word of Allah? No one. And to attempt such "hypocrisy" is punishable by death.

Moderate Muslims are secular. There is nothing moderate in Islam, and this is the deception that must be unveiled. It will take an earthquake of catastrophic proportion to "reform Islam," but it certainly cannot and will not happen if the West continues to appease and surrender in installments.

Get involved. Go to rallies and protests. Support your belief system. Support your peers. Go rain or shine, as I have. Cover them on your personal blogs, whether there are fifteen people or fifteen hundred. Pamela Hall, another AFDI/SIOA board member, is a great role model. She goes to everything and documents it all. She is recording history.

You can't be at everything, but go when you can. Your people need you. If you are heckled, stand proud, march, sing the National Anthem, stand for your greatness. Be the proud bearers of your civilization. I have been videoed by Revolution Muslim while they were screaming, "Filthy whore!" "Prostitute!" A member of the extreme hate group, Islamic Thinkers Society, would shout, "Cover your tits!" These incidents only fortified me. The more they heckled, the more determined I became. And I began to organize rallies and demonstrations, and the people came.

Any one of you can do the same. You need nothing but love and will. If you need help, I am happy to consult and help organize similar demonstrations all over the country.

Get involved. Join SIOA. Check the Web sites for events, action alerts, and upcoming legislation that needs your phone calls and letters.

Support candidates who understand the threat.

Be the eyes and ears in your community. Stay on the wall. When you see something, start something.

It's up to you to stop the Islamization of America, and to save the Land of the Free and the Home of the Brave.

"On strategy: In order to live...act; in order to act...make choices."
—Ayn Rand

ACKNOWLEDGMENTS

I wish to thank my colleague, partner, and friend, Robert Spencer, for his meticulous hand in editing this essential guide. It is a joy to fight alongside one of this war's leading lights. And a special thank you to John Jay, a wonderful sounding board, whose intellectual fidelity to our founding principles as well as to *The Federalist Papers* is indispensable.

Of course, this book would not be possible without the affection and unconditional support of my patient and loving family, for whom I do it all.

Lastly, and most importantly, I wish to thank all of my Atlas readers, Facebook "friends," and fellow Tweeters who spread the word, send letters, go to rallies, write their congressmen, get involved in the election process, and ask the questions that inspired this book. You are the foot soldiers in this war. *You* will save the free world.

ENDNOTES

Introduction

1 Mohamed Akram, "An Explanatory Memorandum on the General Strategic Goal for the Group in North America," May 22, 1991, Government Exhibit 003–0085, U.S. vs. HLF, et al. 7 (21).

2 Corky Siemaszko, "Southern Poverty Law Center Lists Anti-Islamic NYC Blogger Pamela Geller, Followers a Hate Group," New York Daily News, February 25, 2011.

3 Robert Spencer, Stealth Jihad, Regnery, 2008, p. 73–100.

4 Robert Spencer, Stealth Jihad (Regnery, 2008).

5 Mohamed Akram, "An Explanatory Memorandum on the General Strategic Goal for the Group in North America," 7 (21).

6 Art Moore, "Did CAIR Founder Say Islam to Rule America?" WorldNetDaily, December 11, 2006.

7 Minneapolis Star Tribune, April 4, 1993, quoted in Daniel Pipes and Sharon Chadha, "CAIR: Islamists Fooling the Establishment," Middle East Quarterly, Spring 2006.

8 Jagan Kaul, "Kashmir: Kashmiri Pundit View-point," Kashmir Telegraph, May 2002.

9 Ahmed ibn Naqib al-Misri, Reliance of the Traveller: A Classic Manual of Islamic Sacred Law [Umdat al-Salik], translated by Nuh Ha Mim Keller (Amana Publications, 1999).

10 Pamela Geller, "US Treasury Submits To Islam," AtlasShrugs.com, November 4, 2008.

Chapter One: The Awakening

11 Ralph Blumenthal and Sharaf Mowjood, "Muslim Prayers and Renewal Near Ground Zero," New York Times, December 8, 2009; Pamela Geller, "NY Times Scrubs Imam Rauf's Controversial Islamic Supremacist Ground Zero Mosque Remark, 'New York Is the Capital of the World, and This Location Close to 9/11 Is Iconic,'" AtlasShrugs.com, August 18, 2010.

12 Robert Spencer, "SIOA at Manhattan Community Board Meeting on the 9/11 Mosque—the Fix Was In," Jihad Watch, May 25, 2010.

13 Justin Elliott, "How the 'Ground Zero Mosque' Fear Mongering Began," Salon, August 16, 2010.

14 Pamela Geller, "Fox News: Geller vs. CAIR," AtlasShrugs.com, May 30, 2010; Pamela Geller, "911 Mega Mosque: Pamela Geller vs Islamic Supremacist Liar on CNN Sunday Morning June 6, 2010," AtlasShrugs.com, June 6, 2010.

15 Pamela Geller, "CNN Ground Zero Mosque Debate: Geller vs. Muslim American Society," AtlasShrugs.com, July 15, 2010; Pamela Geller, "VIDEO Round 2: Geller vs Ramey, Muslim American Society Debate the Ground Zero Mega Mosque," AtlasShrugs.com, July 19, 2010.

16 MISSING

17 Pamela Geller, "RLTV VIDEO: Pamela Geller vs 'Palestine Center' Rap Artist, Debate Staten Island Mosque Victory, 'Mosques in America,'" AtlasShrugs.com, July 25, 2010; Pamela Geller, "RLTV Video: 911 Mega Mosque Debate: Pamela Geller vs Robert Salaam," AtlasShrugs.com, June 8, 2010; Pamela Geller, "RTV VIDEO: Pamela Geller on Ground Zero Mega Mosque Landmark Decision," AtlasShrugs.com, August 3, 2010; Pamela Geller, "Pamela Geller on Bill O'Reilly Rebuts CAIR's Fallacious Accusations," AtlasShrugs.com, August 4, 2010; Pamela Geller, "Unindicted Co-Conspirator Hamas-linked Muslim Brotherhood Front CAIR Smears Pamela Geller on O'Reilly," AtlasShrugs.com, August 4, 2010.

18 Pamela Geller, "911 Mega Mosque: The Joy Behar Show with Pamela Geller and Daisy Khan," AtlasShrugs.com, May 26, 2010.17 Pamela Geller, "Fox and Friends: Pamela Geller vs Nicole Neroulias on Ground Zero Mosque and Bus Campaign," AtlasShrugs.com, August 11, 2010.

19 Pamela Geller, "Hannity: Ground Zero Mosque Debate Pamela Geller vs David Lane, Liberal Lawyer," AtlasShrugs.com, August 12, 2010; Pamela Geller, "HANNITY: Geller vs Gross on Ground Zero Mosque," AtlasShrugs.com, August 23, 2010.

20 Pamela Geller, "Hamas-linked CAIR on FOX: Hate Sponsor Ibrahim Hooper Soils Himself with Geller Obsession," AtlasShrugs.com, August 17, 2010.

21 Pamela Geller, "CNN on Ground Zero Mosque: It's All Geller's Fault!" AtlasShrugs.com, August 18, 2010.

22 Pamela Geller, "FOX Business TV Appearance: Geller on the Dove Church Qur'an Burning," AtlasShrugs.com, September 7, 2010.

23 "Sean Hannity Show: Pamela Geller Debates Michael Ghouse (Muslim American Congress) 911 Mega Mosque," YouTube, May 13, 2010.

24 "BBC Radio: Ground Zero Debate Geller vs Shahed Amanullah," YouTube, August 15, 2010.

25 Pamela Geller, "Here's the Geraldo Hit Job Video," AtlasShrugs.com, September 12, 2010.

26 Pamela Geller, "Fox Business: Pamela Geller vs. Black Panthers Leader Malik Shabazz on Money Rocks," AtlasShrugs.com, September 12, 2010.

27 Pamela Geller, "FOX Business: Hate Sponsor CAIR on Steroids, Waterboy Bob Beckel Squeal and the Ground Zero Mosque," AtlasShrugs.com, September 27, 2010.

28 "Rauf's Group Claims Credit for 'Training' NY Times Reporter," IPT News, September 20, 2010.

29 "Memo to Media: Pamela Geller Does Not Belong on National Television," Media Matters, July 14, 2010.

30 Pamela Geller, "Atlas TV Alert: Hardball Tonight UPDATE: HARDBALL CANCELS," AtlasShrugs.com, July 14, 2010.

31 Luisita Lopez Torregrosa, "Why Christiane Amanpour Is Bombing on ABC's 'This Week,'" Politics Daily, September 30, 2010.

32 Hana Levi Julian, "New Yorkers Plan to Fight Mosque Near Ground Zero," Israel National News, May 25, 2010.

33 Sayyid Qutb, Milestones, The Mother Mosque Foundation, n.d. 263.

34 Feisal Abdul Rauf, "Sharing the Core of Our Beliefs," Washington Post, March 27, 2009.

35 Feisal Abdul Rauf, "Conflicting Cultural Norms Require Respect, Restraint," Washington Post, May 5, 2010.

36 Robert Spencer, "SIOA at Manhattan Community Board Meeting on the 9/11 Mosque—the Fix Was In."

37 "AP Standards Center Issues Staff Advisory on Covering New York City Mosque," Associated Press, August 19, 2010.

38 "Role Players & Contributors of the Perdana Global Peace Organisation," Perdana Global Peace Organization, http://www.perdana4peace.org/agenda.aspx?x=3.

39 Perry Chiaramonte and Cathy Burke, "Mosque 'Slumlord,'" New York Post, August 30, 2010.

40 Peter J. Sampson and Jean Rimbach, "Imam in Mosque Debate Has History of Tenant Troubles," The Record, August 29, 2010.

41 Pamela Geller, "Dear Imam Rauf and Daisy Khan....A Heartfelt Appeal," Big Government, June 28, 2010.

42 Walid Shoebat, "Ground Zero Imam: 'I Don't Believe In Religious Dialogue,'" Pajamas Media, May 27, 2010.

43 Pamela Geller, "Reuters Coverage: NYC 'Leaving Islam' Freedom BusesPamela Geller vs. 911 Mega Mosquer Daily Khan," AtlasShrugs.com, June 3, 2010.

44 Maggie Haberman, "Rudy: GZ Mosque Is a 'Desecration,' 'Decent Muslims' Won't Be Offended," Politico, August 2, 2010.

45 Michael S. James and Lara Setrakian, "'Ground Zero Mosque' Imam Says Project Must Go Forward in the Interest of National Security," ABC News, September 9, 2010.

46 Pamela Geller, "Waiter Sharif El Gamal's Exercise and Stress Relief Regimen," AtlasShrugs.com, August 16, 2010.

47 Pamela Geller, "Sharif El-Gamal, Thug Developer in Ground Zero Mega Mosque, Evicted," AtlasShrugs.com, September 15, 2010.

48 Pamela Geller, "Ground Zero Deadbeat Thug Sharif El-Gamal Owes 224G Tax," AtlasShrugs.com, August 29, 2010.

49 Kathianne Boniello, "More Trouble for Mosque Man," New York Post, October 17, 2010; Kathianne Boniello, "Bank Sues Mosque Man," New York Post, December 3, 2010.

50 "Imam's Wife Tells of Death Threats," New York Times, October 3, 2010.

51 Wafa Sultan, "A Mosque at Ground Zero Equals Victory," Hudson New York, May 19, 2010.

52 "Remains of 72 People Found at World Trade Center Site," Telegraph, June 23, 2010.

53 Erica Blake, "Fitzgerald Wreck Site Gets Added Protection," Toledo Blade, February 8, 2006.

54 Pamela Geller, "The Mad Rush to Build the Ground Zero Mega-Mosque," Big Peace, July 9, 2010.

55 David Seifman, "Bloomberg Defends Ground Zero Mosque as Freedom-of-faith Issue," New York Post, May 29, 2010.

56 Pamela Geller, "Palin KO's Bloomberg on Ground Zero Mosque: 'This Is Nothing Close to "Religious Intolerance," It's Just Common Decency,'" AtlasShrugs.com, July 21, 2010.

57 Kathleen Lucadamo and Erin Einhorn, "Bloomberg's Aides Provided Political Support for Ground Zero Mosque, ReleasedEmails Show," New York Daily News, December 23, 2010.

58 Pamela Geller, "The Fix Was In: 911 Mega Mosque Community Board Farce, Board Votes Yes for Mega Mosque," AtlasShrugs.com, May 25, 2010.

59 "Mayor Bloomberg's Office Spearheaded Drive for Ground Zero Mosque Approval According to Documents Uncovered by Judicial Watch," Judicial Watch, December 2010. http://www.judicialwatch.org/news/2010/dec/mayor-bloomberg-s-office-spearheaded-drive-ground-zero-mosque-approval-according-docum.

60 Linda Young, "Judicial Watch Sues Bloomberg Seeking 'Ground Zero Mosque' Documents," All Headline News, December 9, 2010.

61 Pamela Geller, "95-Year-Old St. Nicholas Church at Ground Zero Sues for Right to Rebuild While Bloomberg Lobbies for 911 Taxpayer Dollars for Ground Zero Mosque Supremacists," AtlasShrugs.com, December 8, 2010.

62 Pamela Geller, "WPIX: 'What's More Insulting and Offensive—That Image of Truth, or a15-story Mega-mosque Looking Down on the Sacred Ground of Ground Zero?'" AtlasShrugs.com, August 9, 2010.

Chapter Two: All Mosques are Not Created Equal—A Handy Guide to Fighting the Muslim Brotherhood

63 "Turkey's Charismatic Pro-Islamic Leader," BBC News, November 4, 2002.

64 Sarah Honig, "Another Tack: A Masjid Grows in Brooklyn," Jerusalem Post, July 3, 2008.

65 Pamela Geller, "Selling Out Staten Island to Stealth Jihadists: Muslim Brotherhood aka MAS Takes Over Convent," AtlasShrugs.com, June 10, 2010; Pamela Geller, "Fighting Moe Hood in the Hood," AtlasShrugs.com, June 28, 2010; Christopher Logan, "Tennessee: Hundreds to Fight Against 52,000 sq ft Islamic Center- Video," Logan's Warning, June 19, 2010; Christopher Logan, "UPDATE Wisconsin: Board Gives Conditional Approval for Mosque-Video," Logan's Warning, May 17, 2010.

66 Mohamed Akram, "An Explanatory Memorandum on the General Strategic Goal for the Group in North America," May 22, 1991, Government Exhibit 003–0085, U.S. vs. HLF, et al. 7 (21).

67 Mohamed Akram, "An Explanatory Memorandum on the General Strategic Goal for the Group in North America," May 22,1991, Government Exhibit 003–0085, U.S. vs. HLF, et al.

68 James Lafferty, email to Pamela Geller, April 4, 2011.

69 James Lafferty, email to Pamela Geller, April 4, 2011.

70 James Lafferty, email to Pamela Geller, April 4, 2011.

Chapter Three: A Primer for Protest

71 Daniel Pipes and Sharon Chadha, "CAIR's Hate Crimes Nonsense," FrontPageMagazine. com, May 18, 2005.

Chapter Four: War Games in the Information Battlespace

72 Ayn Rand, "'Extremism,' or The Art of Smearing," in Capitalism: The Unknown Ideal, 1967, http://www.aynrand.org/site/PageServer/News2/feed/PageServer?pagename=ari_ayn_rand_ extremism.

73 Society of Professional Journalists, "Guidelines for Countering Racial, Ethnic and Religious Profiling," https://www.spj.org/divguidelines.asp.

74 Society of Professional Journalists, "Guidelines for Countering Racial, Ethnic and Religious Profiling," https://www.spj.org/divguidelines.asp

75 Society of Professional Journalists, "Guidelines for Countering Racial, Ethnic and Religious Profiling," https://www.spj.org/divguidelines.asp

76 Society of Professional Journalists, "Guidelines for Countering Racial, Ethnic and Religious Profiling," https://www.spj.org/divguidelines.asp

77 "President Obama Addresses Muslim World in Cairo," Washington Post, June 4, 2009.

78 Society of Professional Journalists, "Guidelines for Countering Racial, Ethnic and Religious Profiling," https://www.spj.org/divguidelines.asp

79 Curt Anderson, "Muslim Girl in Oklahoma Can Wear Head Scarf to School," Associated Press, May 19, 2004.

80 "Victims of Hezbollah Terrorist Rocket Attacks File Lawsuit Against Al-Jazeera TV in New York Federal Court," PRNewswire, July 13, 2010.

81 "Columbia University Awards Top Journalism Prize to Al Jazeera English," FoxNews.com, May 5, 2011.

82 Sarah Baxter, "Rumsfeld's Al-Jazeera Outburst," The Sunday Times, November 27, 2005.

83 "Columbia University Awards Top Journalism Prize to Al Jazeera English," FoxNews.com, May 5, 2011.

84 "Muslim Groups Nervous about King Hearings," Politico, January 11, 2011.

85 "Keith Ellison's Slurs," IPT News, April 13, 2011.

86 "King Hearing Falls Short, As Predicted," Investor's Business Daily, March 14, 2011.

87 Pamela Geller, "Jasser's Jihad," AtlasShrugs.com, May 13, 2009.

88 Pamela Geller, "Clarion Call or Dangerous Deception? Justification of Jasser," AtlasShrugs. com, May 20, 2009.

89 Hans A. Von Spakovsky, "Radicalizing Civil Rights," National Review, March 9, 2010.

90 Curt Anderson, "Muslim Girl in Oklahoma Can Wear Head Scarf to School," Associated Press, May 19, 2004.

91 Jerry Markon, "Justice Department Sues on Behalf of Muslim Teacher, Triggering Debate," Washington Post, March 22, 2011.

92 Thomas Kaplan, "Hearing on Terror Includes Heated Debate on Islam," New York Times, April 8, 2011.

93 Marcela Rojas and Brian Howard, "State Sen. Ball Targeted with Package 'Full of Hate,'" Poughkeepsie Journal, April 13, 2011.

94 Bat Ye'or, "Geert Wilders and the Fight for Europe," National Review, February 16, 2009.

95 Pamela Geller, "Muslim Death Threat for US Cartoonist: Marked for Death: 'Everybody Draw Mohammed Day' Artist Forced to Change Identity," AtlasShrugs.com, September 16, 2010.

96 Robert Spencer, "Why Jihad Watch?," Jihad Watch, October 20, 2003.

97 Claire Berlinski, "Moderate Muslim Watch: How the Term 'Islamophobia' Got Shoved Down Your Throat," Ricochet.com, November 24, 2010.

Chapter Five: Litigation Jihad

98 Patrick Poole, "(PJM Exclusive) Did Obama and Holder Scuttle Terror Finance Prosecutions?" Pajamas Media, April 14, 2011.

99 Pamela Geller, "The Muslim Brotherhood By Any Other Name is Still Hamas-Linked; Muslim Groups Get Little in the Way of Ruling," AtlasShrugs.com, October 26, 2010.

100 Pamela Geller, "Call For DOJ Prosecution: Preponderance of Evidence to Establish Unindicted Co-Conspirator Status for CAIR, ISNA, ICNA, NAIT et al," AtlasShrugs.com, November 22, 2010.

101 Robert Spencer, Stealth Jihad (Regnery, 2008), 100.

102 "Profile: Muwafaq Foundation," CooperativeResearch.org, http://www.cooperativeresearch. org/entity.jsp?entity=muwafaq_foundation; Mark Steyn, "The Vanishing Jihad Exposés," Orange County Register, August 5, 2007.

103 "Governor Paterson Signs Legislation Protecting New Yorkers Against Infringement of First Amendment Rights By Foreign Libel Judgments," New York State Governor's Office, May 1, 2008.

104 http://www.smartbus.org/Smart/mktg/advertise.aspx.

105 "Detroit Transit Sued for Nixing 'Leaving Islam?' ad," Washington Times, May 27, 2010.

106 Pamela Geller, "Detroit Free Speech Lawsuit Status: Eight Months Later Still No Decision," AtlasShrugs.com, March 14, 2011.

107 Pamela Geller, "Detroit Lawsuit: Awaiting Judge Hood's Ruling," AtlasShrugs.com, July 13, 2010.

108 Pamela Geller, "Rifqa Bary Death Threat: Exhibit A, The Document: FATWA (Death Penalty) for Apostasy," AtlasShrugs.com, September 21, 2009.

109 Daniel Pipes, "CAIR Backs Down from Anti-CAIR," FrontPageMagazine.com, April 21, 2006.

110 Pamela Geller, "Rifqa Hearing: Judge Rules for Rifqa! Keep Rifqa's Cards Coming!" AtlasShrugs.com, December 22, 2009.

111 Sarah Karush, "Hamtramck Vote a Victory for Those in Favor of Allowing Mosques to Broadcast Islamic Call to Prayer," Associated Press, July 20, 2004.

112 Pamela Geller, "US Jihad School OK After Promise to Revise Textbooks," AtlasShrugs.com, June 15, 2008.

Chapter Six: Cultural Jihad

113 Jerome Corsi, "White House Linked to Flotilla Organizers," WorldNetDaily, June 5, 2010.

114 Rick Stanton, "FBI Raid in MN Reveals New Global Terror Alliances (PJM Exclusive)," Pajamas Media, October 12, 2010.

115 Pamela Geller, "'Unpacking the Jews,'" AtlasShrugs.com, April 4, 2011.

116 Pamela Geller, "ATLAS EXCLUSIVE: Imam Rauf's Sharia Puppets: Madeleine Albright 'Is Now Pushing [My] Ideas in Many Places, She Is in Constant Communication with Me, and on the Issue of Hamas, America Should Really Engage with Them.'" AtlasShrugs.com, August 26, 2010.

117 "ALA Joins CAIR to Oppose Radicalization Hearings Sponsored by Congressman Pete King," Safe Libraries, March 9, 2011, http://safelibraries.blogspot.com/2011/03/ala-joins-cair-to-oppose-radicalization.html.

118 Pamela Geller, "CAIR'S Jihad on the West: Robert Spencer Silenced," AtlasShrugs.com, July 11, 2009.

119 Naomi Wolf, "Behind the Veil Lives a Thriving Muslim Sexuality," Sydney Morning Herald, August 30, 2008; Jamie Glazov, "Why Naomi Wolf Loves the Burqa," NewsRealBlog, September 2, 2009.

120 "Muslim Employee Accuses Disney of Discrimination," Orange County Register, August 18, 2010.

121 Bob Egelko, "Muslim Defendant Can Sue over Hijab Removal," San Francisco Chronicle, March 16, 2011.

122 Ginnie Graham, "Teen at Center of Rights Suit," Tulsa World, September 18, 2009.

123 "Clinic Apologizes for Telling Muslim Doctor She Can't Wear Headscarf," FoxNews, November 2, 2009.

124 "Justice Department Files Religious Discrimination Lawsuit Against Essex County, New Jersey," DailyLawBlog, June 9, 2009, http://www.dailylawblog.com/justice-department-files-religious-discrimination-lawsuit-against-essex-county-new-jersey/.

125 "N.J. Woman Given $25K in Suit over Muslim Garb," Associated Press, November 12, 2010.

126 "Target Shifts Muslims Who Won't Ring Up Pork," Associated Press, March 18, 2007.

127 "Swift Fires 130 Muslim Workers after Ramadan Dispute," Rocky Mountain News, September 10, 2008.

128 David Migoya, "EEOC: Swift Acted with Bias: Muslims Were Discriminated Against by the Meatpacker, the Federal Panel Determines," The Denver Post, September 1, 2009.

129 "Civil Rights Complaints Have Been Filed in Greeley, CO," Refugee Resettlement Watch, June 30, 2009.

130 "Gold'n Plump Settles Worker Lawsuits," Star Tribune, November 10, 2008.

131 Dan Frosch, "Immigrants Claim Wal-Mart Fired Them to Provide Jobs for Local Residents," New York Times, February 8, 2010.

132 Katherine Kersten, "Teacher Breaks Wall of Silence at State's Muslim Public School," Star Tribune, April 9, 2008.

133 Megan Boldt, "TiZA Charter School in Inver Grove Heights Countersues State's ACLU

Chapter, Claims Defamation," Pioneer Press, July 29, 2009.

134 Katherine Kersten, "TiZA vs. the Search for Truth: The School—Public, Mind You—Tries to Intimidate All Who Would Challenge It," Star Tribune, October 16, 2010.

135 Pamela Geller, "KGIA: NY Public School Madrassah Is Moved for 3rd Time," AtlasShrugs. com, April 1, 2008.

136 Gilbert T. Sewall, "Islam in the Classroom: What the Textbooks Tell Us," American Textbook Council, June 2008, 18.

137 Ibid, 6.

138 Ibid, 23.

139 María Rosa Menocal, The Ornament of the World: How Muslims, Jews, and Christians Created a Culture of Tolerance in Medieval Spain, Little, Brown, 2002, 72–3.

140 Gilbert T. Sewall, "Islam in the Classroom: What the Textbooks Tell Us," American Textbook Council, June 2008, 9.

141 Ethan Cole, "Texas Edu Board Approves Ban on 'Pro-Islam' Textbooks," Christian Post, September 25, 2010.

142 "SBOE Adopts Resolution Regarding Islam," KXAN.com, September 24, 2010.

143 Kari Huus, "Texas School Board Debates 'Pro-Islamic' Bias in Textbooks," MSNBC, September 23, 2010.

Chapter Seven: The Erosion of Women's Rights in America

144 "Al-Azhar University Scholars Argue over the Legitimacy of Female Circumcision Practiced in Egypt on Al-Arabiya TV," Middle East Media Research Institute, March 1, 2007.

145 Gail Gartrell, email to Pamela Geller, December 7, 2008.

146 Gail Gartrell, email to Pamela Geller, December 7, 2008.

147 Bud Gillett, "Friends: Murdered Teens Were Afraid of Their Dad," CBS 11 News, January 2, 2008.

148 Glenna Whitley, "American Girls: Crossing Between American and Egyptian Cultures, the Said Girls Made One Deadly Misstep: They Fell in Love," Dallas Observer, June 19, 2008.

149 Ibid.

150 Ibid.

151 Gail Gartrell interview with Pamela Geller, July 1, 2008.

152 Glenna Whitley, "American Girls: Crossing Between American and Egyptian Cultures, the Said Girls Made One Deadly Misstep: They Fell in Love."

153 Gail Gartrell email to Pamela Geller, December 7, 2008.

154 Ibid.

155 Glenna Whitley, "American Girls: Crossing Between American and Egyptian Cultures, the Said Girls Made One Deadly Misstep: They Fell in Love."

156 Gail Gartrell email to Pamela Geller, December 7, 2008.

157 Tanya Eiserer, Scott Farwell and Scott Goldstein, "Lewisville Cab Driver Had Been Investigated for Previous Abuse," Dallas Morning News, January 9, 2008.

158 Ibid.

159 Wendy Hundley, "Lewisville Cabdriver Sought in Slayings of 2 Teen Daughters," Dallas Morning News, January 2, 2008.

160 Glenna Whitley, "American Girls: Crossing Between American and Egyptian Cultures, the Said Girls Made One Deadly Misstep: They Fell in Love."

161 Tanya Eiserer, Scott Farwell and Scott Goldstein, "Lewisville Cab Driver Had Been Investigated for Previous Abuse."

162 Glenna Whitley, "American Girls: Crossing Between American and Egyptian Cultures, the

Said Girls Made One Deadly Misstep: They Fell in Love."
163 John Jay, email to Pamela Geller, June 1, 2008.
164 Gail Gartrell interview with Pamela Geller, July 1, 2008.
165 Gail Gartrell email to Pamela Geller, July 1, 2008.
166 "Murder in the Family: Honor Killing in America," FoxNews, August 22, 2008.
167 Gail Gartrell, email to Pamela Geller, April 4, 2009.
168 Gail Gartrell email to Pamela Geller, December 7, 2008.
169 Glenna Whitley, "American Girls: Crossing Between American and Egyptian Cultures, the Said Girls Made One Deadly Misstep: They Fell in Love."
170 Ibid.
171 Rod Dreher, "Was This an Honor Killing?" Dallas Morning News, January 13, 2008.
172 Source needed. Gail
173 Glenna Whitley, "American Girls: Crossing Between American and Egyptian Cultures, the Said Girls Made One Deadly Misstep: They Fell in Love."
174 Ibid.
175 "Muslim Arizona Man Arrested After Allegedly Running Down 'Westernized' Daughter," MyFoxDetroit.com, October 30, 2009.
176 Dustin Gardiner, "Woman in Suspected 'Honor Killing' Dies," Arizona Republic, November 2, 2009.
177 Pamela Geller, "Germany: Honor Killing Victim's Face 'Beaten Beyond Recognition,'" AtlasShrugs.com, March 11, 2009.
178 "Killed for Falling in Love with Wrong Man," YouTube, June 11, 2007.
179 "Schoolgirl 'Was Tortured by Her Father' Before She Was Murdered in Honour Killing," Daily Mail, October 12, 2009.
180 Phyllis Chesler, "Worldwide Trends in Honor Killings," Middle East Quarterly, Spring 2010.

Chapter Eight: Outlawing the Barbaric and Unspeakable

181 Robert Spencer, "Oklahoma judge sides with Hamas-linked CAIR, Issues Permanent Injunction Against Sharia Ban," Jihad Watch, November 30, 2010.
182 Maryclaire Dale, "Pa. Bigamist Slain Hours Before Trip," Associated Press, August 8, 2007.
183 Noor Javed, "GTA's Secret World of Polygamy," Toronto Star, May 24, 2008.
184 Barbara Bradley Hagerty, "Some Muslims in U.S. Quietly Engage in Polygamy," National Public Radio, May 27, 2008.
185 Robert Spencer, "Oklahoma judge sides with Hamas-linked CAIR, Issues Permanent Injunction Against Sharia Ban," Jihad Watch, November 30, 2010.
186 David Yerushalmi, "Criticism of the Oklahoma Amendment Banning Shariah from State Courts: Legitimate or Ill-considered?, Center for Security Policy, November 29, 2010.
187 David Yerushalmi, "Criticism of the Oklahoma Amendment Banning Shariah from State Courts: Legitimate or Ill-considered?, Center for Security Policy, November 29, 2010.
188 http://www.oklegislature.gov/BillInfo.aspx?Bill=HB1552&Tab=1.
189 Pamela Geller, "CAIR Fights Oklahoma Anti-Sharia Law, Not Jihadis," Human Events, October 14, 2010.
190 "CAIR Oklahoma Will Fight Oklahoma's New Anti-Sharia Law!" YouTube, November 4, 2010.
191 Pamela Geller, "Sharia (Islamic) Law in New Jersey Court: Muslim Husband Rapes, Beats, Sexually Abuses Wife, Judge Sees No Sexual Assault Because Islam Forbids Wives to Refuse Sex," AtlasShrugs.com, July 24, 2010.

192 Pamela Geller, "The ABA's Jihad," American Thinker, February 22, 2011.
193 Pamela Geller, "The ABA's Jihad," American Thinker, February 22, 2011; "Correction to Information on Section of International Law Task Force," ABANow, February 22, 2011.
194 Pamela Geller, "Spin, Damage Control and Backpedaling on the ABA Sharia InitiativeGeller Responds to Official Statement," AtlasShrugs.com, February 24, 2011.

Chapter Nine: The Muslim Brotherhood Project in America

195 Sahih Bukhari, vol. 4, bk. 52, nos. 267–269, http://www.usc.edu/schools/college/crcc/engagement/resources/texts/muslim/hadith/bukhari/052.sbt.html#004.052.267.
196 Robert Spencer, Stealth Jihad, (Regnery, 2008), p. 174–175.
197 Mohamed Akram, "An Explanatory Memorandum on the General Strategic Goal for the Group in North America," May 22, 1991, Government Exhibit 003–0085, U.S. vs. HLF, et al.
198 Mohamed Akram, "An Explanatory Memorandum on the General Strategic Goal for the Group in North America," May 22, 1991, Government Exhibit 003–0085, U.S. vs. HLF, et al.
199 Imam Muslim, Sahih Muslim, Abdul Hamid Siddiqi, trans., Kitab Bhavan, revised edition 2000, book 19, no. 4294.

Chapter Ten: Infiltration

200 http://www.kptv.com/local-video/index.html?grabnetworks_video_id=4444265.
201 Robert Spencer, "Dayton 'Islamophobic Hate Crime' Hoax Police Report: 'Victim' Blamed 'Black Males,'" Jihad Watch, October 23, 2008; Pamela Geller, "Muslim Arrested in Mosque Arson Case," AtlasShrugs.com, July 8, 2010.
202 "Study: 3 in 4 U.S. Mosques Preach Anti-West Extremism," WorldNetDaily, February 24, 2008.
203 "ISNA Admits Hamas Ties," IPT News, July 25, 2008.
204 Pamela Geller, "US State Department Spending 100s of Millions on Mosques in Middle East," AtlasShrugs.com, February 24, 2011.
205 Pamela Geller, "US State Department Spending 100s of Millions on Mosques in Middle East," AtlasShrugs.com, February 24, 2011.206 Pamela Geller, "Obama's State Department Submits to Islam," American Thinker, August 18, 2009.
207 "History," U.S.-Muslim Engagement Project, http://www.usmuslimengagement.org/index.php?option=com_content&task=view&id=14&Itemid=43.
208 Frank Gaffney, Jr., "Shariah's Brotherhood," Center for Security Policy, March 16, 2009, http://204.96.138.161/p17940.xml.
209 Report of the Leadership Group on U.S.-Muslim Engagement Project, Changing Course: A New Direction for U.S. Relations with the Muslim World, Second Printing, February 2009, 6.
210 Ibid., 5.
211 The Brookings Project on U.S. Relations with the Islamic World, The Doha Compact: New Directions: America and the Muslim World, Saban Center at Brookings, October 2008, 4.
212 Report of the Leadership Group on U.S.-Muslim Engagement Project, 6.
213 Ibid., 5.
214 Ibid., 61.
215 The Brookings Project on U.S. Relations with the Islamic World, 16.2
216 Report of the Leadership Group on U.S.-Muslim Engagement Project, 77.
217 The Brookings Project on U.S. Relations with the Islamic World, 16.Chapter Eleven: The Real Threats to Freedom

218 Corky Siemaszko, "Southern Poverty Law Center Lists Anti-Islamic NYC Blogger Pamela Geller, Followers a Hate Group," New York Daily News, February 25, 2011.

219 "Dallas Target: Texas Resident Arrested on Charge of Attempted Use of Weapon of Mass Destruction," The33TV.com, February 24, 2011.

220 Jerry Woodruff, "SPLC: America's Left-Wing Hate Machine," The Social Contract Press, Volume 20, Number 3 (Spring 2010).

221 Pamela Geller, "The President's War on Free Speech," AtlasShrugs.com, September 9, 2010.

222 "Geller, Jones Amp Up Anti-Muslim Hate Rhetoric," Southern Poverty Law Center Intelligence Report, Winter 2010, Issue Number 140.

223 Pamela Geller, "Un-indicted Co-Conspirator, Hamas-tied CAIR Hails Crushing Defeat of Free Speech in SIOA Miami Bus Campaign," AtlasShrugs.com, April 16, 2010.

224 Pamela Geller, "SPLC Redefines 'Hate': Islamic Jihadists Good, Pammiecakes Bad," AtlasShrugs.com, August 29, 2010.

225 "Charges Against 'New Black Panthers' Dropped by Obama Justice Dept.," FoxNews.com, May 29, 2009.

226 "New Black Panther Party," Discover the Networks, http://www.discoverthenetworks.org/groupProfile.asp?grpid=7556.

227 Bat Ye'or, "OIC and the Modern Caliphate," American Thinker, September 26, 2010.

228 Bat Ye'or, "OIC and the Modern Caliphate," American Thinker, September 26, 2010.

229 Ekmeleddin Ihsanoglu, "Speech of Secretary General at the Thirty-fifth Session of the Council of Foreign Ministers of the Organisation of the Islamic Conference," June 18, 2008.

230 John Esposito and Ibrahim Kalin, Islamophobia: The Challenge of Pluralism in the 21st Century (Oxford University Press, 2011), xix.

231 "TNR's Peretz Cropped Transcript to Support His Smear of Soros as 'A Young Cog in the Hitlerite Wheel,'" Media Matters, February 5, 2007.

232 "George Soros—A Jewish Nazi Sympathizer?" Rense.com, March 21, 2011.

233 "Insider Trading Conviction of Soros Is Upheld," New York Times, June 14, 2006; "George Soros' Agenda for Drug Legalization, Death, and Welfare," Forbundet Mot Rusgift, January 15, 1997; "OSI Sues USAID over Dangerous Public Health Policy," Open Society Foundation, September 23, 2005; Pamela Geller, "Obama's Puppetmaster, George Soros, Made Buko Billion Talks Down the Economy," AtlasShrugs.com, March 25, 2009; Matthew Russell Lee, "At UN, Susan Rice Is Asked About Obama Order for CIA in Libya: Were Council Resolutions & Members Skirted?" Inner City Press, http://www.innercitypress.org/icglobal.html.

234 Pamela Geller, "Terror Pig Gets 28 Months in Pen," AtlasShrugs.com, October 16, 2006; Pamela Geller, "Massive Democrat Election Fraud," AtlasShrugs.com, August 30, 2007; Thomas Lifson and Ed Lasky, "Soros-related Firm Raided by FBI (updated)," American Thinker, October 25, 2007.

235 Pamela Geller, "Viciously Anti-Jewish 'J' Street Funded by George Soros," AtlasShrugs.com, September 25, 2010.

236 Eli Lake, "Jewish Lobby Group Admits Soros Support," Washington Times, September 26, 2010.

237 Pamela Geller, "Soros Stealing America," AtlasShrugs.com, August 29, 2006.

238 Isi Liebler, "J Street's 'Pro-Israel' Stance is Phoney," Guardian, October 26, 2009.

239 Philip Klein, "Obama National Security Adviser to Speak at Anti-Israel Conference," American Spectator, October 16, 2009.

240 Pamela Geller, "Obama: Sleeping with Dogs (Many)," AtlasShrugs.com, January 23, 2008; Bob Unruh, "Obama Lawyers Want More Secrecy at White House," WorldNetDaily, May 1, 2010.241 Pamela Geller, "J Street Is a Dead End as Rats Jump Ship," AtlasShrugs.com, October 20, 2009.

INDEX

WND Books has a history of publishing provocative, current-events titles, including many *New York Times* bestsellers.

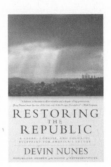

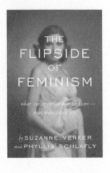

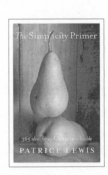

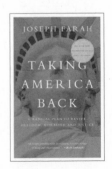

WND Books • a WND Company • Washington, DC • www.wndbooks.com

Follow intern Chris Gaubatz as he courageously gains the trust of CAIR's inner sanctum, working undercover as a devoted convert to Islam, and blows the whistle on the entire factory fueling the wave of homegrown terrorism now plaguing America.

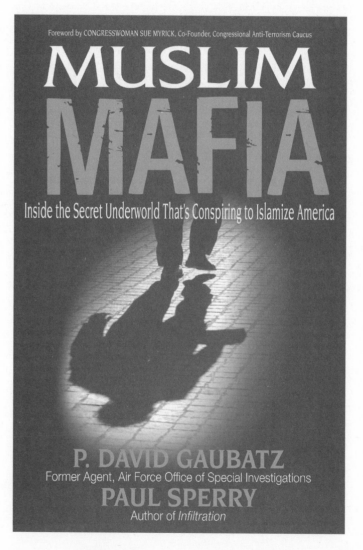

Foreword by CONGRESSWOMAN SUE MYRICK, Co-Founder, Congressional Anti-Terrorism Caucus

MUSLIM MAFIA

Inside the Secret Underworld That's Conspiring to Islamize America

P. DAVID GAUBATZ
Former Agent, Air Force Office of Special Investigations
PAUL SPERRY
Author of *Infiltration*

WND Books • a WND Company • Washington, DC • www.wndbooks.com

Aaron Klein, WND's Jerusalem bureau chief, confronts terrorists whose stated goal is the annihilation of the United States and Israel, and narrates his interviews from the unique perspective of a Jew meeting with his enemy.

AARON KLEIN

SCHMOOZING WITH TERRORISTS

From Hollywood to the Holy Land, Jihadists Reveal their Global Plans—to a Jew!

WND BOOKS

WND Books • a WND Company • Washington, DC • www.wndbooks.com

In this groundbreaking work, Aaron Klein will show how Israel is often its own worst enemy. And how Hamas, Iran and Palestinian terrorists are poised to end the democracy once and for all.

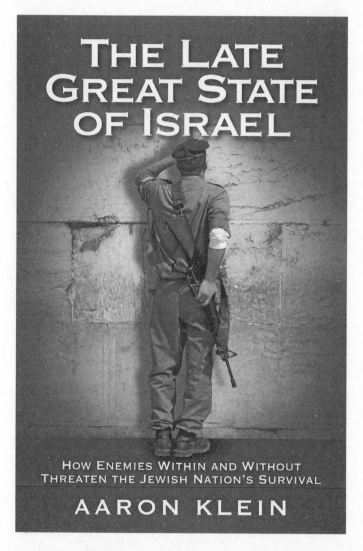

THE LATE GREAT STATE OF ISRAEL

HOW ENEMIES WITHIN AND WITHOUT THREATEN THE JEWISH NATION'S SURVIVAL

AARON KLEIN

WND BOOKS

WND Books • a WND Company • Washington, DC • www.wndbooks.com